FORECAST

FORECAST

WHAT PHYSICS, METEOROLOGY, AND THE NATURAL SCIENCES CAN TEACH US ABOUT ECONOMICS

MARK BUCHANAN

B L O O M S B U R Y

NEW YORK · LONDON · NEW DELHI · SYDNEY

Published by Bloomsbury USA, New York

All papers used by Bloomsbury USA are natural, recyclable products made
from wood grown in well-managed forests. The manufacturing processes
conform to the environmental regulations of the country of origin.

LIBRARY OF CONGRESS CATALOGING-IN-PUBLICATION DATA

Buchanan, Mark.
Forecast : what physics, meteorology, and the natural sciences
can teach us about economics / Mark Buchanan.—1st U.S. ed.
p. cm.
Includes bibliographical references and index.
ISBN 978-1-60819-851-1 (alk. paper)
1. Equilibrium (Economics) 2. Business cycles. 3. Financial crises.
4. Economics—Mathematical models. 5. Economic forecasting. I. Title
HB145.B83 2013
330—dc23
2012028070

First U.S. Edition 2013

1 3 5 7 9 10 8 6 4 2

Typeset by Westchester Book Group
Printed in the United States by Thomson-Shore, Inc. Dexter, Michigan

For Kate

Contents

Preface   ix

1. The Equilibrium Delusion   1
2. A Marvelous Machine   24
3. Notable Exceptions   45
4. Natural Rhythms   70
5. Models of Man   89
6. Ecologies of Belief   112
7. Perils of Efficiency   133
8. Trading at the Speed of Light   156
9. Twilight of the Idols   178
10. Forecast   203
Acknowledgments   225
Notes   227
Index   251

Preface

There is nothing like a revolution, the British historian Edward Hallett Carr once said, to spark an interest in history. And nothing like a global economic crisis to stir wide interest in just what lies behind the mysterious turbulence of our financial markets and economic lives. Since the beginning of the financial crisis of 2007–2008, I've read probably twenty or thirty books on the topic, many of them wonderfully informative as well as amusing and, of course, infuriating—Michael Lewis's *The Big Short*, John Lanchester's *Whoops!*, and Gillian Tett's *Fool's Gold*, for example. These books all explore the nature of the global financial system, how it has changed in recent years, and how various (mis)incentives in the decade before the crisis led nations, financial institutions, and individuals to take on huge risks. These books also explored the psychological and institutional factors that kept almost everyone from seeing the looming disaster right up to the days before it finally unfolded.

In all these books, I felt one thing was missing—an examination of the peculiar concepts of economic thinking, of the atmosphere of ideas of modern economic theory, which swayed many people to believe that the tumultuous history of economics and finance, a history of almost continual crises and disruption going back four hundred years, had somehow come to a miraculous end in our era because of the markets' self-regulating nature and tendency towards "equilibrium." I've written this book to help fill this gap, and also to explore more constructive ideas for building a more realistic and more natural understanding of economic systems.

Economic theory today is highly mathematical, and economists have often been accused of having "physics envy," of using imposing mathematics to give their field the same prestige and apparent certainty as one finds (sometimes) in physics and in other natural sciences. I think this is misleading. If economic theorists have tried to mimic physics, they've only done so, I would argue, on a false and distorted view of physics. This book is an examination of how a more authentic use of some ideas and concepts coming from physics can be very helpful in putting our understanding of economic and financial systems on a more natural basis. Most certainly, they can help correct the dangerous view that markets are somehow inherently stable and self-regulating.

Many scientists have been generous with their help in refining the ideas in the following pages; I've listed them in the Acknowledgments on page 225.

Mark Buchanan
November 9, 2012
London, England

The Equilibrium Delusion

Economics is a discipline for quiet times. The profession, it turns out, . . . has no grip on understanding how the abnormal grows out of the normal and what happens next, its practitioners like weather forecasters who don't understand storms.

—Will Hutton, journalist
The Observer, London

I think physicists are the Peter Pans of the human race. They never grow up and they keep their curiosity.

—Isidor Rabi, physicist

LIKE MANY TOWNS SPRAWLED ACROSS the great flat expanses of the mid-western United States, Overland Park, Kansas, is no stranger to extreme weather. Each year, in spring and early summer, warm, moist air sweeping in from the Gulf of Mexico slips under sheets of colder air tumbling in over the Rockies. "Warm air rises," that banal phrase of folk physics, here takes on life: gravity drives vast plumes of the warmer, lighter air to penetrate the colder layer above and billow upward to a height of ten miles. This is the first ingredient in a recipe for atmospheric violence. The second is surface winds, blowing to the North and from the West, which drive this incipient protostorm to rotate like a turnstile. The result—several billion tons of wet, warm air whipped into an unstable, spinning tower—creates near-perfect conditions for powerful tornadoes, some as much as a mile in diameter, with winds churning to 400 m.p.h.

To most of us, tornadoes seem freakish, unnatural, definitely abnormal. Yet the state of Kansas alone sees hundreds of them every year, and they come about through perfectly ordinary atmospheric processes. Broadly speaking, it's all just part of what happens in the atmosphere: one event builds on another, and then another, and soon an ordinary gray sky becomes a violent, memorable twister. More technically, we could say the atmosphere is prone to what scientists call "positive feedbacks," the consequences of which our human minds find hard to imagine.

Maybe you've heard the term elsewhere. Positive feedbacks are a long-standing concept in science—the process by which small variations in a given system can become increasingly large. They are commonplace in discussions of global warming. Melting glaciers turn white ice to blue water, reducing how much sunlight gets reflected back into the atmosphere; the process could accelerate planetary warming. Positive feedbacks arise in psychology, biology, electronics, physics, computer science, and many other disciplines. Yet even though many of us recognize this notion, we are dreadful when it comes to estimating its impact.

Take $1,000 and invest it in something that earns interest at a rate of, say, 10 percent each year. Leave it there for thirty years with the interest earned feeding back into the account. How much will you have? Well, 10 percent of $1,000 is $100, so you might think the amount should increase by $100 or so each year. Thirty years makes the total gain about $3,000, giving a total of $4,000. Of course, as the amount grows, you'll be getting 10 percent of a growing number each year, so you'd expect something a little more than $4,000. Maybe, without a calculator, you'd guess $5,000 or $6,000? It already starts to feel hopeful to consider $10,000. But human intuition is no match for the mathematics. The actual total after thirty years is a little over $20,000. The amount feeds on itself and grows faster than anyone would expect.

There's more here than a lesson about money; it's a lesson in human thinking and why the world so often surprises us.

As humans, we're terrible at imagining the likely consequences of positive feedback. Take a piece of paper and fold it, and then take that doubled paper and fold it again, and then again, thirty times in all. Actually, don't waste your time. You'll find you can't do it because the result, if you did, would be about seventy miles thick. Ask a friend to give you an apple today, two apples tomorrow, four the third day, and so on, for one whole month (thirty-one days). You'd better rent a large warehouse because on the final day alone you'll get more than 2 billion apples. This is the power of positive feedback: each step not only makes things bigger, but also gears up the process itself, accelerating how fast things get bigger in a way that leads to consequences far beyond our expectations.

Positive feedback matters a lot more than we think, because in one form or another it lies behind almost everything that makes our world rich and surprising, changeable and dynamic, lively and unpredictable. It makes seeds sprout and grow into trees, matches burst into flame, and single cells divide and proliferate into living, thinking human beings. It drives political revolutions and new religions, and it makes perfectly peaceful blue skies give rise, with little warning, to storms of terrifying violence, like those tornado-spawning storms in Kansas. Our brains lack intuition for all this. In meteorology, and in the rest of science, it's taken years of learning from mistakes to recognize how and why positive feedbacks play such a crucial role in causing events we might not otherwise expect.

Yet outside of these areas, an intellectual blind spot to the power of positive feedbacks still holds us back. Nowhere is this truer than in the science of human systems, in social science, and especially economics and finance. Consider what happened, for example, on May 6, 2010.

Four Minutes of Mayhem

In addition to being a frequent site of tornado activity, Overland Park, Kansas, is also home to the headquarters of an important investment company named Waddell and Reed Financial, Inc. Founded on a shoe-string by financiers Cameron Reed and Chauncey Waddell back in 1937, the firm started out with offices in department stores, but today it has grown to handle funds totaling more than $60 billion. It lacks a famous name, but it's big enough to make investment decisions that—with the help of positive feedbacks—can threaten the stability of the entire global economy. In less than five minutes.

In the spring of 2010, a mutual fund run by Waddell and Reed had invested heavily in futures contracts for the Standard and Poor's Stock Index, one of the most widely traded stock futures. Buying such a futures contract means that you agree to buy the S&P 500, not now, but on a certain fixed date in the future. The price you pay, however, is fixed now. They're among the simplest "derivatives" products, which "derive" their values from the value of something else, in this case the S&P 500. If that index rises in value, the value of the future also rises, as it raises the likely future value of the index, too. Waddell and Reed were deeply into these futures as a hedge or balance against other investments they had, and their strategy seemed sound until the early days of May, when financial authorities in Greece admitted (under pressure) that levels of government debt were far in excess of the limits set by the European Central Bank. Suddenly, as European and international bankers met to find ways to keep Greece from defaulting, the future of the European monetary union was called into question. Investors worried. Between the market's opening and noon on the sixth of May, stocks of the Dow Jones Industrials slid downward by 2.5 percent.

At two thirty-two P.M., concerned that troubles in Europe were spreading to the United States, Waddell and Reed requested a broker at Barclays bank to get out of the stock index futures market. Using a computer program to make the trade, the broker began trying to sell $4.1 billion in so-called E-mini stock index futures. Selling has the effect of driving prices down, so the program was designed to work cautiously, selling a little at a time, spreading it over the day. For ten minutes or so, things went smoothly. But then, at two forty-one P.M., something kicked off an explosive chain of events. High-frequency traders, whose computers conduct thousands of trades per second, had been buying most of the contracts as Waddell and Reed sold them. Many of these traders make money as "market makers": their computer programs stand ready to buy or sell at any moment, and they profit from slight differences in the prices they set for buying and selling. But according to the trade-by-trade data for the day, these programs seem to have purchased too many futures contracts, accruing an inventory larger than desired. At two forty-one P.M., one of these programs decided to bail out of market making and started selling aggressively, causing futures prices to drop off a cliff.

The result was a spectacular plunge as positive feedback involving completely automated trading clipped the value of E-mini futures by more than 3 percent in only four minutes. But this was only act 1 of the unfolding drama.

This tumult in the futures market then acted like a detonator to set off act 2—an implosion in the stock market itself. Stock traders soon noticed the sudden drop in futures prices and jumped in to profit by buying up these cheap futures, meanwhile selling an equivalent amount of the same stock.[1] In effect, the S&P 500 five months in the future could be had for a fraction of the index price now; with no particular reason to think the index would rise or fall strongly over those months, investors dumped the current stock in favor of the future. In a few minutes, the sheer volume of trading soared so violently that automatic protection rules for computers trading on the New York Stock Exchange and other exchanges kicked in to shut down trading. Stock prices went into free fall as sellers could find no one willing to buy. The blue-chip stock of Procter and Gamble lost a third of its value in three and one-half minutes; Accenture stock went all the way to less than a penny per share. In all, the Dow Jones Industrial Average lost 9.2 percent of its value in a few minutes—the largest drop in such a short time ever.

Almost as quickly, the markets recovered, closing the day with the Dow and the stocks of most companies back within a few percentage points of where they started. It was as if the markets had, like a jet liner, flown into a pocket of devastating turbulence and plunged several thousand feet in a terrifying death spiral, before recovering, climbing, and carrying on as before.

What happened? In the days and weeks after this "flash crash," popular speculation pointed to a computer error, or perhaps a "fat finger"—a trader hitting the wrong key and initiating a mistaken trade. An article on CNBC's website reported a rumor that someone had typed *b* for billions rather than *m* for millions when making a trade on Procter and Gamble (although one blogger noted that it must have been a very fat and strangely shaped finger to miss *b* and hit *m* without touching the *n* that lies between). Others worried that some powerful financial genius had manipulated the market for his or her own gain, luring the computer traders to cause the crash so they could profit.

Investigations by the Securities and Exchange Commission over the next five months found no evidence to support any of these ideas. What it did find, after sifting through mountains of data detailing trades in many markets during the day, was that the Waddell and Reed trade seemed to be the primary trigger for the turmoil, which then took off with an energy all its own. The SEC-CFTC final report[2] on the event—entitled "Findings Regarding the Market Events of May 6, 2010"—documents a very complicated set of happenings that are nevertheless fairly simple in conceptual outline, if you think in terms of positive feedbacks. The event had two or maybe three principal stages, and, like all positive feedbacks, culminated in consequences far beyond what anyone might have expected.

But perhaps the most interesting thing about the SEC-CFTC report is that it never uses the words "feedback" or "instability," makes no analogy to storms in the atmosphere, or indeed to self-reinforcing processes of any kind. Like a food critic describing a sumptuous meal without mentioning flavor, texture, or color, the SEC report struggles to describe positive feedbacks running through the markets without ever mentioning the basic idea. It's a peculiar but telling contortion, which points to the singular weakness in most current thinking about markets and other economic systems.

There are two reasons why the SEC report doesn't use the natural language of positive feedback. First, doing so would immediately undermine one of the report's principal aims, which was to reassure rattled investors that this event was an unusual and exceptional episode, a one-off freak occurrence unlikely ever to happen again. (In the time since the SEC report, there have been further flash crashes, albeit on a somewhat smaller scale; to take just one example, the stock for the computing giant Apple dropped by 9 percent in five minutes on March 23, 2012. Its share price had already substantially recovered by close of business that day.) Investors would like to hear that an evil perpetrator had orchestrated the whole thing, made millions out of it, but has since been identified and arrested. Or at least they want to hear that it all came out of one big trade and a conspiracy of other events that probably won't come together again. Problem solved. Talk about natural feedbacks and instabilities, explain how the event emerged out of quite ordinary happenings in the market, and you're not likely to do much reassuring, even if you do strike much more closely to the truth.

The financial press for the most part played along with this view. They dutifully reported that the big Waddell and Reed trade had kicked off the crash, and in some vague way had probably caused it, though without ever explaining quite how. LONE $4.1 BILLION SALE, as the *New York Times* reported,[3] LED TO "FLASH CRASH" IN MAY.

The second reason the SEC report failed to mention positive feedback is more fundamental, and so holds more importance for the long run. Economics in general—and finance in particular—have long been based on notions of balance and equilibrium, on the idea that the economy at large and financial markets in particular naturally tend toward a state of balance. Any disturbance or shock is thought to stir forces—negative feedbacks—that will bring the system back into balance. Negative feedback is what makes the water stirred in a cup settle back to rest, as the initial action stirs forces that act against it, slowing the flow and restoring stillness. Markets, economists insist, work similarly. Through a long and circuitous path, the idea goes back to Adam Smith's famous notion of the invisible hand, which allegedly leads markets to good outcomes despite the manifold conflicting and typically selfish motivations of the people involved. The notion of positive feedbacks is rarely, if ever, considered in potential explanations of economic happenings.

The SEC report on the flash crash doesn't use the most natural language to talk about the event because that language goes against the core concepts of mainstream economic thinking, especially as it has developed over the past few decades.

Instead, it follows a very different approach, not really trying to explain at all. The report documents how the Waddell and Reed trade led to the flash crash through a plausible chain of events, one causing the next, never once asking *why* such an explosive chain of events was possible on this particular day, *why* this one large but hardly unusual trade could have sparked it off, or *why* anyone should think it was unlikely to happen again, possibly with much more severe consequences. After all, had the trade been made a couple hours later, the market might have closed at the end of the day down one thousand points, triggering similar crashes all around the globe.

Equilibrium thinking is so deeply ingrained for most economists that they find it difficult to think in other terms. Standard economic analyses always begin by identifying the aims of the relevant parties involved in some situation, and what they stand to gain or lose from taking various possible actions. The economist then works out mathematically—and the mathematics are basically always the same[4]—the details of the balance point or equilibrium that will supposedly emerge out of the competition between all these parties. Almost all economic policy advice comes from such exercises, as economists analyze how the properties of the supposed equilibrium would change if the government raises taxes, for example, or changes regulations on CO_2 emissions—or how the financial markets would quickly adapt to a new stable equilibrium if a trader in Kansas suddenly starts selling lots of futures. But what if, rather than settling back into a nice equilibrium, the markets instead fall into a condition more akin to a rag soaked in gasoline or like the atmosphere in summertime Kansas, inherently prone to stormy chaos? There is nothing in all the usual calculations to account for that.[5]

Belief in equilibrium confers a sense of safety and predictability, and reflects a firm belief in the triumph of human logic over nature. The assumption of equilibrium sharply restricts the kinds of things economists can imagine happening in the world. This limitation most likely explains why the SEC for months sought to explain the flash crash as the result of something exceptional and abnormal, from a mistake in the market, a fat finger, or computer glitch, because it just *couldn't* have come from the ordinary, internal workings of the market, which are always supposed to remain in stable equilibrium.

Except when they don't. What is most troubling about the story I've told here is that it could be told just as well about the recent global financial crisis, which also emerged from natural positive feedbacks, or the Internet stock bubble of the late 1990s, or any of the other financial crises large or small that have struck markets and economies over the past several hundred years. The history of economics is largely a history of surprises that have emerged out of positive feedbacks. Since the flash crash, U.S. markets have experienced numerous "mini flash crashes" as the stocks of individual companies have mysteriously plummeted to less than a penny in a few minutes, only to recover afterward. A company called Nanex records data on all kinds of market activities, and their studies suggest that events of this kind are now simply endemic to the market. In the first three months of 2011, for example, individual stocks showed perplexing moves in 139 cases, rising or falling about 1 percent or more in less than a second, only to recover. Nanex detected[6] 1,818 such occurrences in 2010 and 2,715 in 2009. The May 6, 2010, crash simply seems larger than similar events taking place all the time.

Even so, most economists persist in the belief that economic systems are inherently stable and self-regulating, that they always tend toward a state of balance, and that they don't have any *interesting weather.*

In this book, I'm going to argue that this really is a crazy state of affairs, something more or less equivalent to physics in the Middle Ages, and that financial crises of all kinds, from short shocks like the flash crash to global economic meltdowns, really are closely akin to storms in the socioeconomic system. As with storms in the atmosphere, the key to understanding lies in identifying the positive feedbacks and instabilities that lead to fast and surprising changes. These positive feedbacks are the most important elements in all markets; they're not exceptional in the least. I'll also argue that it would be utterly astounding for it to be otherwise, for instabilities driven by positive feedbacks affect almost everything in the universe, from stellar supernovae to planetary ecosystems and our climate to the movement of the earth's crust, and from the flow of electronic traffic through the Internet to the growth of cities.

We'll never understand economies and markets until we get over the nutty idea that they alone—unlike almost every other complex system in the world—are inherently stable and have no internal weather. It's time we begin learning about the socioeconomic weather, categorizing its storms, and learning how either to prevent them, or to see them coming and protect ourselves against them. As I'll explore, the ideas and concepts required to do this—or at the very least to make a good start—are already available in other areas of science, especially in physics. The idea of a "physics of finance" isn't strange at all, but perfectly natural—perhaps even unavoidable.

Market Meltdown

In the first few hours of trading on Wednesday, the first of August 2007, the Medallion Fund of James Simons and his firm Renaissance Technologies was earning money as usual. It was the beginning of another great day for Simons's hedge fund, which over the past year had raked in upward of $3 billion. By the norms of Wall Street, they'd deserved it, as they'd taken real risks and held their nerve. Medallion relied on smart people using mathematics to spot small and temporary market opportunities, and borrowed heavily from banks to leverage and amplify their profits. It was a recipe that couldn't fail it seemed—until around ten forty-five A.M. on this particular Wednesday, when something went dreadfully wrong.

Over the next forty-five minutes, everything that had been working before—for that week, as well as in the months leading up to it—abruptly stopped working. In less than an hour the fund lost all the gains it had made in the entire *year* to that point. As they soon learned, other hedge funds trading on similar principles—including well-known funds run by AQR Capital Management and Goldman Sachs—were losing staggering sums of money at the very same time. Just as abruptly, things went back to normal for several days until Monday of the following week, when the market opened at eight A.M. and it happened again. This time the trouble lasted longer and was even worse. By the middle of the day Medallion had lost nearly $500 million for the week.

In these two brief episodes, a handful of the most sophisticated and successful hedge funds in the world suffered unprecedented losses. Some went out of business, while others lost enormous sums. Goldman Sachs's Global Equity Opportunities Fund lost 30 percent of its total value. Nothing had seemed easier than making money, and then, suddenly, nothing seemed harder than not losing it. What happened?

This spectacular collapse has come to be known on Wall Street as the "quant meltdown," and what happened turns out to be fairly simple. Hedge funds don't just invest their own money, they also borrow heavily from banks to "leverage" their positions, thereby amplifying their potential gains. The funds compete to attract investors, and if one fund gives higher returns by using more leverage, others will soon follow along; they have to or they'll lose investors. It is far from obvious, but this competition has an unexpected consequence: it ties the funds together into a loop of positive feedback that if sparked by the right event will trigger a fierce financial storm.

That event occurred on August 1. The precise details remain unknown due to the proprietary secrecy of hedge funds, but the likely scenario is clear from subsequent research. Around ten thirty A.M., something—perhaps a chance, momentary dip in stock prices—forced at least one of the hedge funds to sell off some stock they owned to raise cash. This was not a matter of choice: the banks that loan to hedge funds demand that those funds keep their debts below a specific percentage of their overall worth. So when a hedge fund's stocks lose value, they are forced to make an automatic payment (a "margin call") back to the banks in order to shrink their debt. But here's the rub: in order to free up cash to pay the bank, the hedge funds often need to sell off some of their stock, and this very sale will drive the value of that stock down further. On this day, sales of this kind in turn lowered the total wealth of several other hedge funds that owned the same stock. And the feedback cycle was on. These funds faced margin calls of their own, which they met by selling stock, pushing values down again, and so on in a deadly spiral from which escape was barred by contract.

The gist of the story is this: the competition between hedge funds to attract investors leads in a natural way to increasing leverage, which in turn drives the market into an unstable situation in which the right accident can spark an explosive sequence of events. Once started, the process runs more or less mechanically and there's not a lot people can do to escape. Random market fluctuations in the first week of August 2007 were, on two occasions, strong enough to spark chain reactions of this kind.

It would be unfair to say that economists aren't familiar with such events. The economic literature on "liquidity crises" is extensive and explains how, in the right circumstances, everyone can be driven to bail out of a market like people fleeing from a burning building. But the standard economic perspective of such events, crafted in equilibrium terms, doesn't explain at all why and how this instability arises and develops quite naturally, or why it can persist for a long time without being set off. Indeed, the explanation I've related here hasn't emerged from traditional economic research, but from the efforts of two physicists working with one economist to model this market much the way meteorologists model the weather, with computer simulations following the natural interactions among banks, hedge funds, and investors. When I originally wrote about this work (in an article in *Nature* in August 2009),[7] *Nature*'s editor asked me to give some context on all the other work of economists modeling this kind of situation. He quite understandably assumed, given the crucial importance of financial markets to our economy, that economists must have studied thousands of models examining the dynamic interactions among hedge funds, banks, and investors, tested them with data, and achieved a detailed theory of the spiraling feedbacks to which they can lead. It turns out, however, that there are *no* other models, at least none going much beyond the acknowledgment that such things may happen from time to time, and that leverage may make them more likely.

Of course, we're used to the weather doing interesting things, from thunderstorms to windstorms, tornadoes, and hurricanes. Finance and economics have an equally wide variety of stormlike events that emerge out of the ordinary activities of human beings. The quant meltdown hit only a handful of hedge funds using similar strategies; it might be likened to an intense local thunderstorm that hit the North Shore of Boston but didn't extend more than a few miles away. The flash crash hit the stock and stock futures markets hard, but only for a few minutes, and they recovered; it was like a brief but powerful burst of atmospheric turbulence. And the subprime catastrophe and the global economic crisis to which it has led looks more like an unusually powerful hurricane that was brewing and gaining strength and approaching landfall for half a dozen years while economists—their textbooks on financial weather dealing only with the theory of calm blue skies—insisted that everything was fine.

An Atmosphere of Ideas

Greedy bankers have taken a lot of the blame for the recent financial and economic crisis, and I personally think they deserve most of it. Read widely about the crisis, its origins, and aftermath, and it's hard not see a nucleus of greed and plain old corruption. The group Transparency International does an annual ranking of levels of corruption in different nations. In 2000, it ranked the United States number 14; as of 2010 the United States had fallen to number 22. You can understand why the ranking fell when banks such as Goldman Sachs and J. P. Morgan were ignoring laws on a vast scale, yet not a single person from these institutions or any of the other large banks has gone to jail. *Rolling Stone*'s Matt Taibbi put it most eloquently:

> Nobody goes to jail. This is the mantra of the financial-crisis era, one that saw virtually every major bank and financial company on Wall Street embroiled in obscene criminal scandals that impoverished millions and collectively destroyed hundreds of billions, in fact, trillions of dollars of the world's wealth—and nobody went to jail. Nobody, that is, except Bernie Madoff, a flamboyant and pathological celebrity con artist, whose victims happened to be other rich and famous people.[8]

He is right. Lots of greed and corruption have gone unpunished. But putting those vices to one side, I'm going to argue that economists and the theories they've developed bear a deeper and more profound responsibility for the crisis. I certainly don't intend to attack all economists; some do truly important work, teasing out the subtle factors that make poverty so hard to eradicate in Africa and India, for example, or gathering data to test the success or failure of government policies. I do very much intend to criticize the main body of economic theory—generally referred to as neoclassical economics—which represents the mainstream of economic thought on issues ranging from the potential benefits of deregulation to monetary policy.

"Both when they are right and when they are wrong," as the economist John Maynard Keynes once noted, "the ideas of economists and political philosophers are more powerful than is commonly understood. Indeed the world is ruled by little else." The prevailing ideas of economics produce the atmosphere in which most business decisions and government policy making takes place. Here the problem is not that contemporary economists have failed to understand economic systems—an exceedingly difficult task, everyone should admit—but that they have not been honest about their failure. We've all been brainwashed into thinking the economists know more than they actually do.

Over the past three decades, the thrust of mainstream economics has been to encourage governments worldwide to privatize their industries and to deregulate markets; they've generally argued that everything should work better if left to the wisdom of the market. This advice, economists often claim, rests firmly on sophisticated mathematical theories developed initially in the 1950s and improved continuously since then. Like many other physicists, I took an interest in theories of finance and economics about two decades ago when many physicists began branching away from their traditional subject matter and applying the physics way of thinking far more broadly. In looking into the basis of economic theory, I fully expected to find a body of thought and mathematical theory that had been developed with the same commitment to scientific honesty as you find in, say, physics, aeronautical engineering, neuroscience, or social psychology.

The truth is disturbingly different. If you study the economic theorems claiming to explain how markets work, and look closely at the conditions under which those theorems might hold, and then consider what they imply about real markets, you will find a jaw-dropping discrepancy between economists' claims and reality. Again, this does not apply to all economists, but to an awful lot of them. It's as if you began exploring the details of Einstein's theory of relativity and found that actually, despite its reputation as one of the most profound and well-tested theories, despite how physicists rave about it at every opportunity, there were in fact almost no reason to believe it. Your trust in physics and science would rightly be undermined. So it is with economics—at least as it is applied to markets.

This doesn't mean, of course, that markets aren't useful or don't have interesting properties; but it does mean that many economists have perpetrated something tantamount to scientific fraud in presenting economic ideas to the public. It's when economists speak among themselves that the state of economic understanding becomes more apparent. In the spring of 2009, the Ninety-Eighth Dahlem Conference in Dahlem, Germany, brought together a number of economists for five days of discussion on the economic modeling of financial markets. After the meeting, they issued a statement on the economic profession's failure either to see the financial crisis coming or to judge its ultimate severity. The lack of understanding, they suggested in the conference report,[9] can by explained by "a mis-allocation of research efforts in economics. We trace the deeper roots of this failure to the profession's insistence on constructing models that, by design, disregard the key elements driving outcomes in real-world markets. The economics profession has failed in communicating the limitations, weaknesses, and even dangers of its preferred models to the public."

In the following chapters I'm going to explore a little of the history of how economics got itself into the weird position of trying to ignore the most important events that determine market outcomes, especially the most dramatic events. But what matters more is learning how we can do better, and how economic science might be turned into something more deserving of the label "science." The crucial thing, I'll argue, is getting past the archaic fixation on equilibrium, and adopting concepts from the science of "nonequilibrium" systems, of which the earth's atmosphere and ecosystems are natural examples. Beyond mere metaphor, there are deep reasons to think that financial crises really are closely analogous to atmospheric storms and related natural upheavals in physical systems. Understanding such events means grappling with the concepts of positive feedback and natural instability. These ideas find their fullest treatment in physics, so at least part of what we need, I'll argue, is a way of thinking that comes from physics.

This may seem strange. How can physics have anything to do with financial crises?

The Physics of Finance

Say the word "physics" and most people think of Albert Einstein and the theory of relativity, the famous Higgs boson, or maybe the Hubble Space Telescope taking pictures of strange galaxies across the immense distances of the universe (that'd be astrophysics). Physics explores the very edge of what is known, or what is even possible. It's Stephen Hawking talking about black holes and warped space-time, or string theorists asserting that pure mathematics suggests our universe has at least eleven dimensions, although most are hidden to us. Indeed, all of this is a part of physics.

But here's a little secret: physics is changing, profoundly and rapidly, and most physicists today aren't working on any of these things. Look in the journals of physics over the past two decades and you'll find research on the patterns of e-mail use, on the evolution of language, and the way fashions sweep across human populations. You'll find others on genetic signaling networks, the growth patterns of business firms, the structure of the Internet, and the dynamics of the human heart—or the statistics of financial markets. Physics doesn't look like it used to.

What's happened is that physicists have been hit by a revelation.

Today's physicists have inherited from past generations an enormously rich set of mathematical tools and concepts for studying and understanding the physical world. In recent years, they have discovered that many of the same tools and concepts are also uncannily well suited to understanding things elsewhere, in biology and ecology, and in social science. At the deepest level, physics isn't at all just about things that are physical. Rather, it turns out to be a science attuned to answering fundamental questions about order, organization, and change, about forms and their natural patterns of transformation—whether the order and form exists in a collection of molecules, galaxies, genes, bacteria, people, or investors interacting in a market. More than any other science, physics is well placed to understand how lots of pieces or parts or components, in interaction, give rise to often-surprising collective patterns or behaviors in an overall system. The pieces, parts, or components don't have to be electrons or atoms; they might be almost anything.

Here's one simple everyday example. When the curtain closes at any stage theater, the audience bursts into applause. It's usually a few clappers who tentatively start on their own, and then others join in. Applause is a funny thing in which each person tries to give credit to the performers, but also tries to blend into the crowd; you don't want to clap before everyone else, or to go on after others have stopped. In fact, if you study it, you'll discover there is a pronounced pattern in the way an audience goes from silence to full volume of applause. Recordings at theaters around the world show that the pattern transcends different cultural habits and that different crowds all follow one universal curve showing how the sound rises over several seconds. Even more remarkably, this curve is absolutely identical to a curve known from physics that describes how a group of atoms or molecules collectively go from one kind of behavior to another, rapidly and abruptly, because what one does depends very strongly on what others nearby do. They aren't really independent at all.[10]

Applause isn't such an important social phenomenon. But this pattern of collective behavior, changing from one condition (silence) to another (full applause) isn't so different from what happens in a financial market when something new comes along—the Internet, a housing boom—and everyone piles in largely because they see and hear others piling in.

It's this surprising link between physics and patterns of collective behavior that has triggered an incursion of physicists into finance and economics. To be clear, I'm not talking about those physicists—and there are many—who were hired by Wall Street firms to do calculations to price financial instruments in an effort to make money. I'm talking instead about physicists who have looked at markets and economies as natural systems to be understood in the same way we try to understand the earth's crust, or the workings of a living cell. They have been exploring how markets work in normal times, why they plunge so frequently and seemingly as a matter of course into crises, and why economists seem so hapless in seeing them coming.

The short answer that emerges from this work is that the British journalist I quoted at the beginning of this chapter is largely right in saying that economists are "like weather forecasters who do not understand storms."

This book is an exploration of the new vision of markets and economies that is currently emerging from such work. It's my attempt to distill the principal elements of this physics-inspired perspective that takes instabilities and positive feedbacks as a starting point. If you want to understand the most interesting and important elements of the weather—the storms and hurricanes, the rains and clouds and weather fronts and convection cells that make everything happen—you have to go beyond assuming the sky will be blue every day and being surprised when it's not. Natural scientists did so long ago in every other area of science ranging from chemistry to evolutionary biology. Today's economics remains ineffective largely because its only concepts are those based on the notion of balance, while in reality the most important things arise from just the opposite—from forces that stir up imbalance, and whip up whirlwinds and turbulence.

To go further, we have to appreciate just how rapidly markets can get very far out of balance, and how violent financial storms can emerge quite naturally out of what appears to be very fine economic weather. We need to embrace disequilibrium thinking and see economic reality as the outcome of ceaseless change driven by innovation and countless unstable feedbacks. This conceptual shift should be as radical as that ushered in by Adam Smith's metaphor of the invisible hand, and turn much of what we have been taught about markets on its head.

Beyond Equilibrium

As I'll show, disequilibrium thinking transforms our understanding of how markets work—even in "normal" times. If equilibrium economics asserts that markets harness the wisdom of crowds to give an efficient assessment of the true, realistic value of things like stocks, bonds, derivatives, mortgages, and other assets, including houses (this is the so-called efficient market hypothesis), the disequilibrium view of markets dismisses this as a fantasy. Markets price stocks and other assets through the disorganized actions of millions of individuals, firms and funds, traders, brokers, market makers, long- and short-term investors, sophisticated financiers, starry-eyed gamblers, and (increasingly) computer algorithms, all of which influence the flow of information through the market, without any guarantee of anything like a "wise" outcome. The actions of "sophisticated" Wall Street investors often amplify trends rather than correcting them (indeed, following such trends is a popular investing strategy). Anything this complex, depending on the actions of many capricious human beings, cannot be expected to reach a miraculously efficient and stable state of balance.

Rather, the normal state of the market is something more akin to the ever-shifting and changing patterns in the global weather in which new disturbances and storms and patterns emerge in a natural but highly irregular and unpredictable way. I'll examine this in considerable detail in the context of the flash crash, the quant meltdown, the subprime crisis, the crash of 1987, and the Long-Term Capital Management fiasco of 1998, as well as from history. As we'll see, physics-inspired models of financial markets account for these natural fluctuations much more accurately than any theories from economics.

Indeed, disequilibrium thinking transforms our fundamental understanding of cause and effect in markets. We're all used to thinking that dramatic events should have equally dramatic and significant causes. We think a sudden event like the market plunge on May 6, 2010, must have been triggered by a *big* mistake—a fat finger, major computer glitch, or something similar, perhaps the nefarious activity of some brilliant and evil market manipulator.

But disequilibrium systems don't work this way. They follow a natural rhythm in which long periods of relative calm are occasionally shattered by periods of great upheaval. The disequilibrium view suggests that the crashes of May 6 or of 1987 or of 2007–2008 weren't any more abnormal than last year's earthquake in Japan or the 1906 quake in San Francisco. Models developed by physicists show that extreme events can arise quite easily from the shifting patterns of beliefs, expectations, and mood among investors—especially those pertaining to the likely beliefs, expectations, and moods of other investors. Market economies are self-propelling and self-referential systems strongly driven by perceptions and expectations, and these systems routinely develop explosive amplifying feedbacks.

This implies that current thinking about markets rests on an arbitrary and misleading division of events into normal and abnormal, a division with no true basis. This way of thinking makes authorities look for special reasons for big events, while they should (at least in many cases) be looking to the ordinary workings of markets as they're currently set up. The Federal Reserve and other institutions currently charged with forming economic policies think like early man, seeing in storms and lightning the acts of angry gods. Embracing the reality of disequilibrium means coming to terms with the truth of how violent and unusual events nevertheless have perfectly ordinary origins.

I'll also examine how disequilibrium thinking provides the right concepts to explain why it is that crises always seem to surprise us. One of the key concepts of disequilibrium thinking is the notion of "metastability," which explains how a system can seem stable, yet actually be highly unstable, much like the sulfurous coating on a match, ready to explode if it receives the right kind of spark. Inherently unstable and dangerous situations can persist untroubled for very long periods, yet also guarantee eventual disaster. Metastability appears to be the key to explaining the quant meltdown, for example, and it plays a major role in the bursting of any economic bubble, whether in Internet stocks, mortgages, or foreign investment. It is difficult to predict the moment when a bubble will collapse, and equilibrium economics has concluded, therefore, that bubbles aren't real. The disequilibrium view accepts at face value the overwhelming evidence that bubbles do exist—economic history is a veritable champagne glass full of them—yet explains in simple terms why the moment of collapse is so hard to predict: the arrival of the key triggering event is typically a matter of random chance. The deeper lesson is that to understand bubbles we need to identify the conditions that lead to the growth of dangerous feedbacks in the economic system.

In distinct contrast to the restrictive equilibrium view of markets, disequilibrium thinking calls for a "weather manual" for markets. The weather is rich and variable and full of endless surprises. There is no simple and universal "theory of the weather." Instead we have a profusion of associated models and concepts and theories that meteorologists find useful for understanding different aspects of the weather—one for thunderstorms over the plains, another for hurricanes developing over the sea, and another still for fog forming at the earth's surface. Similarly, a science of markets and economics should not seek a universal theory, but rather an assortment of related models and theories attuned to specific phenomena—to rapid market fluctuations driven by high-frequency trading, or to daily movements driven by trend-following speculators, or to instabilities forming over months or years due to larger social changes, such as the trend in subprime lending.

What should unify them all is a focus on how the most important economic phenomena emerge out of feedbacks in the interactions of individuals, firms, governments, and other economic actors. As with the weather, the most significant events in economic systems involve violent shifts from one condition to another (bull to bear market, credit crunch to credit expansion, etc.), shifts that always are driven by positive feedbacks. The disequilibrium view of markets doesn't give immediate answers to any question on markets, any more than basic physics spells out every detail of how the weather works. But it does outline the path to understanding market dynamics by focusing on what really matters—the feedbacks that lead to instability and dramatic change. The task is to identify when and where such feedbacks are likely to become active, how we can detect their presence, and, if it is warranted, take steps to defuse their energy.

As I'll examine in detail, disequilibrium thinking is now beginning to transform our understanding of topics ranging from the stability (or instability) of banking networks to the role of derivatives in markets and the benefits (and costs) of high-frequency computer trading. Banking networks, for example, pose a far greater risk to the financial system than problems on (or off) the balance sheet of any one institution. Banks and other financial firms have grown increasingly interlinked in the past few decades, especially through the proliferation of derivatives instruments. This has introduced an explosion of new kinds of potentially dangerous positive feedbacks. International authorities have recently proposed new banking regulations (the so-called Basel III accords), but these still depend on equilibrium theory and so do nothing to monitor the patterns of linkages between institutions that cause dangerous and destabilizing positive feedbacks.

The past two decades of finance were dominated by a belief that the proliferation of derivative instruments should only make markets more "complete" and therefore more efficient and stable. This pillar of finance theory is based on the equilibrium perspective, but disequilibrium thinking shows that the opposite is true. Derivatives often increase market instability and drive markets toward the edge of trouble. This has policy implications for the regulation of derivatives to protect market function, from which everyone benefits as a public good.

High-frequency computerized trading is the newest threat to the stability of financial markets. Computers that trade thousands of times per second now account for more than half of all trades, and we know virtually nothing about whether there are positive feedbacks between the actions of different computers that could drive markets out of control. The May 6, 2010, event in which the NYSE fell five hundred points in five minutes was an early warning. We will only begin to understand the dangers and threats when we launch a serious effort to model the feedbacks between interacting trading strategies.

Finally, and at the level of metaphor, the disequilibrium view makes it obvious that markets don't "know best." Metaphors affect our worldview more than we generally think, and false metaphors can be especially dangerous. The equilibrium delusion has given false support to the movement to organize as many social activities as possible—including education and basic utilities such as water and public transportation—through private, market-based enterprise. This shift has been defended by reference to equilibrium theories that claim such market-based systems should supply needed goods with greater efficiency. Yet these theories totally ignore positive feedbacks that often lead to very different, and sometimes disastrous, outcomes.

To take one example, the electricity shortages and surging prices afflicting California in the summer of 2000 were puzzling for equilibrium economists. The deregulation of the electricity markets in the mid-1990s had been expected to lower prices by increasing competition, forcing firms to lower their charges to attract more customers. Instead, the market never settled into any equilibrium. Firms such as Enron realized they could manipulate the flow of electricity and make huge profits by causing sharp temporary shortages in some parts of the state and then raising prices. In effect, Enron learned how to create market storms to their own benefit and the citizens of California suffered the consequences. When electricity prices spiked—increasing by 800 percent in a few months toward the end of 2000—this was a surprise only to economists wearing equilibrium blinkers.

More generally, blind faith in the benefits of privatization has had negative social consequences, including the deterioration of overall social trust, the dissolution of traditional nonmarket relations based on social norms, and the replacement of cultural incentives to "to do a good job" with purely monetary incentives. These worrying trends have been documented by political scientists such as Harvard's Robert Putnam in his landmark *Bowling Alone*, or Francis Fukuyama in his book *Trust*. More recently, a host of sociologists and economists have shown how the ascendency of market norms based on competition has often led to the displacement or "crowding out" of beneficial social norms based on cooperation. As a result, policy makers pushing market incentives because of their supposedly superior efficiency have often caused unintended damage by eroding the influence of social norms that long supported the cohesion of communities.

Forecasting?

We need disequilibrium thinking to make intelligent policy. It has emerged out of physics and chemistry, biology and ecology, atmospheric science and geology. The movements of the continents drive earthquakes and the growth of mountain ranges, and ecosystems evolve continually in response to our ever-changing climate. The biggest shift in scientific thinking of the past fifty years has been the movement to understand these "out of equilibrium" systems, which have rich dynamics, never settle into any lasting state of balance, and kick up perpetual surprises and novelties. Alongside this shift in scientific focus has come a shift in methods, as timeless equations akin to those of classical physics are ill suited to describing systems in which ongoing change plays such a distinguishing role.

This movement has helped to bring into stark relief the conceptual problems of contemporary economics, especially its (seemingly intentional) blindness to self-reinforcing feedbacks. In examining this movement, I will by necessity explore some of the details of today's economic theories, and their shortcomings, but I aim to focus primarily on the new insights emerging from creative and groundbreaking work that reaches far beyond these older theories. We are at a truly revolutionary moment in the history of economics, and science, and I hope by reading this book you'll come to see the tremendous opportunities this moment presents. It's ironic, but the recent economic crisis could in the long run be a positive event for the science of economics and finance. With the help of ideas from modern physics, and other sciences, we finally have the chance to slip free of the intellectual straitjacket fitted by economic tradition and to replace it with something much better.

I've given this book the title *Forecast* for a simple reason—knowedge brings with it the ability to predict. Our understanding of the earth's atmosphere and the instabilities and positive feedbacks that drive it has grown gradually over several centuries, and has led to an ability to make forecasts and predictions. Of course, nothing is as fickle and prone to surprises as the weather, but weather science has built up methods for predicting at least the likelihood of various outcomes in different circumstances. Partial accuracy, even simple knowledge of what is possible, can be immensely valuable. I certainly don't think that anyone will soon be making perfectly accurate predictions of the economic or financial future, but we can hope to do some things—forecasting problems likely to emerge under certain conditions, and exploring how they might be avoided. We can be prepared with the knowledge that visions of equilibrium stability are largely illusory, and that we should expect a much more tumultuous ride. I'll take a look at what we might hope to do, and how, in the final chapter.

For five years, we've been swimming in commentary, analysis, and re-analysis of the subprime crisis. We've seen congressional testimony of bankers and financial experts, and been subjected to innumerable newspaper op-eds and blog posts about how it happened and whose fault it was. Numerous books and articles on the episode mostly tell a similar story of how persistently low interest rates in the years following 9/11 fueled the housing bubble, which attracted Wall Street bankers who made enormous profits selling complex derivative products concocted out of increasingly risky subprime mortgages that they sold to gullible investors around the globe, all of which reinforced the bubble itself. Regulators looked the other way.

But this story, true as it may be, is not the most important one. The story behind the story, a more fundamental story of science and ideas and of what went wrong long before the crisis, demands to be told.

2

A Marvelous Machine

Stock price movement represents the aggregate knowledge of Wall
Street and, above all, its aggregate knowledge of coming events.
The stock market represents everything everybody knows, hopes,
believes, anticipates, with all that knowledge sifted down to . . . the
bloodless verdict of the market place.

—William Peter Hamilton, editor, *New York Times*,
The Stock Market Barometer, 1922

The most important single central fact about a free market is that no
exchange takes place unless both parties benefit.

—Milton Friedman

IMAGINE A MARVELOUS COMPUTING machine, a magical device into
which we could inject all the desires of everyone in the world, all their
wishes and worries, knowledge, aims, hopes, expectations, and fears.
Imagine that this machine would devour and digest all this information,
grind and hum, while carrying out a calculation of unimaginable complexity, and then send out explicit instructions to everyone about what
they should do today, where they should work and what they should produce, how much they should sell it for and to whom.

Imagine that scientists had studied this machine and learned how it
worked, and that mathematicians had been able to prove with absolute

certainty that it gave the best possible plans for how to satisfy all our collective wishes and avoid our collective fears. Imagine they had proven that no effort by any group of wise individuals, even if those individuals had infinite intelligence and worked for the lifetime of the universe, could do any better.

This would be a truly miraculous machine, a solution to virtually every societal problem you could dream up. But in fact, you don't have to imagine it. The free market, if you take seriously the theories developed by economists over the past two hundred years, really is a machine of just this sort. Sure, the markets may lurch up and down in unpredictable stomach-churning undulations; they may occasionally cause states to default, banks to fail, and innocent grandmothers to lose their pensions; they may even encourage corruption and fraud and theft. But behind all that chaos, as first suggested by the Scottish economist Adam Smith, there really is a mechanism of amazing power, an "invisible hand," leading the market to wise outcomes for all. The market, many economists claim, is efficient in gathering all the available information there is about the future, information hiding in disorganized fragments in the minds of billions of people, and puts it together to guide human investments and steer our activities in the best possible way.

Is this true? Can markets really be such amazing machines for deciding how to allocate, as economists like to say, our scarce resources and capabilities?

There is indeed something kind of amazing about markets and their ability to organize, even in the absence of any organizer. For the Apple iPhone and iPad there are now more than a hundred thousand available "apps"—software applications designed to carry out tasks that range from booking last-minute travel to recognizing stars in the sky. As of April 2012, one of the more popular apps is Plants vs. Zombies, a bizarre game in which players try to defend their homes from invading zombies with the aid of zombie-killing plants. Developing a new app isn't child's play. Apart from the vision and inspiration of the basic idea, a developer needs to have considerable skill in writing computer code in Objective-C, the language that runs apps on Apple devices, and deep familiarity with a range of software techniques for storing data, laying out the app for ease of use, and so on. The wonder of the market is that no team of Apple engineers had to write and debug the millions of lines of code that make up this ever-growing population of apps, nor did Apple marketers need the genius to foresee a public craving for a game of plants against zombies. An army of unknown individuals from around the world responded quite spontaneously to the opportunities created by the iPhone and iPad, filling every niche and need. The market crafted an exquisite plan—without any planner.

Even so, I am going to argue that the idea of markets as a marvelous self-regulating and stabilizing machine, as developed in economics, is mostly a fantastic dream, and that our understanding of how markets work is actually quite primitive. Economics hasn't really kept up with, and benefited from, the most important new ideas in science and mathematics over the past half century, and today stands to learn a lot from the rest of modern science, physics especially, but also computer science, ecology, and evolutionary biology. Yet lots of smart people have been enthralled by the ideas and mathematics of markets, and they shouldn't be dismissed lightly. So I want to begin in this chapter with an exploration of the economists' vision of the market as a marvelous machine, a vision that has so excited and energized theorists over the past two centuries, and encouraged them to build market theory into the form it takes today.

Of course, even economists don't really believe that the markets are quite as amazing as the machine I've described above; markets often fail in a variety of ways and so fall short of the theoretical ideal. They fail when people lack good information about what's available, or its quality; they get ripped off by the shady garage selling used batteries as if they were new. Markets fail when buyers or sellers have few competitors and can effectively fix their prices; people have no choice but to pay the lone water utility or broadband provider the outrageous sums they demand. Markets fail when it's not easy to switch from one seller to another, or if people have perverse incentives to take on crazy risks because they profit now and won't be the ones who suffer when things go bad. The study of market failures is a small industry in economics.

But the ideal market many economists carry in their heads, the one typically described in their theories, really is like that machine, and it forms the basis for a great deal of thinking—and policy making—about real markets. It's the vision economists hold in their heads for markets in the absence of any failures. We need to begin with a clear picture of what has been accomplished in the way of market theory, and why most economists think the markets often really do possess an amazing efficiency. So, how does this marvelous machine work?

Two Geniuses

Probably the most potent word in market economics over the past fifty years is the word "efficiency." In science and engineering, efficiency means doing something well with minimal waste. An automobile engine is a device for turning the raw chemical energy locked in petroleum fuels into useful, purposeful motion, and an efficient engine loses as little of that energy as possible to friction, waste, heating, and so on. You might expect that economic efficiency would work, more abstractly, on fairly similar principles, referring to the conversion of resources (such as wheat or coal or hot spring water) into salable goods and products with as little waste as possible. That's almost right, but not quite.

Alongside Karl Marx, the Scottish philosopher Adam Smith has the most famous name in economic history. In his 1776 book *The Wealth of Nations*, Smith tried to explain the key factors driving economic realities during the Industrial Revolution. Among other things, he pointed to the division of labor in any nation—based on specialized skills linked to technology or industry—as the factor most responsible for increased production and wealth. Smith saw the Industrial Revolution taking off around him; in 1743, while he was studying at Oxford University, a mill opened in nearby Northampton that employed the parallel operation of fifty spinning machines that turned cotton into threads. In his analysis, Smith hit on the metaphor that has ever since been the guiding light for modern economics— the notion of the invisible hand. In a phrase that has been burned into the memory of students of economics over the past century and more, Smith noted that the typical individual in his or her economic actions

> intends only his own security; and by directing that industry in such a manner as its produce may be of the greatest value, he intends only his own gain, and he is in this, as in many other cases, led by an invisible hand to promote an end which was no part of his intention. Nor is it always the worse for the society that it was not part of it. By pursuing his own interest he frequently promotes that of the society more effectually than when he really intends to promote it.[1]

We may all be selfish and greedy, in other words, typically seeking only our own ends. Even so, our actions often produce products or provide services that end up benefiting others and the community as a whole as well.

Economists love talking about Adam Smith, and for good reason. His profound arguments cut through age-old prejudices and changed the world with a counterintuitive idea—that less control and conscious design of what people do can actually improve economic organization and outcomes. As Alan Greenspan noted in a 2005 speech when he was chairman of the Federal Reserve Board:

> Smith, on remarkably little formal empirical evidence, drew broad inferences about the nature of commercial organization and institutions that led to a set of principles that would profoundly influence and alter a significant segment of the civilized world of that time. Economies based on those principles first created levels of sustenance adequate to enable the population to grow and later—far later—to create material conditions of living that fostered an increase in life expectancy . . . Most of Smith's free-market paradigm remains applicable to this day."[2]

But Greenspan and other modern economists aren't smitten with Smith's invisible hand merely because they think he knew what he was talking about, or because famous economists over the past two centuries from David Ricardo and Alfred Marshall to Friedrich von Hayek and Milton Friedman have celebrated those ideas. Their conviction comes from more than two hundred years of further development in which economists have put hard mathematical theory behind Smith's prose and metaphor. Ironically enough, it all got started in the late nineteenth century when economists tried to adapt their own field to the latest ideas of physics.

The notion of a state of balance or equilibrium dates to prehistory and the cosmological assumptions of the earliest religions. The equilibrium of the body has been at the center of medical thinking since the time of the Greek physician Hippocrates, and the Greek physicist and inventor Archimedes used the idea of an equilibrium balance to understand the action of levers and other simple machines. But the idea of equilibrium became more than metaphor after Isaac Newton's publication in 1678 of *Principia Mathematica*, or *The Mathematical Principles of Natural Philosophy*, in which he described his theory of gravitation and laws of motion for the planets, as well as for ordinary objects and machines. In Newton's theory, unbalanced forces acting on any object—a rock, a bird, or a planet—will cause it to accelerate, and this acceleration will continue until the force stops acting, or until other forces come into play to balance against it.

The result, when forces balance, is equilibrium—a rock resting stably on the ground, or the many pieces of a great bridge locked in a stable and self-supporting structure.

There is, of course, nothing wrong with this idea of equilibrium; it is a concept of the first order of genius, and explains many things. Think of the atmosphere as a pile of air just resting in equilibrium and you get reasonable numbers for the pressure at the earth's surface, and how it falls off with increasing height—by a factor of about ten every thirteen miles or so. In the latter part of the nineteenth century, as Newtonian physics came to dominate all science and engineering, sparking the Industrial Revolution, it took on exceptionally elegant mathematical form in the works of Joseph Lagrange and William Rowan Hamilton, among others. Lagrange, in particular, showed that the laws of mathematical physics then known implied a principle of "least action"—that the motions of things in the universe, no matter how complex they appear, always act to minimize a certain quantity. It's as if the universe itself has a principle of maximum efficiency.

The French mathematician Antoine Augustin Cournot, like many others at the time, felt sure that a similar mathematical science of society could not be far behind, and applied the idea of equilibrium balance to analyzing supply and demand, pointing out, in particular, the high prices one should naturally expect in the presence of a monopoly. Aside from Cournot, economics was then still dominated by verbal arguments, without any mathematics, but Cournot's efforts inspired others, especially Léon Walras—the son of a French economist who had some early training in engineering—to change that. In 1874, in a book called *Elements of Pure Economics*, Walras showed how the notion of mechanical equilibrium could be used as a conceptual template to build an analogous theory of economics, and to give a precise mathematical expression to Smith's invisible hand.

The Mathematics of Equilibrium

Every introductory economics text begins with the basic idea of supply and demand. Prices of heating oil and gasoline in the United States aren't set by acts of Congress or presidential decree, but rather by supply and demand on an international oil market. Most people think the supply comes mainly from Saudi Arabia and other nations in the Middle East, and this is true, but Russia supplies more than 10 percent and the United States nearly 10 percent, with other significant suppliers including China, Canada, Mexico, Brazil, and Venezuela. All of this oil gets sold to energy companies on commodities exchanges, principally the International Petroleum Exchange in London. As the price of oil rises, people generally want or demand less of it, turning their thermostats down or driving less. At the same time, producers want to make or supply more of it, in the hope of greater profits. If civil war or international conflict disrupts production, prices will naturally rise. They will continue to rise until demand falls sufficiently so that at one unique price supply and demand will be equal. At this equilibrium point, producers won't be supplying too much, leaving a surplus, or too little, with lines of unsatisfied customers. At this point, supply equals demand and economic forces balance.

This basic story was already well known in Walras's time, and simple enough to think about for one good—oil or wrenches or hiking boots. But any real economy has thousands or even millions of goods and different markets for fruit, shipbuilding, haircutting, and so on. Walras tried to show mathematically that the same kind of balance of supply and demand might naturally come to hold in the more complicated case with a vast range of distinct markets in different goods. He thought he had achieved it, writing to a colleague, mathematician Paul Matthieu Hermann Laurent, that "all these results are marvels of the simple application of the language of mathematics to the quantitative notion of need or utility . . . You can be sure that the economic laws that result from it are just as rational, just as precise and just as incontrovertible as were the laws of astronomy at the end of the 17th century."[3]

Another economist at the same time—Englishman William Stanley Jevons—independently came up with much the same idea. Walras and Jevons's equilibrium theories put a crude workable mathematical model behind the invisible hand, but there was an important limitation: in the language of mathematics, their conclusions weren't absolutely proven, merely suggested.

As a result, Smith's tantalizing notion had to wait for its Isaac Newton until 1954, when two economic theorists—Kenneth Arrow and Gérard Debreu—finally accomplished what many economists took to be the economic equivalent of Newton's *Principia Mathematica*, wrapping a vast quantity of deep insight into a few elegant lines of mathematics.

Arrow and Debreu's theory is as laden with mathematics as any calculation in Newtonian physics, and to extend the simple idea that supply equals demand to an economy with a huge number of different goods and markets they turned to a theorem proven by Dutch mathematician Luitzen Brouwer in 1912. To get an idea of how Brouwer's theorem can be used to prove some counterintuitive things, consider the following: take a U.S. map and lay it down flat on the ground somewhere in the United States. Put it anywhere you like. Brouwer's theorem proves that there will be a point on that map that lies exactly, directly over the real corresponding spot on the earth. This is a mathematical fact, but it is certainly not obvious.

Working from Brouwer's theorem (whose principles extend to many subjects besides maps), Arrow and Debreu were able to prove something crucial. In an abstract model of an economy with many consumers and producers, they showed, a set of prices must exist that like the invisible hand act to organize everyone to make mutually compatible choices. This was exactly what Walras and Jevons had supposed. How this set of prices might come to be—in the helter-skelter buying and selling of the marketplace—Arrow and Debreu couldn't say; Brouwer's theorem let them steer around the messy problem of how people actually make decisions. But the marketplace could in principle organize and coordinate an immense complexity of conflicting goals and demands through a single set of prices; this they proved.

For economists of the time, it was a stunning achievement. As economist John Geanakoplos of Yale University put it later in a 1987 review article on the Arrow-Debreu result, "The most striking feature of the general equilibrium is the juxtaposition of the great diversity in goals and resources it allows, together with the supreme coordination it requires. Every desire of each consumer, no matter how whimsical, is met precisely by the voluntary supply of some producer. And this is true for all markets and consumers simultaneously."[4]

Now, Arrow and Debreu did have to take a giant leap into the abstract in proving their result. Economic goods in their model economy are not simply things like apples or tires. Rather, a good has to be specified by where and when it exists, as well as by the "state of the world" at the time. An apple on a sunny day in Oregon in 2012 following a bountiful harvest is a totally different good, with totally different economic value, from an apple, even the identical variety, in a Parisian street market in wartime

1942. They also had to assume that it is always possible for people to exchange such goods, even if those people live in different economies and in different centuries, that no barriers of space or time or anything else get in the way of carrying out any conceivable trade.

But by invoking this level of mathematical detail, Arrow and Debreu could prove more than the existence of market equilibrium. They were also able to prove that this perfect "competitive equilibrium" between supply and demand in all goods should be "efficient" in the sense that all resources would be put to the most productive use in satisfying the demands of consumers. The equilibrium would be what economists call "Pareto optimal," in that no conceivable fiddling with prices or the quantities of various things being produced, even by some infinitely intelligent central planner, could lead to a better overall result without at least one individual or firm being made worse off. That is, there is no direction for pure improvement. These results go under the name of the "welfare theorems" of economics, and have exerted a huge orienting influence on all subsequent research and thinking. These welfare theorems, MIT economist Franklin Fisher has noted, "provide the rigorous justification for the idea that free markets are desirable (although they say nothing about fairness or any other attribute other than Pareto efficiency). It is not an overstatement to say that they are the underpinning of western capitalism."[5]

Guided by the invisible hand, the market, it seemed, really does know best. This is one sense in which economists have shown—under various assumptions required to let the mathematical proofs go through—that markets are efficient. But it's not the only way they use this word. To understand what economists mean by "efficient," we have to consider another meaning, too.

Predictably Unpredictable

There is an alluring elegance to all these concepts. In principle, Arrow and Debreu's equilibrium theory applies to supply and demand in the financial markets just as it does to any other market. The goods in the financial markets are stocks, bonds, and all the other exotic instruments sold by governments, investment banks, insurance companies, and so on. We can buy and sell and trade them with confidence—mathematical certainty, in fact—that our actions are in the best interests of the society or world in which we are economic actors. Yet, doesn't this inspiring vision of calm repose in perfect equilibrium with optimal efficiency seem rather out of joint with the perpetual helter-skelter turmoil of real financial markets? How on earth can perfect equilibrium possess an unending capacity to surprise us?

Late on Friday, August 5, 2011, and for the first time in its history since 1917, the credit ratings agency Standard and Poor's downgraded the credit rating of the United States government, moving it from AAA to AA+. The downgrade, the agency explained, "reflects our view that the effectiveness, stability, and predictability of American policy making and political institutions have weakened at a time of ongoing fiscal and economic challenges."[6]

On the following Monday, August 8, Wall Street had its worst day since the 2008 financial crisis. By the end of the day, all three major U.S. stock indices had lost between 5 percent and 7 percent of their value. Surely, one might think, Tuesday would be even worse. But it wasn't. On Tuesday, the markets shot right back up close to where they'd been at the weekend. The tumult then continued through the week, with the Standard and Poor's 500 Index—a weighted average of the stocks of five hundred leading U.S. companies—posting alternating gains and losses of more than 4 percent on four trading days in a row, another historic first.

Unpredictable movement is the most obvious feature of stock markets, and there's a good reason for that. Let's do a thought experiment, which I'll call the 5 percent problem. Suppose that on Tuesday morning everyone knew for sure that the markets would recover, stocks gaining 5 percent (on average) in a big rally in the final half hour at the end of the day. Everyone in the market would expect this rise, and lots of people on that morning would be eager to pay up to 5 percent more than current values to buy stock, as they would profit by selling at the day's very end. Knowledge of the coming afternoon rise would make the market rise immediately in the morning, violating the assumption we made to start this thought experiment; the prediction of a late rally would be wrong. The idea of a predictable market is simply self-contradictory, as an American agricultural researcher named Holbrook Working pointed out in 1949. "If it is possible under any given set of circumstances to predict future price changes and have the predictions fulfilled, it follows that the market expectations must have been defective; ideal market expectations would have taken full account of the information which permitted successful prediction of the price change."[7]

If what Working argued is true, then we can predict that markets will be unpredictable, by definition. And this odd fact is why ordered equilibrium and perpetual chaos can be seen as two sides of the same coin.

Working knew of a number of prominent studies in the 1930s and 1940s showing that the stock market forecasts of the supposed experts—stock forecasting companies, prominent newspaper analysts, and so on—weren't actually superior to stocks picked just by flipping a coin. In one study, for example, Alfred Cowles had examined the success of stock picks made by roughly fifty statistical stock analysis services, insurance companies, and forecasting letters, and found their success to be "little, if any, better than what might be expected to result from pure chance."[8]

Working wondered if this failure might actually point to something inherently positive in the dynamics of the market, a tendency for investors' actions to bring all information into the market as quickly as possible, thereby destroying any predictable patterns. As he wrote, "[The] apparent imperfection of professional forecasting . . . may be evidence of perfection of the market . . . The failures of stock market forecasters . . . reflect credit on the market."

This was simple conjecture, plausible as it may have sounded. But in 1965, economist Paul Samuelson of MIT put Working's argument into mathematical form in a paper entitled "Proof that Properly Anticipated Prices Fluctuate Randomly." Essentially, Samuelson used mathematics to consider how intelligent, rational investors would respond in the presence even of some very weak market predictability—say, a known probability of just over 50 percent that if IBM stock fell last week it would instead rise this week. Playing out this little experiment, he reached the same conclusion shown by the 5 percent problem: if investors acted rationally and used all information available, their actions would change the dynamics of the market, in effect wiping out that very predictability.

What all this shows is that if people really do act rationally and use all information available, stock movements should be unpredictable. At the end of Samuelson's paper, he was careful to point out that he was only doing mathematics, exploring an if-then linkage between certain assumptions and their logical implications, and that nothing he said implied anything at all about real markets, because he didn't pretend to know how real people behave:

One should not read too much into the established theorem. It does not prove that actual competitive markets work well. It does not say that speculation is a good thing or that randomness of price changes would be a good thing. It does not prove that anyone who makes money in speculation is ipso facto deserving of the gain or even that he has accomplished something good for society or for anyone but himself. All or none of these may be true, but that would require a different investigation.[9]

Even so, this one piece of pure logic was enough to stir another young economist, Eugene Fama of the University of Chicago, to go further. In his 1964 dissertation thesis entitled "The Behaviour of Stock Prices," then later in a famous paper in 1970, Fama introduced what has come to be the most influential of all ideas in finance. Fama took Samuelson's mathematical theorem and asserted that something like it is true for real markets: it's not only a theorem of mathematics, but also a theory of the real world.

The Efficient Market Hypothesis

The world's first stock market took shape in the first decade of the seventeenth century when Dutch investors began trading shares of the United East India Company—originally chartered in 1602 with a monopoly on Dutch trade with the East—first in open-air markets and then later in the specially built *Beurs*. By the end of the century, when a Spanish merchant named Joseph de la Vega chronicled the character of these early markets in a book entitled *Confusion of Confusions,* he noted that those in the markets weren't always upright, moral, or well-intentioned. The business of the market, as he described it, is "at once the fairest and the most deceitful in Europe, the noblest and most infamous in the world, the finest and the most vulgar on the earth. It is a quintessence of academic learning and a paragon of fraudulence; it is a touchstone for the intelligent and a tombstone for the audacious, a treasury of usefulness and a source of disaster."[10]

But de la Vega also noted the extreme lengths to which traders would go to find scraps of information giving them an advantage. In the early markets of Amsterdam or later in London, prominent investors hired dozens of young men to hang around the docks, talking and inquiring, seeking gossip from travels—the world's first stock tips. In 1815, according to legend, the London financier Nathan Rothschild had carrier pigeons released following the battle of Waterloo, which then flew to London and gave him news of the outcome before anyone else. He made a mint buying British bonds, and selling soon after when their value rocketed. For this and other ruthless actions he earned a reputation among contemporaries as a man of inhuman cunning, who appeared to lack a soul. As one described him, "Eyes are usually called the windows of the soul. But in Rothschild's case you would conclude that the windows are false ones, or that there was no soul to look out of them. There comes not one pencil of light from the interior, neither is there one gleam of that which comes from without reflected in any direction. The whole puts you in mind of an empty skin."[11]

Today, of course, the perpetual search for information is just as important as it was then, and furthered just as much by technology. A subscriber to the Bloomberg Professional Service offered by Bloomberg News, for example, can learn in a few seconds about an oil discovery, a rumor of a firm in financial distress, or anything else influencing the fate of a company, market, industry, or government.

Next to unpredictability, this is the second most obvious thing about markets: investors seek information ravenously and the markets revolve around it. As Samuelson suggested, this information seeking and the random movements of markets are not independent; rather, the former tends to enforce the latter. Fama suggested that this might be the most important sense in which markets are efficient—as gatherers and processors of information. As he noted in his thesis, nothing in the market is as obvious as the mass scramble for information:

> Although some people may be primarily motivated by whim, there are many individuals and institutions that seem to base their actions in the market on an evaluation (usually extremely painstaking) of economic and political circumstances. That is, there are many private investors and institutions who believe that individual securities have "intrinsic values" which depend on economic and political factors that affect individual companies.[12]

Equally obvious, Fama pointed out, was that market prices really do move randomly, or at least in a way that is very hard to predict. Apart from Working's or Samuelson's arguments, that idea had actually been around since the Ph.D. thesis of the French physicist Louis Bachelier in 1900, who, in a work entitled *Théorie de la Spéculation,* developed a mathematical model to describe market prices moving randomly, taking small steps up or down at each moment, with subsequent movements being independent of one another, the entire process lacking predictability.

Putting this all together, Fama proposed a satisfying synthesis of how markets work—the efficient market hypothesis, he called it—with information at the center. Of course, it's important that it was not a fact but a *hypothesis*, a proposed truth based on plausible inference and observations. Fama's hypothesis asserts that markets move randomly, and do so precisely because of the voracious information gathering of investors. The result is good or efficient: all the information very rapidly (even instantaneously, in the ideal picture) comes to be reflected in market prices. There's no bit of information known by someone and implying a significant change in the value of a stock that the market hasn't already incorporated.

In this view, a market is a vast crowd of investors with diverse interests and skills all working hard to gather information on every kind of manufacturing company, bank, nation, technology, raw material, and so on. They use that information to make the best investments they can, jumping on any new information that might affect prices as it comes along, and using that information to profit. They sell currently overvalued stocks, bonds, or other instruments, and buy undervalued ones. These very actions act to drive the prices back toward their proper, realistic, or "intrinsic" values, as Fama put it at the time (usage has subsequently changed and economists now use the term "fundamental" rather than "intrinsic").

Hence, greed on the part of individuals has a miraculous effect—just as Adam Smith suggested centuries ago. New information is always coming along, perturbing the market, which then adjusts to a new equilibrium. It always returns to equilibrium because people seeking profits naturally drive it there. Moreover, market movements are necessarily random and unpredictable because investors acting to use all available information make it so. The result, Fama later wrote when revisiting the idea in 1970, was that markets really are efficient:

The primary role of the capital market is allocation of ownership of the economy's capital stock. In general terms, the ideal is a market in which the prices provide accurate signals for resource allocation: that is, a market in which firms can make production-investment decisions, and investors can choose among the securities that represent ownership of firms' activities under the assumption that security prices at any time "fully reflect" all available information. A market in which prices always "fully reflect" available information is called "efficient."[13]

Again, it is important to note that the word "efficient" as it is used here isn't quite the same as the word "efficient" in the work of Arrow and Debreu. For Fama, the market is efficient in terms of how it uses information, what he refers to as "information efficiency." As finance professor Andrew Lo of MIT notes, informational efficiency has a "Zen-like, counterintuitive flavour to it." The more efficient the market, "the more random the sequence of price changes generated by such a market, and the most efficient market of all is one in which price changes are completely random and unpredictable. This is not an accident of nature, but is in fact the direct result of many active market participants attempting to profit from their information."[14]

The efficient market hypothesis, like any other hypothesis, required testing. Since Fama wrote his breakthrough paper, thousands of researchers have refined his original idea and gathered a wealth of empirical evidence that many real markets seem to be information efficient or fairly close to it. There seem to be few predictable patterns in markets, especially patterns resilient enough to be used to make profits. When new information arrives in the market it really does impact prices quickly and does so in the way the efficient market hypothesis suggests.

For example, in March 2012, Greg Smith, an executive director in charge of derivatives at Goldman Sachs, announced his resignation in a prominent and instantly infamous op-ed in the *New York Times*. Smith complained about a progressive erosion of values at the investment bank in his time there over the past twelve years:

> I can honestly say that the environment now is as toxic and destructive as I have ever seen it . . . In the simplest terms, the interests of the client continue to be sidelined in the way the firm operates and thinks about making money. Goldman Sachs is one of the world's largest and most important investment banks and it is too integral to global finance to continue to act this way. The firm has veered so far from the

place I joined right out of college that I can no longer in good con-
science say that I identify with what it stands for.[15]

Within a day, the price of Goldman Sachs stock shares fell 3.5 percent,
wiping more than $1 billion off the firm's value, as investors apparently
concluded that the views expressed by Smith would either hurt Goldman's reputation with clients, or reflected ugly truths about its culture
that would undermine its future prospects.

All in all, the idea of market efficiency fits with common experience
and explains why, in practice, it is so damned hard to beat the market
consistently: anything you can do it can do better. There are zillions of
smart people with vast resources out there gobbling up every piece of
useful information, then buying or selling stocks based on it. Hence the
prices of stocks and bonds and houses and other things should always be
just about right, because the market acts to make them so.

The Spiral to Efficiency

There is one final step in understanding just what economists mean when
they claim, as they often do, that markets today are "more efficient than
ever before." Arrow and Debreu's remarkable proof showed how markets
are efficient in one sense: they ensure optimal allocation of resources
(e.g., wheat) across competing uses (bread, flour, beer). The efficient market hypothesis asserts something quite different—that markets are "information efficient" and act very rapidly to incorporate any new information
(e.g., news of a drought that kills wheat crops) into prices (lowering stock
in agribusiness). Is there any way to link these two different meanings?
Or are they just entirely distinct?

If the two forms of efficiency are truly unrelated, then we have a serious
threat to the vision of the invisible hand. Arrow and Debreu's theory—
as we'll see in a little more detail next chapter—is highly abstract and
its ideal doesn't obviously reflect what might go on in real markets. The
theory talks of producers and consumers, but it doesn't even mention financial markets. Fama's version of efficiency does seem to hold for real
markets, at least roughly, and yet information efficiency could easily be
less than what it seems. In principle, the market might absorb and reflect
all information very rapidly, but reflect it in a very bad way, yielding an

entirely inaccurate and damaging allocation of resources that is anything but optimal.

Not to worry. In the 1960s and 1970s, other economists—notably Roy Radner, now at New York University, and Robert Lucas of the University of Chicago—picked up where Arrow and Debreu left off. As they noted, Arrow and Debreu hadn't really dealt in any fundamental way with uncertainty and expectations, with those aspects of the world that really drive financial markets and make them interesting and dynamic. Doing so meant ratcheting up the mathematics and extending Arrow and Debreu's framework to apply to an infinite sequence of markets, one for each moment in time, in a setting where real happenings in the world, weather, inventions, wars, and so on, change prospects and people try to respond by buying and selling not only physical things but financial instruments that let them express their expectations, optimistic or pessimistic as they may be. The resulting theory of "rational expectations equilibrium" did demonstrate that a theory like Arrow and Debreu's really does imply the truth of Fama's efficient market hypothesis. Hence, there is a link between the two meanings, and the efficiency of Fama can indeed be the efficiency of Arrow-Debreu—efficiency that implies automatically optimal outcomes.[16]

This was the final step to proving that markets are indeed the marvelous machines we dreamed of at the beginning of the chapter. The mathematics also came with a lesson—that markets should work best if they are what economists call "complete." Roughly speaking, this means that every kind of deal has to be possible and there can be no impediments to people making any kind of trade or bet at any moment. A complete market is an ideal market in which investors have access to a vast array of financial instruments that they can use to profit from any piece of information, no matter how obscure or specialized.

Suppose, for example, that it is spring of 2004 and the global housing and credit bubble has been inflating rapidly for a decade. Your friends are saying "housing prices always go up," but you've been doing mountains of research and come to the conclusion that financial Armageddon lies just in the future. You've seen advertisements for "interest-only, negative-amortizing, adjustable-rate subprime mortgages," meaning a buyer has the option of paying nothing at all for a time, just adding interest to the principal balance. You know, because you've been doing your homework, that this is fine if prices *do* always go up and the house can be resold for profit in the future; but it's a disaster if housing prices ever fall. In this situation, you might want to buy—as hedge fund manager Michael Burry did—investments that would pay off if and when the housing bubble burst. That product is what is known as a credit default swap on subprime mortgage bonds—essentially an insurance policy that pays off if the bond goes into default. Burry bought roughly $1 billion of such insurance contracts and ended up making $100 million for himself and $725 million for his fund's investors.[17]

A complete market makes it possible for any kind of information to get expressed in the market.

Today's markets aren't complete, not by a long shot. Indeed, when Burry first wanted to buy credit default swaps on subprime mortgage bonds such things did not exist. He had to convince Goldman Sachs and Deutsche Bank to create the products to sell to him, something that few people without his insider knowledge and contacts could have done. This incompleteness explains one of the most direct influences market theory has had on government policy, because the theory implies that a clear way to make markets more efficient is by eliminating every last obstacle to trading arising from market incompleteness. In practice, this means two things. First, it means market deregulation: a market can become more complete only by removing any legal barriers preventing people from engaging freely in trades if they think they can benefit. Second, it also means more derivatives: after all, derivatives such as options and all their more exotic cousins are simply tools for making any kind of trade or exchange possible, human imagination being the only limit.

The ultimate vision of efficiency through completeness has been among the key forces driving the massive financial deregulation of the 1980s and 1990s, as well as the explosive growth in the derivatives industry. Both trends can be seen as pushing markets ever closer to the ideal of completeness. The result, as economists Robert Merton and Zvi Bodie argued in 2005, is markets that are not only pretty efficient, but that grow ever more efficient with time, because the innovations making the market more efficient are precisely those paying off. As investment banks and brokers and insurance companies and hedge funds dream up ways to put together ever more finely crafted trades, said Merton and Bodie, "[the] success of these trading markets and custom products encourages investment in creating additional markets and products, and so on it goes, spiralling toward the theoretically limiting case of zero marginal transactions costs and dynamically complete markets."[18]

And just as derivatives have made markets more complete, financial deregulation has removed barriers to the efficient flow of information, letting anyone who has information express it in markets across the globe very quickly. Many people still think of the U.S. stock market as the New York Stock Exchange, but the market has been utterly transformed following deregulation in the 1990s. Indeed, computers have so transformed the stock markets that close to 80 percent of all stock shares traded in the United States now get exchanged by computers running algorithms. On these exchanges there are no harried traders shouting and screaming while swimming in paper debris. The trading hub of Direct Edge—an exchange accounting for nearly 10 percent of all U.S. stock trades—sits in an unassuming warehouse in a business park off the New Jersey Turnpike, where a bank of computer servers carries out millions of trades per second for Wall Street banks, hedge funds, and brokerage firms. The time it takes an investor to learn some valuable bit of information and trade on it has fallen to seconds, or even less. The fastest trades now happen in less than one ten thousandth of a second.

The pistons of the marvelous machine are firing ever faster.

As a result of all this—speed, deregulation, more derivatives, and so on—markets, many economists argue, have become ever more efficient. This vision of the invisible hand, dreamed up originally by Adam Smith, has been backed up by Arrow and Debreu, Samuelson, Fama, and finally Radner and Lucas, not to mention thousands of other economists. Empirically, the markets appear to be unpredictable just as market efficiency implies they should be, apparently because information flows quickly and efficiently into the market where it gets reflected in an optimal allocation of investment funds.

Perhaps it is no accident, then, that stocks in the United States over the past thirty years have outpaced those of any other Western nation, reflecting the greater efficiency of investments flowing out of an efficient capital-market-oriented U.S. system.

The Markets Know Best

The history given in this chapter is intended to give only the crudest picture of how economics, and especially the economics of markets, has evolved. I've left out a huge amount and many brilliant characters, but I think it's easy to see, given all these theoretical advances, why econo-mists were so satisfied with market evolution, at least prior to the sudden crisis in 2008. Their confidence was based on a lot of hard work by some very intelligent people.

The vision expressing everything economists thought they had estab-lished about markets and their automatic efficiency was clearly expressed in a 2004 report authored for Goldman Sachs by economists R. Glenn Hubbard of Columbia University and William Dudley, then at Goldman Sachs. Market theory, they claimed, had made markets much more effi-cient, especially in the United States and the United Kingdom where that theory had been taken most seriously.[19] "The ascendancy of the US capital markets—including increasing depth of US stock, bond, and derivative markets—has improved the allocation of capital and of risk throughout the US economy . . . The same conclusions apply to the United Kingdom, where the capital markets are also well-developed."

And the spiral toward market efficiency wasn't just helping bankers and the financial industry, but everyone:

> The development of the capital markets has provided significant ben-efits to the average citizen. Most importantly, it has led to more jobs and higher wages . . . The capital markets have also acted to reduce the volatility of the economy. Recessions are less frequent and milder when they occur. As a result, upward spikes in the unemployment rate have occurred less frequently and have become less severe.

What about derivatives—things like options and futures and credit de-fault swaps? In making the markets more complete, these, too, were mak-ing them ever more efficient, in part by helping investors spread their risks more effectively:

> The development of the capital markets has helped distribute risk more efficiently. Part of the efficient allocation of capital is the transfer of risk to those best able to bear it—either because they are less risk averse or because the new risk is uncorrelated or even negatively cor-related with other risks in a portfolio. This ability to transfer risk facili-tates greater risk-taking, but this increased risk-taking does not destabilize the economy. The development of the derivatives market has played a particularly important role in this risk-transfer process.

Finally, not only was the steadily improving efficiency of markets de-livering excellent economic and financial outcomes, but it was also hav-ing a salient effect on the political system. In the most optimistic discussions of the spiral to efficiency, markets spill outward into every-thing else, including politics, where leaders can make better decisions only if they look to the efficient markets for inspiration:

> By providing immediate feedback to policymakers, the capital markets have increased the benefits of following good policies and increased the cost of following bad ones. Good policies result in lower risk pre-mia and higher financial asset prices. Investors are supportive. Bad policies lead to bad financial market performance, which increases in-vestor pressure on policymakers to amend their policy choices. As a result, the quality of economic policymaking has improved over the past two decades, which has helped improve economic performance and macroeconomic stability.

For the enthusiasts, at least before everything went so very sour, his-tory and the science of finance really did seem to be leading to greater efficiency in the economists' sense, a financial technology with very little waste driving an optimal allocation of resources.

Following the crisis of course, we may wonder if all these geniuses, and all this math, might not have a fatal flaw.

Notable Exceptions

With notably rare exceptions (2008, for example), the global
"invisible hand" has created relatively stable exchange rates,
interest rates, prices and wage rates.

—Alan Greenspan, former chairman of the
Federal Reserve Bank

With notably rare exceptions, Germany remained largely at
peace with its neighbors during the 20th century.

With notably rare exceptions, Alan Greenspan
has been right about everything.

—Comments on the blog *Crooked Timber*

FIVE YEARS LATER, WE KNOW BETTER. DESPITE decades, even centuries, of influential economic theory, the global economic crisis has been a very expensive disproof of the idea of the self-regulating market equilibrium. Estimates of the monetary costs linked directly to the crisis come to about $4 trillion for the United States (more than $10,000 for every last individual), £140 billion for the U.K. with comparable losses in Europe and elsewhere.[1] Indirect costs point to global figures reaching perhaps $50 trillion. That's just so far.

But let's be charitable and push the current crisis to one side. Some people insist that the crisis had nothing to do with bad economics, that the banks behaved responsibly, that everything on Wall Street helped the economy rather than hurt it.[2] A determined mind can fit almost any event into a preferred interpretation. Does the scientific evidence, otherwise, support the idea of efficient market equilibrium? The answer, as I'll show, is an overwhelming no, at least if you interpret "efficient" in any meaningful and interesting way. Alluring as it may be, the picture I presented in the preceding chapter is little more than a fanciful illusion. This argument begins with the famous mathematical theorems of Arrow and Debreu, which don't have the massive explanatory power they've been ascribed. We can look to the simplest physics of everyday objects to understand why.

Conjure an image in your mind: a pencil resting on a small table, perhaps next to a notebook. Now, quickly: what position did you imagine the pencil in? Lying on its side, right? Why not upright, with either the eraser or the graphite tip touching the table and the rest pointing into the air? In terms of strict physical forces, it's possible to position a pencil this way. But we never see it happen—and thus never worry about imagining it— because even the tiniest vibration, from the rumble of someone tapping the table to a slight shift in air currents, will knock it over.

The upright pencil is in what's called unstable equilibrium, a state of being that can exist if unperturbed, but that will change rapidly if given the tiniest shock from the physical world, which is of course inevitable. By contrast, a pencil lying on its side is in stable equilibrium. Blow on it, even slam your fist on the table, and the pencil will stay in that position, or bounce around momentarily and then go back to it. In this position, the pencil is immune to the small forces that would cause it to fall from the upright position.

Stable equilibria are generally more important than unstable,[3] because things in such states stay there. Whether we're thinking of physical forces affecting a pencil or economic forces affecting the Dow Jones Industrial Average, we can expect something to stay near a stable equilibrium, but to wander away from an unstable one. So whenever we consider a state of equilibrium, we've got to ask whether or not it's stable. The general equilibrium of Arrow and Debreu, or of its rational expectations generalizations as developed by Lucas and others, is really only worth thinking about if there's reason to believe that it is stable, so that an economy might actually get itself into this special state, and then hang around close to it. Mathematical economists knew this very well, and proving the stability of the Arrow-Debreu equilibrium became the primary grand challenge for theoretical economics from 1954 on.

The field had to wait two decades, until the mid-seventies, when economist Hugo Sonnenschein, with additions from Debreu and Rolf Mantel, established a definitive result by thinking about the process by which supply might come to be equal to demand.[4] Before that ultimate moment of balance, there must in some cases be more demand for certain products than there is supply; this "excess demand" could drive some people to create more of that product. You might think that the process should be relatively simple, pushing an economy toward an eventual balance. In contrast, the mathematics showed that—given plausible differences in peoples' initial wealth and preferences for various products—an economy of the Arrow-Debreu type might have prices that never settle down and could over time follow essentially any crazy pattern you like.

This discovery came as a massive blow to many economists at the time, as economist Alan Kirman notes in his book *Complex Economics*. Writing in 1994, economist Werner Hildenbrand looked back and recalled how utterly shattering these results were to the vision of gaining a solid understanding of economics through equilibrium:

> When I read in the seventies publications of Sonnenschein, Mantel and Debreu on the structure of the excess demand function of an exchange economy, I was deeply consternated [*sic*]. Up to that time I had the naive illusion that the microeconomic foundation of the general equilibrium model, which I admired so much, does not only allow us to prove that the model and the concept of equilibrium are logically consistent, but also allows us to show that the equilibrium is well determined. This illusion, or should I say rather this hope, was destroyed, once and for all, at least for the traditional model of exchange economies.[5]

All efforts since then to show that a realistic economy might actually reach something like the Arrow-Debreu equilibrium have met with continuing failure.[6] Theorists haven't been able to prove that even trivial, childlike models of economies with only a few commodities have stable equilibria. There is no reason to think that the theoretical general equilibrium so prized by economists is anything more than a curiosity.

The original theory of Walras was simple, but the real economy isn't.

As economist Donald Saari notes, Walras's equations are "sufficiently elementary to be taught in a first course on vector calculus. So, we must wonder what a nice, simple model is doing in a complex place like this." His answer is that the Walras model, and its extensions in Arrow-Debreu and other models, have mostly been useful for telling a convenient story, not due to their actual scientific merits. "I have no idea whether Adam Smith's invisible hand holds for the 'real world,' but, then, no one else does either. This is because, even though this story is used to influence national policy, no mathematical theory exists to justify it."[7]

Weirdly enough, this ongoing failure hasn't led to the abandonment of the equilibrium theory, but rather to a more or less complete cessation of any research bringing too much attention to the sensitive topic of stability. Occasionally economists revisit the topic, as Frank Ackerman did in 2002,[8] and this aspect of "turning away" is what he found most remarkable. One graduate textbook, Ackerman noted, even claimed that the stability question is simply unimportant for an astounding reason: because, in the opinion of the textbook writer, economics is not concerned with dynamics and change within an economy. "A characteristic feature that distinguishes economics from other scientific fields is that, for us, the equations of equilibrium constitute the center of our discipline. Other sciences, such as physics or even ecology, put comparatively more emphasis on the determination of dynamic laws of change."[9]

But dynamics do matter, like it or not. If economics does not establish the laws of change within economies, what exactly does it do? And if it is concerned only with the "equations of equilibrium," what happens if that equilibrium is so unstable and fleeting that it's unlikely to bear any resemblance to the real world around us? It would be like mathematical meteorologists finding beautiful equations for a glorious atmospheric state with no clouds or winds, no annoying rain or fog, just peaceful sunshine everywhere. In principle, the atmosphere might have such a state, but it tells us nothing about the reality we care about, about our own weather.

Aside from Arrow and Debreu's work, there are other less formal arguments commonly pushed in finance and economics for why markets should be in something like an efficient equilibrium. According to one, markets exploit the "wisdom of crowds," pooling the diverse views of many individuals in a way that cancels out their individual errors. Failing that, another argument holds that if there's a mistake in the market— IBM stock being priced a few percentage points too low, for example—

smart investors will soon jump in and trade to make an easy profit. Their exploitation of pricing anomalies—known as "arbitrage"—will drive the price back to the correct value. Inefficiencies, in effect, kick up forces that should automatically erase them.

As we'll see, empirical evidence suggests that these loose arguments don't support market efficiency and equilibrium either. Markets bounce around far too violently and do too many surprising things to be explained by any story of perfect or near-perfect market equilibrium. But first, let's take another look at the wisdom of crowds.

Efficiency Undermined

In mid to late May 1968, a U.S. nuclear submarine, the USS *Scorpion*, armed with two nuclear-tipped torpedoes, was declared missing with ninety-nine men aboard. The sub was known to be only somewhere within a twenty-mile-wide circle in the Atlantic Ocean. Five months of intensive search led to no result. Finally, navy scientist John Craven asked a group of submarine and salvage experts to guess on the sub's location, and then he averaged the guesses together. The sub was found only 220 yards away from that spot, some five hundred miles or so southwest of the Azores; unfortunately, all the crew had long since perished.[10]

Crowds can indeed be wise.

Behind this incredible power of crowd wisdom lies the statistical averaging of a diversity of views. You may not be able to accurately guess how much an ox weighs; nor can I. But get eight hundred people to take a guess at the weight and the average of their guesses can be within a pound or two of the true answer. The naturalist Francis Galton first noted this phenomenon when reporting on a real contest in 1906.[11] Analyzing the eight hundred guesses in a competition held at the West of England Fat Stock and Poultry Exhibition in Portsmouth, he found that the "middlemost" estimate was within 1 percent of the correct value, despite the lack of skill of most of the participants. "The average competitor," as he observed, "was probably as well fitted for making a just estimate as an average voter is of judging the merits of most political issues on which he votes."

This is precisely what American economist Milton Friedman and many others have argued should happen in financial markets, in which investors essentially "vote" on the true value of this or that stock or other product, by buying or selling it at a price they expect will change. But there are limits to the power of this intelligence.

In his 2004 book *The Wisdom of Crowds*, James Surowiecki took care to note that the effect works only if people are unbiased in their estimates, and if they make different mistakes that tend to cancel out.[12] But psychologists and researchers in the new field of behavioral economics have documented in careful experiments that we all tend to make similar mistakes, and do so quite systematically. Most of us, for example, are overconfident and think we're better than average drivers (or smarter than average or more athletic than average), even though by definition about half of us are not. Our estimates of things are systematically "anchored" or influenced by totally irrelevant factors. Show people the number 100,000 and then ask them to estimate the number of dentists in Manhattan. Their guesses will drop significantly if you first show them the number 233 or 867.

Or here's another guessing puzzle. Suppose you're given a choice between two different subscriptions to the *Economist*: (*a*) an Internet-only subscription for $59 or (*b*) a print *and* Internet subscription for $125. Psychologist Daniel Ariely found that 68 percent of students sampled in an experiment chose *a*, the Internet-only subscription. But then Ariely added a third option: (*c*) a print-only subscription for $125. None of the students tested chose this third option. After all, it offers less for the same payment, as you get no web access. However, the mere presence of this third option totally changed how students chose between the other two. Now only 16 percent of the students chose *a*, the Internet-only subscription.[13]

This weird effect reflects how people judge the values of things not in absolute terms, but in comparison with other things, in relative terms. Adding choice *c*, against which *b* is clearly better, gives a boost to *b*'s value in readers' minds.

If we all make similar mistakes, for the same reasons, then perhaps it's a little naïve to guess that our errors will somehow cancel out. We're all biased in similar ways, and crowds—and markets, as examples of crowds—are likely to be similarly biased. But there's another factor that should actually make the reliability of crowds and markets much worse. Whether in fashion, language, or investment choices, people tend to copy one another. As some recent experiments have shown, this can make committees, crowds—and especially markets—very unwise indeed.

Last year, Jan Lorenz and colleagues from ETH Zürich devised a way to test the wisdom of crowds in conditions in which they could control the level of "social influence"—that is, the amount that one person knows about others' choices and can potentially be influenced by them. They had nearly 150 student volunteers answer questions about things like crime statistics—how many car thefts were there in Zurich last year?—for which the true answers were already known. This made it possible to test how well the crowd did.

Now, in some trials, the students made their estimates knowing nothing about the estimates of others, while in other trials, they were made aware of those estimates either completely or on average. The experimental results show clearly that social influence destroys the wisdom of crowds in several ways.

To begin, Lorenz and colleagues' experiments show how delicate the wisdom of crowds effect is even without social influence. For example, when asked: how many murders were there in Switzerland in 2006, the average response was 838, whereas the true number was 198. That doesn't seem too wise. But it is if you calculate the average in a slightly different way. Psychologists have shown that when people try to estimate numbers for things they know little about, the challenge is really to guess the right scale or magnitude of the answer.[14] Is it roughly 10, 100, 1,000? Assuming the students were doing this, the researchers could average the results according to their magnitude—mathematically, this is called using the geometric mean—and in this sense the group was then fairly wise. The geometric mean gave the answer 174, not too far from 198.

Things got worse with social influence, as merely hearing the others' estimates made students revise their own so as to fit more closely with the group. Unfortunately, the experiments showed, this led to no improvement in the accuracy of the crowd's average estimate. In effect, people think they are sharing information, working together to get a better answer, but they're not. Instead, sharing answers caused everyone's answers to converge; when social influence was allowed, the true answer often lay entirely outside of the group's range of estimates.

This finding is particularly discouraging. Imagine a government trying to use the wisdom of crowds to solve some problem, surveying a bunch of people, hoping to get a range of views and some idea of how much consensus there is on some topic. You would hope that if the crowd's average estimate were *not* accurate, this lack of accuracy would be reflected in a wide range of estimates from the individuals; the wide range would signal a lack of unanimity and confidence. But that's not what happens. Rather, social influence tends to push the crowd toward an inaccurate estimate while also narrowing the range of individual opinions, signaling apparent strong certainty in the result—a recipe for stupidity.

Social influence also creates a truly unpleasant combination of stupidity and increased confidence. The researchers interviewed the students after the experiments, asking them how confident they were in the accuracy of the group's final consensus estimate. Social influence, while it didn't make the crowd's estimate any more accurate, did fill the participants with strong belief in improved group accuracy. Rather than the "wisdom of crowds," we have the "unwarranted confidence of crowds."[15]

It's hard to imagine a more socially influenced environment than modern-day Wall Street. Massive open-plan offices are filled with traders, brokers, and investors making deals face-to-face, over the phone, and online. Rumors fly through the business press and corporate boardrooms, and people take cues on what to buy or sell by looking to what others are doing. Mutual fund managers based in the same city are much more likely to invest in the same companies, even those located halfway around the world, than are those in different cities. The most likely explanation is simple social influence through social contact, gossip, one copying another.[16] Financial analysts may claim to be weighing information independently when making forecasts of things like inflation or company earnings, but a study in 2004 found that what analysts' forecasts actually follow most closely is other analysts' forecasts.[17] There's a strong herding behavior that makes the analysts' forecasts much closer to one another than they are to the actual outcomes, exactly as Lorenz and his colleagues' experiments would predict.

Think 2005, the housing bubble, mortgages with no income and no assets, and so on. Many people, along with the market they comprised, agreed that housing values would continue to rise, and certainly wouldn't fall the way they did. People were confident in the crowd even as the crowd raced toward the cliff. The outcome was anything but efficient.

Does this mean we should abandon our faith in crowds, and thus in the intelligence of markets? Not just yet—economists have another line of defense already prepared.

Greed Is Good—For Me and the Market

Gordon Gekko, the evil financier of the 1987 film *Wall Street*, famously asserted that "greed is good." This is indeed the peculiar idea at the core of Adam Smith's vision of markets—that human self-interest and greed actually act to keep the market in balance. As people profit from ineffi- ciencies, they drive the market back to the efficient equilibrium. The logic of how it works is deliciously simple—and seemingly unavoidable.

The marketplace is a complex ecology of buyers and sellers of every sort, but some of them—think investment banks like Goldman Sachs or Morgan Stanley, or hedge funds such as D. E. Shaw or Renaissance Technologies—have more resources and are undeniably more sophisti- cated than most others. They scour the market for profit opportunities, and jump on anything they find. These firms thrive on the basis of myr- iad strategies that in one form or another are complicated versions of "spot the imbalance."

One instance of this kind of strategy is the classic example of how ar- bitrage is supposed to work. Suppose IBM is temporarily undervalued rela- tive to some similar stock, say, Apple. An investment firm will buy IBM stock, paying for that purchase by selling a similar amount of Apple stock. Then, when the prices move inevitably back into line, the firm will sell its higher-priced IBM stock and buy back its lower-priced Apple stock. The transaction is cost-free aside from small trading fees, because in each case one stock is sold to pay for another, and it is also, if you believe in market efficiency, risk-free. If a stock is undervalued, then the efficiency of the market will cause its price to rise. Thus, arbitrage is a way to make risk-free profits.

Spotting such arbitrage opportunities is one of the most common in- vestment strategies there is. Whether it takes place over months, days, or even seconds, the result, according to the standard argument, should be the same: the arbitrageurs' actions should tend sooner or later to elimi- nate the original price discrepancy and drive the market back into effi- cient equilibrium.[18] In economics circles, theorists have concluded that this process is so instantaneous and effective that, in effect, there is no arbitrage. In other words, any obviously wrong stock price will be so quickly set right that the market is always in perfectly efficient equilib- rium. Hence, there is the old joke about two economists walking down the street. One suddenly says, "Look, a $100 bill!" And the other immediately replies, "No, it's not real, because if it were real someone would already have picked it up."

If this sounds like an improbable state of affairs, maybe it's because it is. The trouble, as economists Andrei Shleifer and Robert Vishny initially pointed out in 1997, brings to mind a famous line from Hamlet: "There are more things in heaven and earth, Horatio, than are dreamt of in your philosophy." In other words, assuming the market will quickly eliminate all arbitrage just doesn't give enough respect to all the world's possible surprises.

Think again of the hedge fund that spots an imbalance between IBM and Apple. The profit seems easy: buy and sell the two stocks, wait a while until the price difference vanishes, and then do the opposite. But what if, after you've made the first trade, the prices don't come together, because a group of ignorant investors out there hears a false rumor about IBM and dumps the stock, making its price plummet? It becomes even more undervalued relative to Apple. This is profoundly irritating to the hedge fund manager, who *knows* the stocks should have equal value, especially because now he or she can't exit the trade without taking a loss. The fund is stuck waiting for the moment—in a day, month, year, who knows—when those idiots will finally come to their senses, if they ever do.

In a formal mathematical argument, Shleifer and Vishny showed that there's no way out of this mess, and that arbitrage, despite being thought of as risk-free, always entails some uncertainties.[19] Coincidentally, one year after Shleifer and Vishny pointed out this problem, it actually caused the most spectacular hedge fund collapse in history. The fund Long-Term Capital Management—the partners of which included financial economists Myron Scholes and Robert Merton, both Nobel Prize winners in economics and firm believers in efficient markets—had made bets that the prices of two kinds of treasury bonds, currently having different values, would converge. After all, a thirty-year bond and a twenty-nine-and-three-quarter-year bond both pay a fixed value roughly thirty years in the future and should be almost identically priced. But investors, panicked by the Russian government's default on its debt, made the prices instead move further apart. LTCM lost more than U.S. $6 billion of its investors' money. Worried about a cascade of failures in the financial system should LTCM fail, the Federal Reserve Bank of New York in 1998 organized a bailout funded by LTCM's major creditors.

The LTCM disaster was a classic case of misplaced faith in the market and in the mechanism of arbitrage. What seemed like a sure bet turned out to be a very risky investment indeed. This is just one narrow example of how crowds aren't always or even often smart; in fact, crowd intelligence may be an exceedingly rare occurrence. Arbitrage is possible, and may often work to drive prices back to fundamental values, but you just can't guarantee it; irrational traders may drive the market further away from the "correct" values, making the arbitrageurs lose. As John Maynard Keynes said, "The market can stay irrational longer than you can stay solvent."

But even this may be too optimistic. Efficient market theorists like to talk about the "fundamental" or "intrinsic" values of stocks and other financial instruments, and they generally get away with it. I've been writing here as if this is perfectly legitimate, as if such values really do exist, even though there really is no way to measure the fundamental value independently. A stock has a value in the market; its hypothetical fundamental value is largely a matter of conjecture. Physicist Jean-Philippe Bouchaud of the hedge fund Capital Fund Management suggests there's really little evidence at all that such true values even exist:

> Maybe smart investors have a slight advantage in their prediction, but not much. In my experience, even with tons of signals, studies and statistics you have at best a 52% probability of success, even for "relative value" trades that compare two prices but don't predict anything on the absolute value. There is so much noise and uncertainty about where the price should go . . . that I strongly believe there is no such thing as the true price.

In any event, whether the idea of fundamental values is fantasy or not, the arbitrage mechanism itself clearly also fails to guarantee market efficiency.

A Category 5 Hurricane

Late in the afternoon of Monday, October 19, 1987, Alan Greenspan stepped off a plane in Dallas, Texas. During the trip from Washington, he'd been revising notes for a speech the next morning at a conference of the American Bankers Association. Markets had been turbulent for several days, so Greenspan wasn't unduly alarmed when an assistant told him that the Dow Jones Index had closed down "five zero eight." He assumed that meant 5.08 percent, worrying, but not unexpected.

Greenspan never did deliver his speech. The assistant had actually meant 508 points, reflecting a drop in the Dow Jones Industrial Average of 22.6 percent—the largest single-day drop in history.

A telephone call soon arrived from President Reagan's White House chief of staff Howard Baker. "You've got to get back here," he said. "I don't know what the hell I'm doing." That evening, a military jet whisked Greenspan back to Washington, where panicked officials feared that an even worse drop on Tuesday could trigger total economic meltdown. At eight forty-one A.M. Tuesday morning, just before markets opened, the Federal Reserve Bank released a statement crafted by Greenspan and others.[20] "The Federal Reserve, consistent with its responsibilities as the nation's central bank, affirmed today its readiness to serve as a source of liquidity to support the economic and financial system."

Banks, hedge funds, and smaller investors relaxed, confident that the Federal Reserve Bank would inject enough money to keep the markets from seizing up. Calamity was averted, and the markets began rising soon after opening.

But what caused the crash in the first place? Twenty-five years later, no one knows for sure. Looking back, market participants such as Robert Hormats of Goldman Sachs recall their total shock and disbelief. "I was stunned. It was almost surreal. It was so rapid. It hit you all at once. I equate it to a category five hurricane."[21]

Except, of course, that hurricanes generally don't strike as sudden, unexpected surprises.

One explanation, offered by economist Richard Sylla of New York University, points to an unusual confluence of global pressures—international disputes about foreign exchange and interest rates, and fears over inflation. The trouble was then amplified, he suggests, by so-called portfolio insurance. To limit losses on suddenly falling stocks, many traders had programmed computers to sell automatically if a stock fell by, say, 10 percent. This effect could have caused a medium-size problem to grow automatically into a large one. This theory has become a component of many explanations of what happened, but it has shortcomings. If all we have to go on are factors like "global pressures" and "fears over inflation," then what explains why the crash happened on October 19 rather than the day before or after?[22]

A more unusual hypothesis is that the crash was actually the result of a self-fulfilling expectation. Many people—including famed hedge fund manager John Tudor Jones—had noted similarities between the market's behavior in the days leading up to October 19 and in the days leading up to the great crash of 1929. Expecting a crash, investors' own expectations could have made it actually happen.[23]

But again—we still don't know. As financial writer John Paul Koning puts it, "The crash of 1987 stands out for . . . its complete lack of explanation. To this day no definite reason for the decline has been isolated. Basic concepts such as cause and effect, predictability, and human rationality melt before the evidence of the record breaking decline. The crash stands like a black hole in 20th century history; unexplainable, fearsome, extraordinary."

The crash of 1987 is also a harsh slap in the face to the idea that markets are efficient and self-stabilizing. According to this vision, any price movement must reflect a real reassessment by investors of financial values in the light of new information. Yet nothing noticeable happened on October 19 that could possibly have caused investors to decide that the stocks of U.S. companies were suddenly worth 22.6 percent less than they were one day before. Unexplainable. Fearsome. Extraordinary.

Or, perhaps, it's not so extraordinary. For its size, of course, the 1987 crash stands out. But soon after the crash, economists David Cutler, James Poterba, and Larry Summers started wondering if the event might just be a particularly violent example of something that actually happens more frequently—big market movements with no apparent cause. If the efficient market theory asserts that markets move only when caused to by new information, it ought to be possible to look at history and see if it is true. This is what Cutler and colleagues decided to do.

They undertook a detailed study of the fifty largest single-day movements since the Second World War, looking to see if anything in news reports at the same time could have been the cause. Studying the *New York Times*, they found that some events do seem to show markets responding to news. For example, the market fell 6.62 percent on the day in 1955 on which U.S. president Dwight Eisenhower had a heart attack, and the outbreak of the Korean War on June 25, 1950, knocked 5.38 percent off the market. Just the same, many events didn't seem to be linked to any plausible news. On June 4, 1962, *New York Times* analysts could only lamely explain a big 3.55 percent drop as a "continuation of the previous week's decline." On October 21, 1987, two days after the crash of 1987, when the markets went up 9.1 percent, this was attributed to the fact that "interest rates continue to fall."

And when markets fell 6.73 percent on September 3, 1946, the normally determined and inventive business press gave up: "No basic reason for the assault on prices."

Cutler and colleagues ultimately concluded that the arrival of news or information could only explain, as they put it, perhaps "half of the variance in aggregate stock prices."[24] Yes, the 1987 crash was bigger than any other, but it doesn't really stand out from other large movements for being strangely inexplicable. Like a hurricane, it's not a random event with no explanation; it's just an unusually fierce example of the kind of storm that happens all the time.

Notably Rare Exceptions

Let's go back to Alan Greenspan's ridiculed remark from the start of this chapter. The invisible hand, he seemed to be saying, is wonderful—except in those cases in which it instead leads us into catastrophe, a position bloggers at *Crooked Timber* took delight in ridiculing. Another nice one from the blog: "With notably rare exceptions, Russian Roulette is a fun, safe game for all the family to play."

Any theory can get high marks if it gets to take credit for any successes, while its failures are considered unimportant "exceptions" to be ignored.

In 2000, economist Ray Fair of Yale University extended the Cutler et al. study by identifying big movements in records of the S&P 500 futures contracts over periods of less than five minutes, and trying to match them to items in newswire reports. He defined "big" to mean at least fifteen times bigger than average size calculated over the whole time period. He then searched for associated news in the Dow Jones News Service, the Associated Press Newswire, the *New York Times*, and the *Wall Street Journal*. The results showed that many large market movements—in fact, most—don't seem to be linked to any plausible information coming from news. In all, of the 1,159 total big events, he was able to find plausible news reports for only 69 of them, less than one in ten.

As Fair concluded:

> Stock price determination is complicated. Many large price changes correspond to no obvious events, and so many large changes appear to have no easy explanation. Also, of the hundreds of fairly similar announcements that have taken place between 1982 and 1999, only a few have led to large price changes . . . and it does not appear easy to explain why some do and some do not."[25]

And we can, of course, go to even shorter times. Since the flash crash of May 6, 2010—itself an unexplained cataclysm—markets have been hit by a flurry of similarly abrupt crashes, if on a somewhat smaller scale. In November 2010, the *New York Times* reported on a dozen "mini flash crashes" in which individual stocks plunged in value over a few seconds, recovering shortly thereafter. In one episode, for example, stock for Progress Energy—a company with eleven thousand employees—dropped 90 percent in a few seconds. There was no news released about the business prospects for Progress Energy either before or after the event.[26]

In the first month of 2011, according to the market data company Nanex, stocks in 139 cases either rose or fell by 1 percent or more in less than a second, then recovered. There were 1,818 such occurrences in 2010 and 2,715 in 2009. On April 27, 2011, Jazz Pharmaceuticals' stock opened at $33.59, fell to $23.50 for an instant, then recovered to close at $32.93. On May 13, Enstar, an insurer, fell from roughly $100 a share to $0 a share, then zoomed back to $100 in just a few seconds.[27]

Markets often do, of course, respond directly to information in news. On October 6, 2011, rumors had been flying that U.S. investment bank Morgan Stanley, the smallest of the big banks, might be close to collapse. Around ten A.M., U.S. treasury secretary Timothy Geithner said publicly that there was "absolutely" no chance the Federal Reserve would let another U.S. financial institution fail[28] and almost immediately, the value of Morgan Stanley stock jumped upward by about 4 percent as investors piled into the stock, apparently believing that the government would step in if necessary to save Morgan Stanley.

But the efficient market theory doesn't just claim that information moves markets. It claims that *only* information moves markets. Prices should always remain close to their so-called fundamental values—the realistic value based on accurate consideration of all information concerning the long-term prospects for the company to persist and profit. We've seen this can't possibly be true for the biggest and most violent market events, many of which happen unexpectedly and on the basis of no information; but it isn't true more generally either, even if one looks at ordinary movements. As Yale finance professor Robert Shiller first showed in 1981, prices in general move up and down too vigorously to be explained as rational prices based on real information.

Shiller's idea was to plot the real prices of the S&P 500 and of the Dow Jones Index (with the upward growth trend removed in each case) versus the real, rational values for those indices. The latter, theoretically, should be the "rationally expected or optionally forecasted" future dividends an owner would receive, which he could calculate from the actual dividends the stocks paid out. Shiller found that the "rational" prices based on dividends stayed fairly smooth (not surprisingly, since the calculation means averaging over many years, which reduces the importance of temporary fluctuations), while the real prices bounced up and down quite wildly.[29] Shiller's argument pointed to "excess volatility"—movement in the markets over and above what you should expect on the basis of markets moving efficiently on information alone. Since 1981, further studies have essentially confirmed this picture.[30]

All in all, there's not much to support the exclusive role of information in driving markets, or the view that markets get prices right, which is really the interesting claim of the efficient market idea. But it's possible to go further still in scrutinizing whether or not it's always information that drives markets. Importing some ideas from the physical sciences helps.

Calming Down—In Two Different Ways

There are plenty of obvious cases of news events driving market prices: a merger, perhaps, or a government bailout, or even, as in the case of Morgan Stanley in 2011, the mere promise of a bailout. With that in mind, perhaps we could speculate that there are two different kinds of market movements: those caused by news or information, as the efficient market theory says, and others caused by something else we don't yet understand—a psychological effect, perhaps, or something else.

Three years ago, a team of physicists led by Armand Joulin and Jean-Philippe Bouchaud set out to test this idea. Bouchaud is an expert in the relaxation properties of physical solids. In the case of solids, relaxation refers to the state of the molecules: the molecules in a piece of paper, for example, become excited when exposed to heat. Expose it for long enough, and the paper will catch fire. But if you take the heat source away before it catches, the molecules will eventually relax back to their normal state as the paper gradually cools. Coincidentally, Bouchaud is also the founder of a highly successful hedge fund, Capital Fund Management, based in Paris. Putting ideas from these two wildly different interests together, Bouchaud, working with graduate students Augustin Lefèvre and Armand Joulin, wondered if markets might be a bit like that piece of paper—stirred up after a big price movement, and then slowly settling back to a normal state. Market data, they found, shows that prices do just that—and what's more, the relaxation happens in either of two very distinct ways, suggesting the market movements really do come in two different types.

They first repeated an analysis similar in spirit to Ray Fair's, but using a far larger volume of data for more than nine hundred stocks listed on the NASDAQ exchange and high-speed news feeds from Dow Jones and Reuters listing more than a hundred thousand news items over a two-year period. Suppose you take all the big movements that do have a clear link to news, and then take all the ones that don't, and in both cases study the market in the hours after these moves happen. Does the market do anything different?

A key statistic they considered was volatility—roughly speaking, the typical magnitude of price movements each day (regardless of their being up or down.) Day to day, markets come with a certain level of volatility, but a sudden big event tends to create a more volatile market. Afterward, it takes some time before the volatility falls back to the norm. In their study, Bouchaud, Lefèvre, and Joulin found a striking result: the market following news events went back to the norm much more quickly than it did following the no-news events. This pattern shows up in diagrams like those on the following page.

The first one shows how market volatility goes back to the norm following a news shock. In this case, the data is for news-related events either four or eight times larger than the norm (eight is the upper curve,

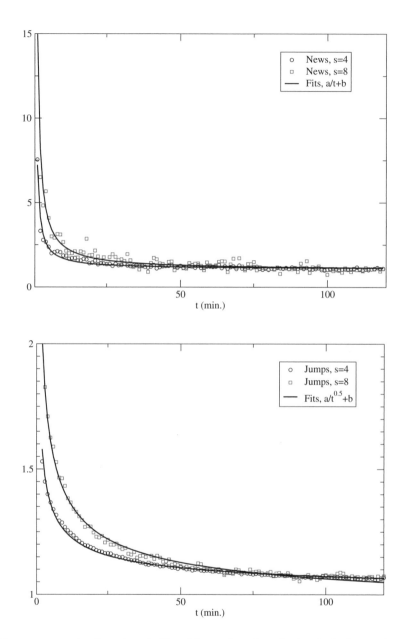

The two curves show how the volatility of the market relaxes back to its background level following a sudden "jump" event. What happens depends strongly on whether the event is clearly linked to outward news. Part A shows that the volatility relaxes quite quickly in the case of news-related jumps. The relaxation in part B, for jumps having no clear link to news, occurs much more slowly. (Figures courtesy of Jean Philippe Bouchaud)

four the lower). The two curves show that within about twenty-five minutes, the market has already gone back into some more or less normal state. In contrast, something very different happens for no-news events, as in the bottom graph on the left. In this case, for shocks of the same size, the market is still digesting the event after twenty-five minutes and hasn't yet returned to the norm. Even after one hundred minutes it still looks slightly high. If you still think that the no-news events might be the same as the news events, only we haven't been clever enough to figure out what the news was, these figures spoil that idea.

The conclusion is that the market relaxes back to the norm much more slowly after a no-news event than after one linked to news.[31]

No one knows why this should be, but Joulin and colleagues made the quite sensible speculation that a jump clearly related to news is not really surprising, and certainly not unnerving. It's understandable, and traders and investors can decide what they think it means and get on with their usual business. In contrast, a no-news event—think of the flash crash, for example—is very different. It is a real shock and presents a lingering unexplained mystery. It is unnerving and makes investors uneasy. The resulting uncertainty registers in high volatility.

So the idea that information, public or private, drives markets to efficient outcomes, doesn't stand up.[32] If the efficient market idea was once considered pretty strong—economist Michael Jensen of Harvard University once called it "the best-established fact in all of social science"—it has crumbled rather spectacularly in the past twenty years.

True Believers

As we've seen, an awful lot of evidence doesn't square too well with the idea of efficient markets. This centerpiece of the economic theory of markets is, at best, a crude partial story. In efficient markets, financial bubbles—episodes of unrealistically overvalued assets—cannot exist. Housing values in the United States in 2005 must have been just about right, as were the values of all the CDOs—collateralized debt obligations—and other derivatives built from mortgage-backed securities. If not, after all, sharp arbitragers would have jumped into the game and forced those values to be realistic "almost instantaneously."

As of 2007, the big banks were better placed than anyone to know the real values of the products they held on their books. Yet as economist Brad DeLong notes, investors in Citigroup ultimately lost 93 percent of their holdings. The numbers for Bank of America and Morgan Stanley were 85 percent and 75 percent. "The senior executives of these banks," DeLong adds, "had no clue they were holding as much mortgage or house price or AIG risk as they were."[33]

But religious conviction admits no failure, and some finance theorists still cling to their theory. Jeremy Siegel of the Wharton School at the University of Pennsylvania, in a talk after the crisis, argued that "our economy is inherently more stable" than it was before—precisely due to the wonders of modern financial engineering.[34] Robert Lucas of the University of Chicago asserted in the *Economist* that the efficient market theory "has been thoroughly challenged by a flood of criticism which has served mainly to confirm the accuracy of the hypothesis."[35] How is this possible?

Well, here's a useful trick. Suppose you want to defend a crazy idea like "the world is always fair." That's a tough sell. But you might try by devising a technical meaning of the word "fair" that is very different from the ordinary meaning. Specialists might define "fair" to mean that the world always follows a certain set of laws—the laws of physics. So now you have two meanings of "fair"—the normal and the technical. If you're talking about the technical meaning of "fair," you can make strong arguments that the world is indeed fair: it does obey the laws of physics. You can write papers about the fair world hypothesis and show reams of data indicating that yes, indeed, the world does seem to be fair. Anyone not paying attention might come to believe that there are strong arguments for the world really always being fair—in the usual sense.

The trick works very well with "efficient," especially in the context of markets in which efficiency might mean all kinds of things. This swindle makes it possible to go on defending the efficiency of markets even in the face of overwhelming evidence.

Starting in the late 1960s, economists have clarified several distinct forms of the efficient market idea. The "strong form" asserts that all publicly available information is very rapidly and appropriately reflected in the prices of stocks or other assets, which then have close to their proper values. As we've seen, this version is clearly false. Markets often get prices quite wrong. A more plausible "weak form" of efficiency merely asserts that asset prices fluctuate in a random way, so there's no information in the patterns of past price movements that can be used to predict future prices. This idea is also false. In their 1999 book *A Non-Random Walk Down Wall Street*, Andrew Lo and Craig MacKinlay documented a host of predictable patterns in the movements of stocks and other assets. For example, stocks tend to rise in January, a pattern known as the January effect. There are hundreds of similar patterns or "anomalies."

Other studies document similar if more subtle patterns. Back in the 1970s, physicist Doyne Farmer and others at a financial firm called the Prediction Company identified numerous market signals or clues they could use to try to predict market movements in the future. The figure below shows the correlation between one such trading signal (a secret one, devised and protected by the the Prediction Company) and market prices two weeks in advance, calculated from data over a twenty-three-year period. In 1975, this correlation was as high as 15 percent, and it was still persisting at a level of roughly 5 percent as of 2008. This signal has long been giving reliable advance information on market movements.

One might argue, based on the chart, that this pattern is gradually ceasing to exist over a period of decades. But if markets were truly efficient, the pattern should have vanished nearly instantaneously once it was established. Remember, the theory insists that any pattern should be discovered and wiped out quickly as investors exploit it, no matter how hard one firm may try to keep it secret. There's not much reason to think

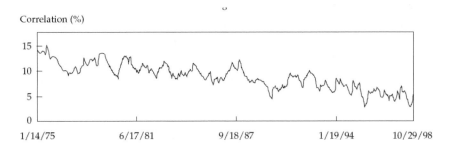

Correlation (%)

The figure shows the historical performance of a proprietary trading signal over a twenty-three-year period. The curve indicates how much each signal was correlated with the movement of stock prices two weeks into the future, thereby providing information that could be used to make predictions. Clearly, the correlation has decayed slowly over time, but it hasn't been wiped out by arbitrage as the efficient markets view would predict. (Figure courtesy of Doyne Farmer)

this pattern will be entirely wiped out for another ten to twenty-five years.

This means that this weaker form of the efficiency hypothesis is also false. Still, you can form a "ridiculously weak" version: "most asset prices are difficult to predict," which seems to be true, and no one doubts it. Note, however, that this should honestly be called the market unpredictability hypothesis, as it has nothing whatsoever to do with efficiency.

Now we come to the rhetorical trick. The strong (and false) form of the efficient market idea says something amazing about markets—that they process information with ruthless efficiency and give wise valuations to the stocks of different enterprises, thereby acting as an invaluable social resource for steering our society. The markets really know best. In contrast, the ridiculously weak form says nothing about the wisdom of markets, merely asserting that markets are hard to predict. This could be true even if markets were driven up and down by monkeys bashing randomly on keyboards,[36] and we obviously wouldn't use the word "efficient" in that case. We have two forms of the hypothesis—one bold and interesting, but false, and another uninteresting and true—and the trick economists often use is to mix these two meanings, defending the interesting one by giving evidence for the uninteresting one.

It's almost breathtaking to see this tactic in action. In July 2009, the *Economist* published a series of criticisms of current economic theory and its role in furthering the crisis.[37] Why, they asked, had economists told us that markets were so stable and self-regulating, so efficient, when—as history has shown—they obviously didn't know that? In response, economist Robert Lucas defended the efficient market theory by arguing that markets are hard to predict. "The main lesson we should take away from the EMH [efficient market hypothesis] for policy making purposes is the futility of trying to deal with crises and recessions by finding central bankers and regulators who can identify and puncture bubbles. If these people exist, we will not be able to afford them."[38]

Of course, the critics hadn't claimed that economists should have predicted the crisis, but had objected to the view, widely pushed by economists beforehand, that there could *be no crisis* because natural market efficiency would prevent it. As we saw in the last chapter, Hubbard and Dudley had argued that capital markets

> reduce the volatility of the economy. Recessions are less frequent and milder when they occur . . . The development of the capital markets has

helped distribute risk more efficiently . . . This ability to transfer risk facilitates greater risk-taking, but this increased risk-taking does not destabilize the economy. The development of the derivatives market has played a particularly important role in this risk-transfer process.

Apparently for Lucas, anyone objecting to this dangerous delusion and asking about who pushed it and why can simply be countered by pointing out that markets are hard to predict—and therefore "efficient" in a warped technical sense having nothing to do with the ordinary meaning of the word.

It's a brilliant, bait and switch maneuver that leaves an opponent dizzy and unsure of what just happened; it's an abrupt claim of victory when in fact no argument has been put forward. In this, it is a little like the idea of market efficiency itself—a trick designed to push economists' ignorance into a box and close the lid, while making that act of turning away never-theless seem scientific, even heroic. As Emanuel Derman, a physicist who worked for many years on Wall Street, put it, "The efficient markets hy-pothesis was a kind of jiu-jitsu response on the part of economists to turn weakness into strength: 'I can't figure out how things work, so I'll make that a principle.' "[39]

Beyond Equilibrium

In these first two chapters I've given an extremely sketchy summary of economic finance. The more detailed history is fascinating, in part, be-cause economics has attracted a great many brilliant people who have built a rich tradition of nuanced thought. But economic history is also in-teresting as a case study of science gone awry, and suffocated by its own ideas and a desire to appear more certain than it really is.

A great deal of economic research over the past fifty years reflects a determined effort to find reasons to believe that markets are naturally efficient and stable, and to provide a mechanism to give optimal solu-tions to problems of economic organization. Yet the mathematical ideas used in economics are strangely primitive. In his address on winning the Nobel Prize in economics in 2004, Vernon Smith of George Mason Uni-versity noted that economic theory—for all its alleged mathematical sophistication—actually has only *one* model, which is adapted, contorted, twisted, and tortured to fit to every circumstance. It is the hammer in search of a nail:

> I importune students to read narrowly within economics, but widely in science. Within economics there is essentially only one model to be adapted to every application: optimization subject to constraints due to resource limitations, institutional rules and /or the behavior of others . . . The economic literature is not the best place to find new inspiration beyond these traditional technical methods of modelling.[40]

The mathematics of these models has a formal appeal: it's as decorated with impressive symbols and curlicues as anything in mathematical physics. But the pretty package often bears little relation to economic reality. As we've seen in this chapter, the real movements of markets, as reflected in the data, don't fit the vision of market equilibrium and efficiency.

Of course, this is also the evidence of history. Before this meltdown of 2008, we had the dot-com crash of 2000–2002, and before that the meteoric rise and fall of the East Asian economies in the 1990s. Economic historians—Charles Kindleberger in his book *Manias, Panics, and Crashes*, for example, or Carmen Reinhart and Kenneth Rogoff in *This Time Is Different*—paint a picture of economic history that is anything but market efficiency and self-organized stability. Kindleberger's list of crises around the world, just in the last 250 years, includes episodes in 1763, 1772, 1808, 1816, 1825, 1836–39, 1847, 1857, 1864–66, 1873, 1882, 1886, 1907, 1929, the 1980s, 1987, the 1990s, and the 2000s.

In these first two chapters, I've barely scraped the surface of the history of thinking about economics and finance. This book isn't a history, and the history of this topic is infinite in detail, but then so is any history— of science or philosophy, medicine, baseball, alchemy or the human weakness for psychotic mass delusions. I've tried not to distort the general ideas, but my view is the view of an outsider—the physicist's perspective on a very different field of inquiry.

The remainder of this book aims to move beyond criticism and toward something more positive. I'm going to argue that the only way we can really understand markets is to understand them from a perspective that reaches beyond equilibrium and considers disequilibrium and imbalance. If we preserve any concept of equilibrium, it will be a concept more akin to the state of our atmosphere or ecosystems, a loose surface balance riding on a deeper torrent of dynamics and fluctuation. Viewing economies and markets this way means viewing them much as science views other natural systems. We might have expected that to be a good idea long ago.

Why, after all, should economics and the markets be so very different from anything else?

4

Natural Rhythms

*It often happens that the universal belief of one age of mankind—
a belief from which no one was, nor without an extraordinary effort
of genius or courage, could at that time be free—becomes to a
subsequent age so palpable an absurdity that the only difficulty
then is to imagine how such a thing can ever have appeared
credible . . . It looks like one of the crude fantasies of childhood,
instantly corrected by a word from any grown person.*

—John Stuart Mill

*The great progress in every science came when, in the study of
problems which were modest as compared to ultimate gains, methods
were developed which could be extended further and further. The
free fall is a very trivial physical example, but it was the study of this
exceedingly simple fact and its comparison with astronomical
material which brought forth mechanics. It seems to us that the
same standard of modesty should be applied in economics.*

—John von Neumann and Oskar Morgenstern

AT TWO FORTY-SIX P.M. LOCAL TIME ON Friday, March 11, 2011, a portion
of the earth's crust located about seventy kilometers off the coast of Japan
underwent what geophysicists call "undersea megathrust." A section of
ocean floor roughly three hundred miles long abruptly slid beneath
neighboring seafloor, in the process causing one of the most powerful

earthquakes of the past century. In all, the Tōhoku earthquake released as much energy as 600 million atomic bombs of the kind dropped on Hiroshima—enough energy to power the city of Los Angeles for two hundred thousand years. The quake also triggered the horrific tsunamis that wiped out villages along the coast of Japan with waves as high as forty meters, ultimately killing nearly twenty thousand people.

The basic mechanism behind megathrust earthquakes is by no means mysterious. Where two plates are sliding together, one being forced under the other, friction causes the plates to get stuck together, storing tremendous energy, which then gets released when they finally slip. Every one of the largest six earthquakes of the past century has been a megathrust earthquake. Yet no one predicted the 2011 Tōhoku earthquake in timing, location, or magnitude. Some of the most powerful events in nature remain impossible to predict, even after centuries of study.

Indeed, the history of earthquake prediction is a history of failure, with more recent predictions no more successful than those of centuries ago. In 1990, an American scientist named Iben Browning predicted that a series of great earthquakes would strike near St. Louis in November of that year, when the alignment of the sun and moon would create unusually large tidal forces. The quakes never came. Around the same time, an army of geophysicists came to believe that an earthquake would certainly strike before 1993 near Parkfield, in Northern California, as quakes had previously struck there like clockwork, roughly twenty years apart. It happened six times in a row dating back to 1857. That earthquake never came either. In this latter episode, it appears that many good geophysicists fell prey to the basic statistical error of seeing patterns even in random noise.

In 1997, when geophysicist Robert Geller of the University of Tokyo wrote a long review article summarizing the state of earthquake prediction, he concluded that no prediction technique anyone has tried has ever really worked. "Earthquake prediction research has been conducted for over 100 years with no obvious successes. Claims of breakthroughs have failed to withstand scrutiny. Extensive searches have failed to find reliable precursors . . . reliable issuing of alarms of immanent large earthquakes appears to be effectively impossible."[1]

Of course, if there's anything more common than failed earthquake predictions, it's failed predictions about markets and economies. The American economist Irving Fisher set a high bar for such failures with his public proclamation, days before the great crash of 1929, that the

markets had reached "a permanently high plateau." Perhaps MIT economist Rudiger Dornbush matched that with his 1998 claim that the then-
current U.S. economic expansion would "run forever: the US economy will
not see a recession for years to come. We don't want one, we don't need one,
and therefore we won't have one . . . we have the tools to keep the current
expansion going."[2] Instead, the dot-com bubble burst just two years later.

Geller's view on earthquakes isn't miles away from the modern economic view that the one thing we know about markets is that their movements are generally unpredictable. But beyond loose analogy, there are
almost spooky mathematical similarities between earthquakes and market fluctuations. In both cases, unpredictability coexists with profound
regularities that emerge in the statistics of many events. And there is a
lot we can learn from these regularities. Being unpredictable is not the
same thing as being random.

Statistical Ultrasound

If you gave a mathematics test to ten thousand randomly selected people,
you would find that their scores fell into a swarm or cluster about some
average. The spread of scores would conform to the so-called normal distribution of statistics, with most scores just above or below the most likely
score. This is the well-known bell curve. Scores far above or below the
middle would be very unlikely—"exponentially" unlikely in mathematical
terms. Any normal distribution curve has a "standard deviation"—a measure of the size of the spread of scores, which you can estimate in practice
with statistical calculations. In the case of a test out of 100 points, the most
likely score might be 70, and the standard deviation perhaps 7 or 8 points.
By definition, in a normal distribution curve, you won't find anyone falling
outside of a few standard deviations in either direction (see figure on the
following page).

But what happens if the test takers are not chosen at random? If half
the test takers were students of mathematics and the other half students
of English literature, the scores would cluster into two bunches centered
on different averages, with the mathematics students generally doing
better. Now you'd have a chart with two bumps rather than one, and they
would each tell you about the two different types within the group. If you

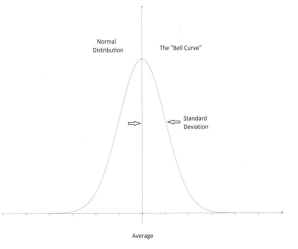

The Gaussian or "normal" distribution—also called the Bell Curve—describes the statistics of test scores, heights, weights, and many other things. It is the usual distribution of anything that reflects the combined action of many chancy independent factors.

noticed a small third bump far to the right, having very high scores, you might suspect that some professional mathematicians sat in on the test as well. A different test—write a short essay on the rivalry between William Shakespeare and Christopher Marlowe—would reveal differences in the group along another dimension of knowledge and ability.

In this sense, statistical analysis is a kind of mathematical ultrasound, able to reveal hidden information. So what kinds of hidden things can we learn about earthquakes? Plot a distribution curve for the magnitude of earthquakes, and you might well expect again to find a series of bumps. Some earthquakes take place deep underground and others at the surface. Some happen in regions where the rocks are hard and brittle, others where it is softer and more ductile. Different kinds of earthquakes— among them the species of megathrust earthquake—should show up as different bumps in the graph, one bump for each of the varieties centered on some typical size or amount of energy released.

Strangely, a graph like this is very much not what earthquake scientists have found. In the 1950s, seismologists Beno Gutenberg and Charles Richter of CalTech carried out an extensive census of earthquakes striking all over the globe over many years. They found no bumps at all.

Earthquakes, it turns out, occur not in clusters by type but obey a very simple rule: stronger earthquakes are consistently less common than weaker ones.[3] This statistical pattern is called a "power law" because the probability is simply proportional to the size raised to some power. Specifically, if you measure the size of an earthquake by the amount of energy it releases, then you find that the number of earthquakes is inversely proportional to the energy squared. Double the energy, and earthquakes become four times (two squared) less frequent. It's as simple as that, holding true from the tiniest tremor up to the greatest mega-quake.[4]

So earthquakes, despite our utter inability to predict them, conform to a surprising statistical simplicity and order. The curve lacks any hint that there are distinct kinds or classes of earthquakes, the way there were kinds or classes of students in the previous example. In particular, there's nothing at all to suggest any essential qualitative difference between the smallest and the largest earthquakes.

Londoners like to joke about city buses: you wait and wait and wait for a particular bus and then, abruptly, three of the same number all arrive at once. This turns out to be more than be a joke: buses really do tend to cluster together.[5] So it is also with earthquakes. For example, seismologists recorded hundreds of aftershocks in just one month following the 2011 earthquake in Japan.[6] Way back in the 1890s, the Japanese seismologist Fusakichi Omori first showed that the frequency of aftershocks decreases in simple direct proportion to the time after the main shock.[7] There are generally twice as many aftershocks in a day one month later as there are two months later.[8]

So the way aftershocks trail in the wake of a main shock also has a lawlike regularity. This is another power law, as the probability decreases as $1/t$ or t^{-1} (for sufficiently large values of t). Power laws of this kind show up all through science: in the complex structure of fractured surfaces on bricks or rocks, in the growth patterns of living organisms, in the way bees and deer forage for food. In each case, the power law points to hidden regularity lying behind apparent randomness, and gives hints about the underlying process.

This is all important—because financial markets appear to work the same way.

Market Shocks

Like the Japanese earthquake of 2011, the stock market crash of October 19, 1987, came as a total shock to most people. Yet the crash wasn't entirely without warning. Five days before, the Dow Jones Industrial Average (DJIA) dropped 95 points, which was then an all-time record. And only two days later it beat that record, closing down another 108 points. In these events, as I've already mentioned, some people thought they saw a parallel to events of 1929. Hedge fund manager John Tudor Jones later recalled:

> The week of the crash was one of the most exciting periods of my life. We had been expecting a major stock market collapse since mid-1986 and had contingency plans drawn up because of the possibility we foresaw for a financial meltdown. When we came in on Monday, October 19, we knew that the market was going to crash that day . . . The previous Friday was a record volume day on the downside. The exact same thing happened in 1929, two days before the crash.[9]

It's not clear if this parallel really meant anything, as Jones believed, or if he was just lucky. But it is true that both the 1929 and 1987 crashes were preceded by significant market rumblings, just like all major earthquakes. In the study I mentioned in the last chapter, for example, Ray Fair found that in the seventeen years from 1982 to 1999 there were roughly twelve hundred times that the prices of S&P 500 futures changed significantly (more than 1 percent) in less than five minutes. More than half of these events look like direct aftershocks of the October 19 crash, taking place in the two or three months just after. There were 109 on October 22 alone, three days after the crash.

This comparison goes far beyond metaphor and analogy. To begin, the statistics of market fluctuations, especially large bubbles and crashes, follow a rule almost identical to the Gutenberg-Richter law for earthquakes.

Consider, for example, how much the prices of stocks and other financial instruments change over a certain time interval—say a few minutes, a single day, or a week. In the early 1960s, French mathematician Benoit Mandelbrot carried out a landmark study of such changes in the prices of cotton, and found that the statistics of large market returns follow an inverse power law very much like the Gutenberg-Richter law. In the simplest of terms, bigger fluctuations are more rare than small fluctuations, following almost exactly the same mathematics as earthquakes. Mandelbrot was able to analyze only a few thousand data points, yet he was on to something.

In 1999, more than thirty years later and aided by the power of modern computers, physicists led by Eugene Stanley of Boston University analyzed hundreds of millions of price changes extending over thirty-five years for sixteen thousand different listed companies and a number of key financial indices such as the S&P 500, the Japanese NIKKEI, and the Chinese Hang Seng. Their data backed Mandelbrot's findings, but also refined them, showing that the statistics of price fluctuations really do follow mathematical regularities every bit as definite as laws of physics. This lawlike pattern holds for intervals varying from a second up to a month, and in different kinds of markets—stocks, foreign exchanges, futures, and so on—as well as in markets in many different countries.

It's quite remarkable that this fundamental law of large market fluctuations has been known for only a decade. Why should it be true? It's as deserving of explanation as anything in science, and finds none at all in traditional economics. The close correspondence with the Gutenberg-Richter law for earthquakes also raises some intriguing questions. The behavior of markets, we tend to believe, rests on the thoughts and emotions and actions of innumerable people, firms, and governments; equilibrium theory insists it reflects the rational nature of human beings. Yet somehow all this thinking and psychology and individual free will don't get in the way of this lawlike pattern. It turns up in the marketplace just as readily as it does in the purely mechanical workings of the earth's crust.

Where does this regularity come from? This is a crucially important question, and it's fair to say no one yet has the definitive answer, although there are some promising ideas, which I'll take a look at. But first, we should explore some surprising implications of this law—as well as some other market laws closely associated with it.

Strange Statistics

The biggest earthquake ever recorded struck in Chile, about 350 miles south of Santiago, on Sunday, May 22, 1960. It swamped the Chilean coast with tsunami waves up to twenty-five meters in height—they were still ten meters high on reaching Hawaii fifteen hours later—and triggered the eruption of the Puyehue volcano, which spewed lava from a fissure more than three miles long. A vast section of the Chilean coastline subsided by five feet.

Most earthquakes aren't nearly this size. Indeed, this is one of the most important things about earthquakes: their sizes vary so much that it stretches our imaginations.

In the final week of December 2011, some 350 earthquakes struck California. Didn't you read about that in the news? No? It's no surprise, actually, as these 350 earthquakes went mostly unnoticed even by the people of California. The biggest, with magnitude 3.0, caused no more vibration than a passing truck.[10]

The great San Francisco earthquake of 1906 (magnitude 7.9 on the Richter scale) released a hundred thousand times as much energy as the very biggest of the 350 earthquakes of the last week of December 2011. To match that energy output, those small earthquakes would have to rumble on continuously for between twenty and thirty years.

Yet all quakes large and small work the same way, as continental plates slide past one another, releasing energy as heat and vibration. How much simply depends on how far the sliding goes, and the surface area involved. The point is that large and small earthquakes aren't essentially different in the way that, say, stars and Ping-Pong balls are essentially different. They're not created by totally different forces. Large and small earthquakes differ only in degree, not quality. That's what the power law implies.

Power-law mathematics causes trouble for our intuition, which is attuned to another way of thinking. The average weight of an adult male in the United States is about 190 pounds. There are a small fraction of men over 300 pounds, some over 400, and a handful pushing the record books at 600 or more. As a child, I was astounded when the Guinness book of records told me that in the 1950s a man named Robert Earl Hughes had weighed more than 1,000 pounds and had to be buried in a coffin the size of a piano case. But you will never find anyone weighing 2,000 pounds, let alone 5,000 or 10,000 or 100,000 pounds. No man has even weighed 1,900 pounds, only ten times the current average.

If peoples' weights worked like earthquakes, then some people would be walking about weighing tens of millions of pounds, as much as ten

Boeing 767 jet liners put together. If weights worked like earthquakes, such people would be big, but not in any sense freakishly big, just big in an expected and ordinary way.

Of course, the nonintuitive character of power-law statistics is now widely appreciated, in good part due to the trenchant argument of Nassim Taleb in his book *The Black Swan*. Power laws reveal the profound and generally underestimated importance of extremes: according to exponential, "normal" statistics, extreme events are so rare they can be disdainfully ignored as they have minor impact. Power-law statistics, which are ubiquitous in everything from the sizes of meteors to the earnings of books or films, mean that extremes aren't so rare and they matter most. (This phenomenon is often described as a "fat tail," a reference to the way the distribution graph looks, with fatter or higher probability for very large events.) In their cumulative effect, these rare but extreme events have disproportionate power. Things like the overall movements of continental plates and markets aren't really driven by a gradual accumulation of the normal and routine, but by the singular, disproportionate impact of a few great tumultuous earthquakes and crises.

Unfortunately, centuries of science and mathematics tradition, focusing on the normal statistics of things like weights, heights, and test scores, has taught us to see the world incorrectly. It was a telling moment on Tuesday, April 27, 2010, when David Viniar, Goldman Sachs chief financial officer, testified to the Senate Permanent Subcommittee on Investigations, which was exploring Goldman Sachs's role in the financial crisis. Viniar graduated from Harvard Business School and is presumably as knowledgeable as anyone about the nature of financial fluctuations. Yet he'd have been more believable in explaining why Goldman Sachs had been unprepared for the financial crisis if he had claimed that Lloyd Blankfein's dog had eaten his homework.

The bank, Viniar claimed, had been perfectly responsible in assessing the prevailing risks, and had simply been hit by an extremely unusual shock. They were profoundly unlucky. "We were seeing things," he said, recalling the tumult of the worst days, "that were 25-standard-deviation events, several days in a row," which is probably the most ludicrous statement ever uttered to any committee in U.S. history. Viniar (or his lawyer) clearly hadn't done the calculation. In Gaussian mathematics, even an eight-standard deviation event is expected only about once in the entire history of the universe. A twenty-five standard deviation event should be expected about once every 10^{135} years—one followed by 135 zeros—which is like the chance of winning a one-in-a-million lottery jackpot about twenty-two times in a row.[11] Among the many reactions to Viniar's silly claim of three such events in a row, one paraphrased Oscar Wilde. "To experience a single 25-standard deviation event might be regarded as a misfortune, but to experience more than one does look like carelessness."

As ridiculous as Viniar sounded before the Senate, we'd do well to consider some context for what he was saying. Stocks over a single day typically change less than about 2 percent, so a movement of even ten standard deviations means a movement of at least 20 percent. While normal statistics says this should happen once every 10^{22} days—again, far longer than the age of the universe—market data shows that it happens essentially every week for at least one of the few thousand stocks in the market.[12] So perhaps we should reexamine our assumptions.

Power laws and fat tails are immensely important for proper risk management, for assessing the likelihood of rare market upheavals with at least some accuracy.[13] But that's not, to my mind, the most important thing. What's of even greater importance is that the power law of market returns helps illuminate a path to theories of finance with greater explanatory power than we've previously seen, because it is a core fact that any theory of markets really has to explain. Just as importantly, it's not the only one.

Even Markets Have Memories

In his landmark 1830 book *Principles of Geology,* the French geologist Charles Lyell argued that scientists would never manage to understand geological phenomena—rock formations, the shapes or mountains and valleys, and so on—if they sought to find in these things the traces of some timeless mathematical order. No one was likely to write down some beautiful equations, do the mathematical work, and wind up explaining the shape of the Swiss Alps. The shape of every planetary orbit is an ellipse. Hang a rope between two trees and its shape is always the same, a curve known as a catenary. Geology, Lyell claimed, is different, as accidents—volcanic eruptions, landslides, floods—leave indelible traces on the future. Landscapes emerge from strings of such accidents, from gradual, evolutionary processes acting over long periods of time. The

Oxford historian Edward Hallett Carr later suggested that Charles Darwin, building on Lyell's thinking, introduced the notion of history into natural science. As he put it, "The real importance of the Darwinian revolution was that Darwin, completing what Lyell had already done in geology, brought history into science. Science was concerned no longer with something static and timeless, but with a process of change and development."[14]

With history, of course, enters the question of future predictability, about which the Gutenberg-Richter law of earthquake science says nothing. The same is true of the statistics of market movements as established by Mandelbrot, and the more recent work of physicists. These laws describe the distribution of types of events. But they say nothing about the order in which they appear. Do small and large changes alternate, perhaps? Or cluster together? Or something else entirely? Maybe the sequence is just totally disorganized and random? Obviously, if you could establish something like an order for these events, the idea of prediction becomes more plausible.

The simplest possibility is that markets behave like a so-called random walk: their movements are totally unpredictable, and what happens today has zero influence on what is likely to happen tomorrow or next week. If you flip a coin and get heads, this makes it neither more nor less likely you'll get a head on the next flip or any other flip. In mathematical terms, this means that each of the coin flips is "independent." Louis Bachelier proposed in 1900 that markets behave this way. As he reasoned, millions of things influence market prices over a day, with some pushing them up and others down. If subsequent influences are (mathematically) independent, then we should expect a normal distribution of price changes—that old bell curve again.

Bachelier's hypothesis, we now know, is definitively false. The distribution of market returns—defined as the fractional price change over an interval—isn't Gaussian and normal, but fat tailed.[15] Bachelier was wrong. But how wrong? Quite aside from the normal distribution, he assumed no history as well, no influence of past moves on future moves, no predictability at all. Are these fair assumptions to make about a market?

One way to test the predictability of a signal (or stock price) that fluctuates up and down is to compute what's called its "autocorrelation," which sounds more complicated than it actually is. It might be better called the "predictability." The idea is to study the relationship between the signal's values at two moments separated by an interval of time, which might be a day or a week or whatever. Over the entire length of the signal you look and see if the first value gives you any hint about the second. Is a positive value now usually followed by a positive value again later? Or instead by a negative value later? Do this exercise enough times, and you can begin to establish predictability: for example, a stock that jumped up 1 percent on Monday could be reliably predicted to move up again on Friday. Or you might find that a 1 percent rise now implies nothing about what happens later, the price later going up as often as down. That's what you'd get for a truly random sequence of prices. By changing the length of the interval, you can test the signal (or price) for predictability over all time periods.

As we saw in chapter 2, the actual future prices of stocks, bonds, futures, and other financial instruments are extremely hard to predict from past prices. Indeed, the efficient market hypothesis claims as much. This should mean that the autocorrelation of price movements should be zero no matter which interval you look at; what just happened tells you nothing about what will happen in the future. This is indeed the case, at least if the time interval you consider is a few minutes or more.[16] The predictability (autocorrelation) of the return signal for stocks, options, futures, or anything else starts out high at $t = 0$—meaning (of course) that the price right now does indeed tell you a lot about what the price is right now. But then, as the interval increases, the autocorrelation rapidly falls off to zero in only a few minutes.

This is a beautiful illustration of market unpredictability. And, if you didn't know any better, it might seem like the end of the story. But it isn't. In 1993, economists Zhuanxin Ding, Clive Granger, and Robert Engle had the clever idea to study not only the record of returns, but also the absolute value of these returns, seeing how much the market moves, regardless of the direction it goes. Is this predictable? It turns out that it is. When Ding and colleagues calculated the predictability of this signal, they found that it persists for a long time, and only decays very gradually. For prices considered on a daily basis, for example, they found that the predictability is well above zero even out to twenty-five hundred days. Given roughly 250 active market days in each year, it seems that the magnitude of returns has positive predictability as far out as ten years.[17]

In plain talk, what this means is that the *amount of price movement* in the market is predictable.

This is an important insight, not only because it literally means you can predict how much change is coming, but also something deeper: for all the erratic randomness of the market, *there is a connection* between what it's doing today and what happened long ago, ten years back and further. Events in the market leave an indelible mark on it, changing it, imprinting it with a memory that lasts for a long time, just as an earthquake shapes the landscape. This long memory shows up in another way, too, which makes the link to earthquakes even closer. Following any big market event—the crash of 1987, for example—the probability of subsequent aftershock events falls off in just the way the Japanese seismologist Fusakichi Omori had found for earthquakes, in direct proportion to the time since the main earthquake.[18] The same is true for significant aftershocks following major policy announcements, such as statements by the U.S. Federal Open Market Committee (FOMC) announcing interest rate changes. The likelihood of big market movements falls in direct proportion to time from the moment of the announcement.[19]

I'm not arguing that markets work precisely and exactly like earthquakes. But the fact that such strikingly similar dynamics arise in two totally different settings suggests that their explanation won't be found in the idiosyncratic details of either one—neither in the detailed properties of rocks and faults and friction nor in the mysteries of investors' behavior and psychology. Blame greed and human fallibility if you want for the proclivity of markets to sudden upheavals and wild reversals. But the very same kinds of surprises arise in the earth's crust and in other natural processes, in systems driven away from equilibrium—things in which history matters, and that never settle down into some state of timeless balance.

The Rice Avalanche

The classical view of the healthy human organism sees it as achieving an ideal balance or homeostasis in a world of fluctuating demands. With exercise, the heart rate rises to pump more blood and supply more oxygen to the muscles. Hormone levels adjust throughout the hours of the daily cycle. In the absence of any outside changes or demands, the body should rest in calm repose, the heart beating regularly and steadily like a clock. This metaphor for balance and equilibrium has often inspired economists who view a market or economy in similar terms.

But here's a surprise: not only does this pattern fail to describe markets, but it also doesn't even describe the human body.

Take a perfectly healthy person at rest and measure the time between his or her heartbeats. It is anything but constant. In a string of studies stretching over twenty years, Ary Goldberger of the Harvard Medical School has shown that the healthy heart has quite vibrant natural fluctuations in the time between beats.[20] These fluctuations also show a long-term memory with subtle links between past and future fluctuations over many hours. These fluctuations aren't random, but instead reflect an inherent organization in the resting heart: rest isn't simple rest, but something far richer. Indeed, Goldberger and colleagues have shown the heart actually becomes more clocklike and predictable, and shows less variability in the aged and in patients with heart diseases. The normal, healthy resting heart just isn't quiet and regular; irregularity and long memory are signs of natural health.

The same is true of the brain. A decade ago, neuroscientist Klaus Linkenkaer-Hansen and colleagues from the University of Helsinki used EEG monitors and other techniques to study neural oscillations at ten and twenty cycles per second in volunteers who were awake but resting. Whether subjects had their eyes closed or open, the network of neurons had a rich storm of activity. People tend to think of "brain waves" as perfectly rhythmic, but in reality they are far more erratic (though not at all random). Despite their erratic appearance, brain fluctuations also show the intricate organization of long-term memory, possessing a high degree of predictability over long stretches.[21]

To a natural scientist, the similarities between earthquakes, the dynamics of the human body, and the financial markets are not coincidental, or even necessarily all that surprising. In the past two decades, scientists have discovered similarly erratic yet highly organized patterns in forest fires and solar flares, in the record of species extinctions in the fossil record, and in fluctuations of bird populations. They're present in the dynamics of the atmosphere and climate. I could go on for pages (and I did in my earlier book *Ubiquity*).[22] All these things share a common character and comprise a class of phenomena within which markets would appear to fall quite naturally. They are all disequilibrium systems—driven out of balance by energy flows, unceasing competition, environmental change, or other pressures.

One reason for the persistence of equilibrium thinking in economics and finance is the power of the metaphors that dominate thinking in these fields. There's an allure to the notion of an economy or market that rests calmly if undisturbed, and responds to an outside shock by readjusting itself as easily as water in a disturbed bucket flows around to restore equilibrium. To build a more powerful science of markets—one able to explain fat tails and long memory in a natural way, and perhaps much else besides—we need equally powerful metaphors for *disequilibrium*, for systems that are out of balance, metaphors showing in a simple way how fat tails and long memory can come about.

With this in mind, let's take another look at that bucket of water. There's no memory in a bucket of water; fill it by adding one drop at a time, and each drop spreads to leave the surface always flat. But what if we replace liquid drops of water with solid grains, say grains of rice, which cannot spread? Imagine building up a pile of rice on a table, adding one grain at a time. We can learn a lot from this experiment.

What would happen in such a pile? At first, of course, the pile would grow very slowly, grain by grain, and get taller and steeper. As grains fall and get locked together, the pile develops a memory: where grains fall now influences how the pile can grow in the future. Occasionally, a dropping grain will trigger an avalanche and some grains will slide down. Eventually, after a long time, the pile will reach a kind of crude steady state in which the number of grains sliding down (and falling off the table edge) will just balance the number being added. This won't happen each time, of course, but on average.

At this point, we might ask the simple question of how many grains we expect to slide in the next avalanche. You might expect there to be some average, say, two hundred grains, but experiments carried out in the 1990s show otherwise. Data show that as you add individual new grains to the pile, the number of grains sliding down in response varies over a huge range (see figure on the following page). The addition of a little memory has led to a system in which the avalanches work just like earthquakes and market movements, varying in size over a tremendous range (in fact, the range is limited only by the size of the table you use).

This is actually a profound experiment that I think Plato or Aristotle would have found most illuminating; it enlarges our fundamental conceptions of the possibilities of how the world can work. After all, because we're controlling the experiment, we can see quite obviously—in a way we can't for complicated real-world things like markets—that the cause of the biggest and smallest events is always exactly the same. It's always the dropping of just one more grain. This is a philosophical experiment, as it illuminates something profoundly wrong with our intuition that large outcomes usually have correspondingly large causes.

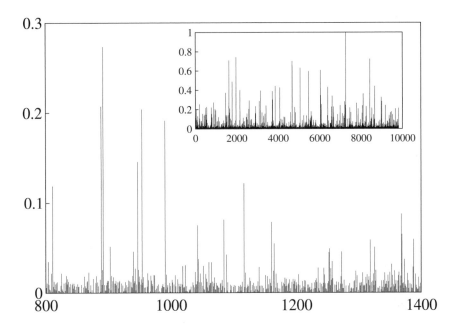

Sequence in time of rice pile avalanches. The height of each line indicates the total energy of that avalanche, reflecting not only how many grains moved but also how far down the slope they went. The pile has extremely erratic dynamics even though each event is triggered by the dropping of one grain. The inset shows the time series over a longer interval. (Figure courtesy of Kim Christensen)

Moreover, the dynamics of this rice pile show a delicate long-term memory with big events tending to cluster together, as we've seen with earthquakes and large market movements. As in those cases, the history of the pile is one of long periods of quiet broken apart sporadically by bursts of violent upheaval. Again, all this even through the driving force could not be more regular and predictable. This philosophical experiment shows that it is very possible for a natural system, driven out of equilibrium, to have much the same kinds of dynamics we see in markets. The mechanisms capable of producing such complexity don't have to be very complicated at all.

Of course, this experiment doesn't prove anything about markets. It's only exploring what is conceptually possible, how things can conceivably work. It teaches that in building models of markets, a little bit of disequilibrium could go a long way.

Of Hurricanes and Hypotheses

So we've seen that the way markets work isn't so weird after all, viewed from the perspective of natural science. I haven't mentioned further similarities between market fluctuations and the chaotic motions of fluid turbulence—the disorderly flow of water in a raging stream—which make the link between markets and the weather very explicit. A theory of finance should explain naturally why markets conform to these big patterns, and why power-law fluctuations and long memory emerge from the behavior of individuals, businesses, and so on.

The equilibrium theories of economics now in fashion don't explain any of this. Worse yet, the nature of equilibrium thinking makes it far too easy to "explain away" any apparent problems. No matter what happens in a market, after all, an equilibrium theorist can always say, "Of course, shocks may cause rare deviations from equilibrium, but the market itself will then act to eliminate this deviation, quickly restoring the efficient equilibrium." They might even claim that this insight is precisely where the theory displays its greatest predictive power.

Take one example. In 1990, Andrew Lo and Craig MacKinlay reported[23] a study of price movements over a period of twenty-five years showing that the present returns of lower-valued stocks were significantly correlated with the past returns of higher-valued stocks. This means that by looking at what has happened recently to higher-priced stocks, investors could predict what will happen to the future prices of cheaper stocks. This clearly contradicts the efficient market hypothesis. Traders in an efficient market should exploit this pattern immediately, buying or selling the cheaper stocks to make a profit, thereby driving the prices of those up or down and destroying the pattern.

An EMH enthusiast, however, can easily counter that this particular predictability has disappeared over the past twenty years, just as the EMH would predict. By 1997, other researchers revisiting the phenomenon needed high-frequency data even to find it at the level of minute-by-minute returns on the New York Stock Exchange. By 2005, when physicists Bence Tóth and János Kertész looked at the effect again, it had completely vanished.[24] Conclusion: the EMH is a shining example of a theory that makes accurate predictions.

But there is something profoundly wrong with this kind of thinking. To see why, let's apply it to another system: the weather. Suppose that some atmospheric theorists argued that the earth's atmosphere is always in a state of equilibrium with the air resting in calm repose. We might call this the efficient atmosphere hypothesis (EAH). Given the total amount of air, its density, and the force of gravity, these theorists would be able to predict things like the air pressure at sea level. The EAH would work pretty well in explaining many aspects of the atmosphere. But following it through the way economists have, the EAH would also make a more controversial claim—that the air pressure at any two places in the atmosphere (at the same altitude) should be identical. (For the purposes of analogy, this would be similar to saying, as any good economist would, that the prices of any two equally valuable stocks should be identical.) After all, any EAH theorist would argue, any pressure differences would create winds carrying air and energy from higher pressures toward lower pressures. That flow of air would lower the pressure in the former place and raise it in the latter, eventually bringing those two pressures back into balance. In other words, any momentary imbalance in air pressure should create forces that quickly act to wipe out that difference.

Obviously, critics of EAH would say this is simply nuts. After all, we observe winds all the time, and sometimes great storms. In the summer of 2011, high winds from Hurricane Irene caused massive flooding up and down the eastern United States. Isn't this obvious disproof of the EAH? On the contrary, the EAH theorists would respond, these observations actually provide further evidence for the theory. Yes, they would concede, the atmosphere does sometimes depart a little from perfect equilibrium, but normal atmospheric forces then drive the system back into equilibrium. After all, if you look at the data on the hurricane after it passed by the United States, you'll see that the immense pressure differences within it were slowly eroded away as the hurricane dissipated energy through its winds. Eventually Irene petered out altogether as the atmosphere was restored to equilibrium. Another victory for the EAH, which predicted just this ultimate fate for such a disturbance.

In the setting of atmospheric physics, of course, no one would take the EAH seriously, as it's obvious nonsense to claim that the gradual disappearance of Irene was evidence for the "increasing efficiency" of the atmosphere, or its return to the equilibrium state. Irene was one very much out-of-equilibrium disturbance, but its disappearance says nothing about whether the atmosphere as a whole has come closer to equilibrium. As Irene disappeared, hundreds of other storms, even protohurricanes, may have been brewing up elsewhere on the planet. Storms are always fading away and others are always growing in the great chaotic maelstrom of the atmosphere, and all of this reflects its condition as a system driven out of equilibrium by energy from the sun.

To show that the atmosphere was actually moving closer to equilibrium over time would require some global study of storms and winds and air pressure differences to see if they were in some general sense progressively getting smaller. What happens to one storm is actually quite irrelevant. Returning to the case of financial markets, the same must be true of a single anomaly such as the one identified by Lo and MacKinlay. Over twenty years, this one has slowly disappeared, as good empirical work has shown. But this doesn't really tell us anything about whether the market as a whole is getting more or less efficient, closer to or further away from equilibrium.

This analogy exposes what I think is dangerous and unscientific about equilibrium thinking: it assumes that markets themselves have no interesting dynamics and are fundamentally different from everything else we know in nature. Economic theory is quite ready to treat the nonmarket part of the world—weather, politics, business, technology, and so on—as a rich thing with infinitely complex dynamics, a thing full of surprises. But the market itself, no sir. It accepts that the rich dynamics of the outside world alter the real, fundamental value of companies and stocks as well as of other financial instruments. But then it insists that the great complex mass of heterogeneous humanity that is the market responds to those changes instantaneously in an extraordinarily simple way to find the new equilibrium that incorporates all information correctly. The market is unlike everything else—an exceptionally simple dynamical thing that simply responds in slavelike fashion to other forces.

This—to me and many others—seems impossible to take seriously. All the patterns we've seen in this chapter suggest that markets do have very rich internal dynamics, which they share with systems throughout the rest of science. They are basic facts about markets, and they need to be explained.

5

Models of Man

The madman is not the man who has lost his reason. He is the man who has lost everything except his reason.

—Gilbert Keith Chesterton

Human beings, viewed as behaving systems, are quite simple. The apparent complexity of our behavior over time is largely a reflection of the complexity of the environment in which we find ourselves.

—Herbert Simon

ANY DECENT THEORY OF FINANCE SHOULD be able to account for the basic mathematical patterns describing how markets work. In the last chapter, we saw two that haven't so far been addressed by mainstream economic thinking. First the power law of market returns reflects markets' wild gyrations—their universal susceptibility to violent movements over periods ranging from seconds to years. Unlike so much received financial wisdom, this is not supported merely by historical anecdote; it finds expression in a kind of mathematical law. And second, the long memory of market fluctuations shows how periods of uncertainty and volatility bunch together in stormlike episodes, calm or upheaval generally portending more of the same.

Besides these two there are yet more market universals,[1] which again point to similarities between markets and processes well-known in physics. Magnify the jagged edge of a small portion of coastline and the result looks much like a larger section. A coastline is a "fractal—a mathematical structure with self-similar properties, in which each fractional part resembles the whole. (For a very simple example, think of a chessboard: it's one big square made up of sixty-four smaller squares; a tiny person with tiny chessmen could subdivide each square into sixty-four minisquares, which could be divided into sixty-four even smaller microsquares, and so on.) Financial price fluctuations also have fractal properties. If you remove the labels from a chart of prices, there is no way to tell from the pattern of up and down wiggles whether it runs over hours, days, weeks, or months, as wiggles on all times look alike. In fact, market fluctuations are even richer than ordinary fractals; they are "multifractals," akin to many fractals overlaid one on another.[2] (This is a more difficult pattern to describe, but multifractals show up in the tangled whirling motions of any turbulent fluid. In a churning stream, for example, large eddies break apart into smaller whirls that in turn break into even smaller ones, in a cascade of structure tumbling all the way down to swirling water molecules. The details are too intricate to be described by one simple fractal; the self-similarity has a more subtle structure.)

Yet another market universal is a link between what a market does now, moving up or down, and the market's subsequent volatility. Studies show that if prices drop now, the market will tend to fluctuate more vigorously in the near future, while rising prices now will tend to calm the market. No one knows why this should be, but the effect is plainly there in the statistics, especially for stock indices.[3]

These patterns are so distinct, and appear so routinely in markets of all kinds—for stocks, bonds, futures and options, commodities, you name it—that they cry out for explanation. Atmospheric physics would be highly suspect if it couldn't explain why hurricanes in the Northern Hemisphere always rotate counterclockwise, while those in the Southern Hemisphere rotate clockwise, or why hurricanes never occur within about five degrees of the equator. It would be suspect if it couldn't give a decent explanation of why tornadoes never emerge directly from calm blue skies, but appear readily in the maelstrom of a thunderstorm. If you were a meteorologist, and your theories couldn't account for these basic facts, what would you do? You'd look for a new theory. The patterns we find in stock markets are every bit as robust as these trends in weather.

Yet none of them find any natural explanation in the efficient market theory or any other equilibrium theory of financial economics.

For physicists and economists studying finance, these mathematical patterns have come to be known as "stylized facts." British economist Nicholas Kaldor introduced this peculiar term in 1961 in an argument over theories of economic growth. Sensibly, he argued that scientists building a theory should begin from a summary of the relevant facts requiring explanation—facts first, then theory. But as Kaldor noted, "facts as recorded by statisticians are always subject to numerous snags and qualifications, and for that reason are incapable of being summarized." Hence, he suggested, theorists would do well to work from "a stylized view of the facts." They should "concentrate on broad tendencies, ignoring individual detail."

Of course, all explanation requires a theory of some sort. But consider all the reasons people make investment decisions: because they heard a tip at a party or read an article online, because they're feeling enthusiastic about Facebook or just got a Christmas bonus. How do you build a theory of the stock market, which is so dependent on the unpredictable thoughts, emotions, and behaviors of millions of complicated human beings? Traditionally, economists have based their thinking on the assumption that people behave rationally. They've argued that people faced with any decision, no matter how complex, choose their action so as to optimize their expected (usually financial) gain. Traders may scream into telephones, pound desks, curse their computers, and make split-second decisions based on what seems like gut feeling, but economists insist they are actually choosing so as to optimize their "intertemporal utility"—their expected gain spread over their entire future—which they can do by solving a complex mathematical equation. You do the same, economists assume, when making any economic decision.

Even a casual observer of human behavior can see that this is insane. But as a mathematical approach it has the miraculous benefit of removing all psychology from the human behavioral equation, reducing human action to a problem in logic or mathematics, making economics a branch of mathematics, and thereby making it easier to build theories. As political scientist Robert Axelrod has suggested, "The reason for the dominance of the rational choice approach is not that scholars think it is realistic . . . its unrealistic assumptions undermine much of its value as a basis for advice. The real advantage of the rational choice assumption is that it allows deduction."[4] Economic theory needn't get dirty with the messy details of reality.

The resulting theories, unfortunately, are as unrealistic as the assumptions going in to them. But what's the alternative? Give up the assumption of perfect rationality, many economists argue, and it is hard to know how to proceed. If we're not rational, then what are we? And besides, many economists believe, there's actually no need to work from realistic assumptions about human behavior. Back in the 1950s, they often argue, the American economist Milton Friedman demonstrated that making wildly inaccurate assumptions is actually quite a sensible way to go about doing science.

This argument is also crazy, of course. But rather than merely dismiss it, I want to look at Friedman's peculiar argument briefly, as his pernicious perspective has brainwashed several generations of economists. It needs to be eradicated if we're to start building better theories of markets.

Milton Friedman's "F-Twist"

Friedman's argument formed the core of one of the most influential economic papers of the past half century—"The Methodology of Positive Economics," published in 1953.[5] In this essay, Friedman argued that economics should have scientific standards akin to those of physics, concerning itself with "what is," and not with "what ought to be." The value of models and hypotheses, he suggested, should also be measured as in the rest of science. "The only relevant test of the validity of a hypothesis," Friedman suggested, "is comparison of its predictions with experience. The hypothesis is rejected if its predictions are contradicted . . . it is accepted if its predictions are not contradicted; great confidence is attached to it if it has survived many opportunities for contradiction."

Most scientists would see this as sensible and very close to their own thinking. Friedman also argued that if several hypotheses make equally good predictions, economists should look to "simplicity" and "fruitfulness" in choosing between them. "A theory is 'simpler' the less the initial knowledge needed to make a prediction within a given field of phenomena; it is more 'fruitful' the more precise the resulting prediction, the wider the area within which the theory yields predictions."

Again, to this point, Friedman's essay says nothing that wouldn't fit into any standard discussion of the generally accepted philosophy of science. But go further, and things get a little weird.

Social scientists, of course, don't have it as easy as do physicists or chemists, who can often take a sample of what they're studying into the lab and subject it to experiments, getting more data in the process to test their understanding. Social scientists typically can't do experiments, and this difficulty, Friedman suggests, poses a special problem as researchers lack new evidence to test hypotheses. The need for such data

> makes it tempting to suppose that other, more readily available, evidence is equally relevant to the validity of the hypothesis—to suppose that hypotheses have not only "implications" but also "assumptions" and that the conformity of these "assumptions" to "reality" is a test of the validity of the hypothesis different from or additional to the test by implications. This widely held view is fundamentally wrong and productive of much mischief.

What Friedman is saying here is what you might call the "it got us to the moon" argument. Who cares where you get the equations you put into a calculator, so long as they result in a spaceship that gets you to the moon? And there's some sense to that. It's never possible for any theory to work from the complete details of reality. Whether in physics or economics, a theory has to start with an *approximate* picture—of the atomic structure of a metal, the key interactions in a market, or what have you— based on simplifying assumptions, including some factors and ignoring others. It then tries to draw out conclusions or predictions that follow logically from those assumptions, in principle producing a skeletal picture of the world capturing interesting elements of reality. In this context, Friedman claims that the choice of assumptions doesn't matter, and that theories should be judged by whether they get you to the moon, which in this case means whether or not they make accurate predictions about economic behavior.

In his enthusiasm, Friedman went on to argue that wildly inaccurate assumptions are the mark of great theories:

> The relation between the significance of a theory and the "realism" of its "assumptions" is almost the opposite of that suggested by the view

under criticism. Truly important and significant hypotheses will be found to have "assumptions" that are wildly inaccurate descriptive representations of reality, and, in general, the more significant the theory, the more unrealistic the assumptions . . . The reason is simple. A hypothesis is important if it "explains" much by little . . . To be important, therefore, a hypothesis must be descriptively false in its assumptions.

Taken at face value, this is a rather amazing conclusion. A theory becomes better insofar as it makes less plausible assumptions. This argument has become known as Friedman's "F-twist"—it was given this name by Paul Samuelson in a critique—and its counterintuitive conclusion has been invoked countless times by economists over the past half century in defending unrealistic assumptions in their theories.

One of the most famous models on finance, for example, is the so-called capital asset pricing model, introduced by economist William Sharpe in 1964.[6] This is a theory of stock prices, which asserts that the return one can expect on a stock in the long run is directly linked to its risk, as reflected in how much its price fluctuates up and down. In a sense, the theory asserts, stocks earning higher returns do so only because they expose investors to higher risks along the way. To come to this, Sharpe had to assume in his arguments that all investors, from the poorest individual right up to Warren Buffett, could borrow funds at the same rate of interest, even though wealthy investors in reality can generally get much lower rates of interest. He also assumed that all investors have absolutely identical views on the prospects of various different investments, even though, if this were true, everyone would want exactly the same thing, and no stock would ever change hands.

"Needless to say," Sharpe admitted, these were "undoubtedly unrealistic assumptions," but he defended his theory with an appeal to the prevailing authority, Friedman. "Since the proper test of a theory is not the realism of its assumptions but the acceptability of its implications, and since these assumptions imply equilibrium conditions which form a major part of classical financial doctrine, it is far from clear that this formulation should be rejected—especially in view of the dearth of alternative models leading to similar results."

Notice that Sharpe here went even further than Friedman, putting the value of the theory not in the *accuracy* of its predictions, but in their mere *acceptability*, which is not the same thing at all. He also defends his theory on the grounds of its tendency to "imply equilibrium conditions" consistent with financial doctrine. If these standards were to be universally upheld, all theories that revised or upended existing financial doctrine would be automatically ruled out. In any event, the absurdity of a theory's assumptions, Sharpe certainly agreed, shouldn't count against it.

Milton Friedman has been called "the greatest debater of all time,"[7] and this argument puts his talents on fine display. Step by step the logic seems unavoidable. But there is something fundamentally corrupt in the proceedings.

The Shifty Switch—Revisited

I argued in chapter 2 that economists often use the word "efficient" in a shifty way, giving evidence for one kind of efficiency (unpredictability) yet claiming another very different kind of efficiency (optimal outcomes). It is a slippery trick supporting a devilish illusion; an amazing claim seems to be established on the basis of quite ordinary and unsurprising evidence. Much the same trick underlies Friedman's argument for the virtues of theories with ridiculous assumptions. As before, the trick pivots on the terms Friedman used and how he used them.

Think about making a theory of the shape of the earth and its surface, a theory useful for navigation. You might start with the assumption that the earth is a sphere. This is an approximate truth, and, quite frankly, among the most profound discoveries in human history. But you could also say that this assumption is "unrealistic," "false," and "inaccurate," as the earth isn't really a perfect sphere. Mountains and trees, rivers and valleys, the vast carved-out volumes of the oceans are all features that mean the earth isn't really a sphere. You can emphasize what the comparison gets right, or what it gets wrong.

Most people would agree that changing our perspective on the earth's shape from flat to spherical was a major breakthrough, with powerful implications. But no sensible person would say it was powerful because it was "descriptively inaccurate." The view is powerful for what it gets right— that the earth is so close to being a sphere, the deviations from that shape being small—not for what it gets wrong. But when Friedman talks about a theory being "descriptively inaccurate" or "false," this is precisely what he means. This twisted usage of words makes his very odd conclusion seem profound, when in fact it is simply not true.

Or consider another example from physics—the motions of the planets as described by the laws of Newtonian physics. In practical application, the theory makes the assumption that two things about planets matter far more to their orbits than anything else—their mass and their distance from the sun. The planets' rotation, temperature, the sizes of their oceans and tides, the amount of sunlight they reflect—none of this matters much at all. The theory ignores all these details, yet makes predictions of remarkable accuracy. This is perhaps the archetypal example in all of science of a successful theory, which works from a boldly simplified assertion of what really matters.

Now apply Friedman's perspective. Is Newtonian physics powerful because it is "descriptively false" in its assumptions? Not at all. It's what the theory gets right, not wrong, that makes it so powerful. Friedman's desires for "descriptively false" theories couldn't be more confused.

What if Newton had somehow read Friedman's paper a few hundred years early, and, inspired by its teachings, sought to make his theory less descriptively accurate? He might have assumed that the nature of the planets' atmospheres mattered most, followed closely by how much sunlight they reflect. He might have assumed that all planets are perfect cubes, with masses in harmonic proportion to the frequencies of the musical scale. Then his assumptions really would have been descriptively false. Obviously, the effect would have been to render Newton's theory of gravity worthless, but let's pretend for a moment that it somehow gave accurate predictions. Then the theory would be nearly impossible to believe, its success as mysterious as planetary motion itself. We'd wonder if we weren't hallucinating, and rightly so.

Friedman's argument would stand up much better as a case for descriptive *simplicity* rather than falseness. Newton's theory of gravity eliminated unimportant variables, but made no attempt to misrepresent reality to the maximum possible extent. But instead we have an exercise in duplicity and dishonest persuasion, and I've explored Friedman's trickery in some detail because this argument has done a lot to warp the shape of today's economic theories.[8] These theories make unrealistic assumptions, achieve mathematical elegance thereby, and yet fail to explain how markets work in the real world. Any respectable theory in economics, as in physics or the rest of science, should aim to build models starting with simple and plausible assumptions, including the factors that appear to matter most. After all, a theory built on believable and testable assumptions might actually teach you something about mechanisms of cause and effect.

So, where do we start? What is "plausible" in the case of financial markets? The actions and decisions of people drive markets, so human behavior is a good place to start, just as understanding the basic behavior of atoms and molecules is step one on building theories of matter. What is perhaps most obvious is that markets aren't made up of people fitting the economists' rational ideal—acting to promote their goals in an "optimal" way. Indeed, as economist Duncan Foley put it in a review of the subject, "The disconfirmation of rational choice theory appears to be one of the few really robust results achieved by the human sciences."[9]

If nothing else, investors (and everyone else) often face situations far too complex for any rational optimization of strategy to be of much use. Friedman's F-twist was a desperate attempt to sidestep the implications of this obvious fact, and to make it okay to go on using convenient theories based on rationality anyway. Moving toward a deeper understanding of markets requires a more honest approach. To begin, it means paying attention to how people really behave in the markets.

The Other Side of Smart

It was the second week of August 2007, and on Wall Street and around the world, the rumors were flying. Over nearly two decades, the famous Medallion Fund run by Jamie Simons had rarely experienced a down month. Yet suddenly, in the span of a few days, it lost nearly 10 percent. The week had brought Goldman Sachs's flagship fund, Global Alpha, down 26 percent for the year, while a prominent fund run by Cliff Asness of AQR Capital Management had lost 13 percent. Other quant hedge funds had done equally poorly, and the rumors suggested that it wasn't over yet; these funds were still hemorrhaging money—and couldn't find a way to stop it.

For any investment fund, of course, rumors of losses are almost as bad as actual losses, as fear has a dynamic all its own, and spooked investors may bolt for the doors. In 2004, Jonathan Bailey and Stephen Coates had won industry awards for the wild success of their just-launched Bailey

Coates Cromwell Fund. But when poor bets the next year took 20 percent off the fund's $1.3 billion portfolio, remaining investors demanded their cash back, wiping the fund out by June 2005.[10]

So in the second week of August, Asness decided it was best to meet the fear head on, which he did in a letter to the fund's investors, explaining how his supersophisticated hedge fund—specializing in trading on the basis of precisely crafted mathematical algorithms—had suddenly run into trouble. "Many of you may have heard rumors concerning us over the last few days. If the rumors are that we've had better weeks, then they are accurate. If the rumors are that we are in some pain over the recent widespread quant stock selection woes, then they are accurate. If the rumors are more severe than that, then they are simply false."[11]

Indeed, Asness admitted, their recent stock selections had been "shockingly bad." Over the previous seven years, AQR's fund had earned 13.7 percent a year on average, after fees. Yet mathematical trading strategies that had been working spectacularly well for a long time had suddenly gone very wrong.

But the letter continued. Despite the abrupt failure of everything he had been relying on for seven years, Asness claimed he wasn't actually surprised, or alarmed. Unpredictable, sudden failures, he suggested are a normal part of business:

> I occasionally hear broad statements like "this just shows computer models don't always work." That's true, of course, they don't, nothing always works. However, this isn't about models, this is about a strategy getting too crowded, as other successful strategies both quantitative and non-quantitative have gotten many times in the past, and then suffered when too many try to get out the same door.

Nothing works always. There's no "free lunch," as economists like to put it, as markets are indeed very hard to predict. This is standard fare as far as Wall Street explanations go, akin to the ubiquitous financial disclaimer that "past performance is no guide to future performance."

But the latter part of this statement says something different and more interesting—that the fund's trouble was brought on at least in part by its own actions, and by the strategy AQR was using getting "too crowded." What did Asness mean by that? He seems to be saying that the fund hadn't merely guessed wrong about the market, the way an NFL fan might guess wrong on a bet on the Super Bowl, an outcome their bet cannot influence. The disaster for the hedge funds, Asness hinted, came about in another way, the actions of the funds themselves setting up the conditions for the trouble.

As Asness was writing, so were others. "Regrettably," wrote Jim Simons of Renaissance Technologies, "we have not had good luck during these last few days of August . . . We have been caught in what appears to be a large wave of de-leveraging on the part of quantitative long/short hedge funds."[12] Minder Cheng of Barclays Global Capital echoed much the same thing to investors. "The past ten days on the whole were very negative," and he, too, pointed to a temporary wave of "deleveraging" as the cause.[13]

All these hedge fund managers were saying the same thing—that their trading strategies had become too similar. Like aircraft flying too close together, the funds had interfered with one another's free space, changed the market, and as a result tumbled together from the sky. (The mysterious "deleveraging," the cause of their demise, I'll explore in detail in a later chapter.) They were, in effect, taking part in a complex game of many players in which what each did influenced the others, whose actions in turn fed back to change their own.

As we'll see in chapter 7, what actually happened to those hedge funds can be explained quite simply; it might even have been predicted by someone with the right data. More important for the moment is what this example says about the way markets work—and how one ought to go about making models of them. The quant meltdown of August 2007 is a dramatic illustration of the inability of anyone to figure out the "game" of the market in some final, rational way, a point most professional traders know from experience. Even the idea of having confidence in one's investment positions, John Tudor Jones suggests, is a recipe for disaster. "The most important rule of trading is to play defense, not great offense. Every day I assume every position I have is wrong . . . If they are going against me, then I have a game plan for getting out. Don't be a hero. Don't have an ego. Always question yourself and your ability. Don't ever feel that you are very good. The second you do, you are dead."[14]

If the market is a game, then it is one in which untold millions of diverse individuals with different histories, beliefs, and aims play against one another, and with one another, at the same time. Investing and taking on the risk of loss is the price of participation.

Economic theory, of course, has a long tradition of thinking about the nature of games and the way people play them. The theory of games has lots of mathematics and a high reputation in economics, which it in part deserves. But game theory as typically used in economics isn't really up to handling the continuous unpredictability inherent in financial markets, as reflected in the quant meltdown of 2007 or countless similar episodes through the ages. The problem, again, is a fixation on equilibrium.

Two Kinds of Games

Several years ago, University of Chicago economist Richard Thaler placed an ad in the *Financial Times* initiating an intriguing competition, open to all comers. The game was very simple. Each entrant had to choose a number between 0 and 100. The winner would be whoever chose the number that turned out to be closest to two thirds of the average of what everyone else chose. Entry cost was $10 and Thaler offered the winner two round-trip business-class tickets from New York to London.

This competition is a game in the usual sense of being something fun to play, but also in the more technical mathematical sense. In game theory, a game is any situation in which multiple individuals interact and fare better or worse depending on both their own actions and those of the others. Invented by physicist John von Neumann and economist Oskar Morgenstern in 1932, game theory has a storied history as a powerful tool for analyzing strategic choices. And in the history of game theory, one insight stands out above all others—that smart players have to assume that they will be playing against others who are also smart, and will try their very best. Assuming anything else is naïve, and likely dangerous.

Take this view very seriously, as mathematician John Nash did in 1950, and it provides the basis of deep insight into strategic situations of all kinds. Nash analyzed not any specific game, like chess or poker or trying to win elected office, but the general *idea* of a game—any number of players, each having a large but finite set of possible strategies or ways to play—and found a general class of solutions. If each person is smart, and thinks hard, and knows others are also smart, and thinking hard, then one logical outcome is a kind of equilibrium stalemate, with each person playing the strategy that gives them the best payoff, on the assumption that each other person will do the same for themselves. In this situation, no player can improve his outcome by unilaterally changing his behavior, if others keep acting the same way.

This is a Nash equilibrium—a simple consequence, it seems, of the capacity of people to be forward thinking and strategic in their actions. The idea of Nash equilibrium is so nice and tidy that it has dominated economic thinking about strategic games ever since. It's been applied fruitfully to bargaining between firms, to evolution, and to the logic of nuclear deterrence. Unfortunately, it also has one major shortcoming: real people often just don't act in the rational way game theory supposes.

Thaler's game, as trivially simple as it is, offers a good example. Each person in the game has precisely the same set of possible actions—choosing any number between 0 and 100. If you're rational, and if you assume everyone else is equally rational, then everyone should come to the same best choice. That best choice should be equal to two thirds of the average of what everyone chooses, which should be that same number. (Remember—everyone is rational, so everyone should make the same choice.) Therefore, the rational answer to Thaler's game is the only number equal to two thirds of itself—0. If everyone chooses 0, then everyone is exactly right: they've chosen two thirds of the average. This is the Nash equilibrium, the consistent rational solution.

The trouble with this mathematical sophistication is that it is psychologically naïve. When Thaler analyzed all the entries, he found that only a few people had actually chosen 0, while quite a few chose 33 and 22. The first is what you would choose if you simply think everyone else will choose randomly between 0 and 100, resulting in an average of 50. The second is what you get if you take the logic one step further—supposing that people will choose 33. People did very different things, thought about the problem differently, and in the end that average was 18.9. The winning entry had chosen 13.

But peoples' failure to act rationally isn't the most serious problem with the concept of Nash equilibrium. As we saw earlier with the Arrow-Debreu proof of an equilibrium for an economy, the mere existence of an equilibrium says little about whether any real economy might actually stumble into such a condition. Similarly, for any game, a collection of authentic human beings with realistic powers of reasoning may well never find a Nash equilibrium, making such states the equivalent of museum pieces with no real-world relevance. It's just as likely that people playing go on changing their styles of play, adapting and responding to one another in a way that leads to ongoing chaos.

No one, after all, not even a grand master champion, plays chess by working out the Nash equilibrium perfect strategy—first, because no human being can possibly calculate what it is, and second, because there's no guarantee your opponent will play that way either.[15] This would seem especially likely in any situation—think financial markets—in which the number of possible strategies is enormous, and it becomes impossible to "solve the problem" of what to do through anything like perfect rational reflection. This theme is as old as human history—probably older. The best laid plans go awry. "No plan," as the Prussian military genius Helmuth von Moltke put it, "withstands contact with the enemy."

This point is obvious enough from world affairs, business, as well as games played by real people, including sports.[16] But it becomes even clearer in experiments with computers playing games. In experiments it's possible to study what happens gradually as games get harder, so that rational behavior becomes ever more impossible. The outcome is that the games begin to look a lot like markets.

The Learning Curve Never Ends

Forget people for the moment. Think strategies. After all, what happens in a game really comes down to the strategies that get played, regardless of the intelligent force behind them, whether it's a person or artificial intelligence or a group of monkeys directing a computer. Whatever happens in complex games with people ought to be reflected in games played by computers. And computers don't get tired, or ask for payment. This is the idea physicists Tobias Galla and Doyne Farmer had a couple years ago—to use computers to explore in a systematic way how intelligent agents playing games fare as games become increasingly complex.

Computers, of course, can't do things people do easily—recognize a friend from a glimpse of the back of his or her head, or parse the complex structures of language. But when it comes to recognizing relatively simple patterns on the fly, computers often do even better than people. Computer scientist Dave Cliff of the University of Bristol has developed several generations of computer trading algorithms that systematically outperform human traders when pitted against them. They do so by using very simple rules, but having the capacity to learn very quickly from their past mistakes.[17] The rise of algorithmic trading in financial markets—it now accounts for well over 50 percent of all trading—reflects the conviction of the biggest trading firms that Cliff and others like him are right: computers can do as well as people.

The advantage of using computers over people is the ability to run hundreds of thousands of experiments very quickly, changing the nature of the games, to see how different levels of complexity influence how players end up playing in the long run. In each of their experiments, Galla and Farmer had two computer players—call them Alice and Bob—compete against one another. Each had N possible strategies to choose from. In game theory, a game is defined by a list of numbers in pairs, showing the payoffs each of the two players get for every possible choice of strategies being played. These numbers, in effect, set the rules of the game, and determine the payoffs for Alice and Bob for every possible choice of their actions. Looking at these numbers, Alice and Bob can decide which strategy they should play.

Now here's the cute idea in Galla and Farmer's analysis. They could have chosen a particular kind of game, one of the thousands studied in the voluminous literature of game theory. But the results would then perhaps apply only to that game or similar ones. To get a much more general result, they instead chose the games randomly, selecting each of the numbers in the list of pairs from a normal distribution curve (explained in greater detail in chapter 1) centered on 0, with most of the numbers being between -1 and 1. For each choice of a game, they then let the two computers play. Each started out making fairly random guesses, but was programmed to learn quickly by playing strategies more frequently if they have worked well in the past. In effect, the computers learn patterns in the competition through trial and error.

Computer scientists know that learning algorithms of this kind, if playing fairly simple games with just a few possible strategies, $N = 2$, 3, or 4, say, very quickly come to coordinate themselves around Nash equilibrium strategies, often learning to play more rationally even than real people. But in more complicated games, Galla and Farmer found, things go quite differently. With $N = 50$, the algorithms failed to settle on any kind of stable behavior, even after a very long time. In a typical run, of course, neither player wins consistently; sometimes Alice does better, and sometimes Bob. In the long run, each has the same average success. But the competition never settles into any repetitive pattern. Bob sometimes wins for an extended period, before Alice reverses the tide. The history is an ongoing chaos of unpredictability, never settling into any predictable pattern.

It is important to point out that game theory itself provides for the possibility that outcomes of a game played many times fluctuate. John Nash proved that all finite games have a Nash equilibrium (meaning not that players or even computers tend to arrive at it, only that such an outcome is *possible*), but some of these may involve the players using so-called mixed strategies—strategies in which they choose their moves with a stable set of probabilities. In this case, the outcome from one game to the next will fluctuate. However, in such a Nash equilibrium, the fluctuations will still be stable and unchanging over time. For argument's sake, think of a chessboard that has been reduced, over time, to just two opposing kings. The kings, which can never venture within one square of each other, can never actually reach an endgame; they can only perform a random, purposeless dance. This is very different from the findings of Galla and Farmer. As long as the game continues, the two agents keep trying to learn optimal strategies, and they often succeed for a time, winning consistently for a while before their opponent can adjust. The process of learning and competing is never over, and neither player can ever settle on a final strategy, even one involving random choice with fixed probabilities. The sheer complexity of the game prevents such outcomes.

This study makes a profound point—that in games of sufficient complexity, the insights coming from equilibrium analyses just don't tell you much about what is likely to happen. The intoxicating notion of Nash equilibrium has little relevance to complex, high-dimensional games. Rather than any balance, the agents never find any equilibrium at all, and the evolution of strategic behaviors simply carries on indefinitely. As Galla and Farmer concluded, "Their strategies continually vary as each player responds to past conditions and attempts to do better than the other players. The trajectories in the strategy space display high-dimensional chaos, suggesting that for most intents and purposes the behavior is essentially random, and the future evolution is inherently unpredictable."

Equally striking, of course, is that these kinds of rich, complex, ongoing dynamics look quite similar to what one sees in real systems, including financial markets, with periods of relative calm punctured by bouts of extreme volatility. Yet, as with the rice pile of the last chapter, there's nothing you can point to that is causing this disruption, no "shocks" to the system, no noise or anything else. It all comes from perfectly natural internal dynamics. And this is in a game with $N = 50$ strategies. Let that grow to 100, 1,000, 10,000, or let there be more players as in the financial markets, and things will likely grow only more chaotic and unpredictable.

The message is that in complex games dynamics really matter and cannot be theorized out of existence, however hard economists may try. Equilibrium is, after all, a way of analyzing a system as if time doesn't matter. If we're going to learn how to model markets effectively, analyzing highly complex games looks like a promising path.

The Other Canon

The economic historian Erik Reinert has written about the Other Canon,[18] a term he uses to refer to those branches of past economic thinking that have fallen out of use and into the history books, pushed aside and forgotten by modern equilibrium theorists. For the economist Joseph Schumpeter, the key to economic progress wasn't free trade leading to exchange and optimal equilibrium, but human creativity and innovation creating perpetual waves of "creative destruction." The Austrian economist Friederich von Hayek celebrated the "spontaneous order" and organization that arises in human societies and its institutions, as people collectively respond to change with novel structures slipping outside the grasp of any simple equilibrium understanding.

The thinking of economists Reinert included in his Other Canon— others were American Thorstein Veblen and the Brit Herbert Foxwell— were all infused with a disequilibrium spirit, as was the great British economist John Maynard Keynes. For Keynes, the markets resembled nothing so much as a beauty contest in which participants aim to choose not the most beautiful entrant, but the one they think most others will choose as the most beautiful. Everyone, ultimately, must guess what others will guess about what others will guess. In the markets, Keynes suggested, we must "devote our intelligences to anticipating what average opinion expects the average opinion to be."[19] This is the market viewed as a game much like Thaler's competition.

In the market, as in the games of Galla and Farmer, there is no "best" strategy, as the success or failure of any strategy depends on what everyone else is doing and the strategies they are using. This is precisely what Cliff Asness learned (or relearned) in the painful episode of the quant meltdown. His strategy worked brilliantly until others began using it and it became "too crowded," disaster ensuing shortly thereafter. Market activity emerges out of an ever-shifting ecology of interacting strategies competing for success in predicting and anticipating the strategies others will be using, and how all will play out together in interaction.

All of this explains, of course, why there's an inexhaustible market for books touting the success of different investing strategies. Some successful investors are "fundamentalists" or "value investors" who study companies and try to identify cheap stocks to buy or overpriced ones to sell short. Famous mutual fund manager Peter Lynch ran the enormously successful Magellan Fund from 1977 through 1990, during which time the fund averaged a 29 percent gain per year. By his own account in his book *Beating the Street*, Lynch didn't rely on complex mathematical analysis or mysterious reading of patterns in price movements ("chart reading"). He relied on old-fashioned hard work and investigation. Lynch typically visited hundreds of companies in the course of a year, talking with top management, strolling manufacturing floors, speaking with engineers. He spoke with managers of a thousand more by telephone. In his view, not everyone should invest in stocks, because there's really no sense if you're not going to do mountains of research. "Millions of Americans should refrain from buying stocks. These are people who have no interest in investigating companies and cringe at the sight of a balance sheet, and who thumb through annual reports only for the pictures. The worst thing you can do is to invest in companies you know nothing about."[20]

But if many investors follow similar strategies, an army of others works instead using so-called technical strategies—methods they claim help them predict future price movements on the basis of past movements. If Japanese yen have risen by 1 percent or more in the past five days, a technical strategy might claim, it will be likely to continue its climb, so it is a good time to buy. Traders in stock, commodity, and foreign exchange markets use such rules widely, following trends, and expecting history to repeat itself as traders react as they have in the past.

As a text on the topic describes the motivation, the technical approach to investment reflects the belief that prices move in trends which are determined by the changing attitudes of investors toward a variety of economic, monetary, political and psychological forces . . . Since the technical approach is based on the theory that the price is a reflection of mass psychology ("the crowd") in action, it attempts to forecast future price movements on the assumption that crowd psychology moves between panic, fear, and pessimism on one hand and confidence, excessive optimism, and greed on the other.[21]

In many cases, traders in such markets also see specific round numbers as points of special dynamics. For example, according to Jorge Rodriguez, director of North American Sales at Credit Suisse, "The 100 yen level for the dollar is still a very big psychological barrier and it will take a few tests before it breaks. But once you break 100 yen, it's not going to remain there for long. You'll probably see it trade between 102 and 106 for a while."[22] Some studies claim that when an exchange rate approaches a round number such as 100 yen to the dollar, it will abruptly reverse its rise, as if repelled. But if the rate manages to burst through that level, it then moves rapidly past it.[23]

Academic studies have shown that such analysis can really work, especially in foreign exchange markets.

Other investors follow still another strategy. Interviewed by Jack Schwager for his book *Market Wizards*, a well-known commodities trader named Michael Marcus suggests that he learned as a floor trader how to identify special moments when the market is prone to large moves, or instead if a strong rally is just about to stall and reverse:

You develop an almost subconscious sense of the market on the floor. You learn to gauge price movement by the intensity of voices in the ring. For example, when the market is active and moving, and then gets quiet, that is often a sign that it is not going to go much further. Also, sometimes when the ring is moderately loud and suddenly gets very loud, instead of being a sign that the market is ready to blast off as you might think, it actually indicates that the market is running into a greater amount of opposing orders.[24]

The legendary financier George Soros based his investment strategy on similar psychological insight. In *The Alchemy of Finance*, he even admits to having bailed out of some positions due to intense back pain, taking this pain as a bodily signal carrying insight his intellectual mind couldn't yet grasp. (This is good to keep in mind when evaluating the claim that human beings are rational investors.)

Again, the market is an ecology of interacting agents. They use an extremely diverse set of strategies. In so doing, they together create their own collective, unpredictable reality.

From *Homo economicus* to *Homo sapiens*

By now, economists have largely conceded the point that people aren't anything like rational when it comes to making decisions, including decisions about investments. Indeed, the very idea of complete rationality doesn't even make sense under close scrutiny; it's a logical contradiction.

Suppose that some unfailingly rational investor faces a decision about whether to sell their holdings in Microsoft, whose stock has been falling for several days. Like Peter Lynch, he or she begins by gathering information and studying reports. But research and deliberation take time and come with costs; Microsoft may still be falling. Getting all the information to make a perfect decision with minimal chance of error may take too long. A perfectly rational investor first has to decide the optimal amount of time to go on studying before making a decision. Before even getting to work, a fully rational person should really solve this preliminary problem.

But this is only the beginning of infinite trouble. This preliminary problem—how long do I spend researching stocks before I make a decision?—is also difficult, and since time is money, a rational individual shouldn't want to waste resources thinking about this one too long either. A fully rational person therefore has to decide on the optimal time to spend on solving this preliminary problem, which presents yet another problem. This chain of problems never ends. Rationality taken to its logical conclusion ends up destroying itself, it's simply an inconsistent idea, an illusion.[25]

Of course, this is an absurd scenario. Any normal person would do some research, and then, when they feel ready, go ahead and make an investment decision. But that's just the point: people behave on the basis not of perfect reason but other more adaptive and flexible principles. Over the past two decades, an avalanche of experiments in psychology have demonstrated that people often make decisions by using simple rules of thumb or "heuristics" rather than hard calculation. Intuitive judgments often give decent results effortlessly and quickly, avoiding costly indecision. In a study in 2006, for example, psychologists found that people facing simple decisions did best with conscious calculation, but that decisions made on "gut feelings" were superior for complex decisions, which involve the conflicting pulls and pushes of many different attributes.[26]

This body of work has stimulated its own revolution in economics, centered on the label "behavioral economics"—economics attuned to how real people behave, rather than a theorists' convenient myth. A principle insight, as described by Princeton psychologist Daniel Kahneman, is that we humans in effect have two minds, not just one. Hold some paper with writing on it in front of a friend's face and they will start reading it, even if you ask them not to; they can't stop themselves, as the urge to interpret written language in our visual field is preconscious. We have a deep instinctive mind that operates automatically and out of our control. This mind often makes errors. It systematically underestimates the likelihood of infrequent risks, for example, and makes us overconfident. But on top of this primitive mind is another very different conscious mind. This mind may not be rational, but at least it takes steps in that direction, using calculation. It takes effort to use, is slow and laborious, but it can correct some of the errors of the instinctive brain. These two types of thinking are the two named in the title of Kahneman's recent bestseller, *Thinking, Fast and Slow*.

This behavioral revolution, in the words of Richard Thaler, is slowly moving economic theorists from their favorite model of people as *Homo economicus*—perfectly rational and greedy—toward a more realistic model of the beast we really are, *Homo sapiens*. But as valuable and necessary as this is, a better picture of individual behavior isn't enough. Many if not most of the surprises in the social world, especially in markets, trace back not to oddities in individual human behavior, but rather to the way the actions of many individuals can feed together—as in the quant meltdown—to create consequences no one intended. This is collective complexity, not individual complexity, and no study of individual behavior on its own can lead us to understand it. It requires a concentrated effort to understand the kinds of patterns that well up naturally in groups of people in interaction.

Last year at a scientific meeting between physicists and economists, I gave a talk arguing this point and using some examples from physics as an illustration. A small metal bead or ball bearing is a simple thing. Put a pile of these into a shallow dish and shake it up and down, and you wouldn't expect to see anything interesting. But the interactions among the beads actually lead to incredible complexity. In experiments, the beads naturally form up to create a wide range of rich patterns, as shown in the figure below. Sometimes the beads form regular gridlike structures, sometimes there is ongoing chaos, and sometimes even isolated structures form and float around on the bead surface as if following aims of their own.[27]

All images show a layer of tiny bronze beads in a vertically shaken container having a diameter of about ten centimeters. The patterns emerge once the acceleration of the beads—which depends on shaking frequency and amplitude—becomes sufficiently high. Which pattern wins out depends on the frequency; for some frequencies the patterns mingle and continue to evolve with time. The figure to the right shows peculiar isolated patterns—known as "oscillons"—that wander around and persist as if they were permanent objects in their own right. (Figures courtesy of Paul Umbanhowar)

I thought this effectively made an important logical point—that the rich dynamics and structures seen in some system of many interacting parts may have nothing whatsoever to do with the nature of the parts. The patterns don't reflect properties of the beads. If you get all this complexity in a thing as simple as a pile of beads, then you should certainly expect to see lots of similar complexity and similar surprises in any system of interacting people such as a market.

But an economist in the audience from the Federal Reserve Bank had an odd response. Economists, he said, don't like surprises in their models. "If an economist presents a model and in the end pulls a rabbit out of a hat," he said, "you can be sure that he will have shown you along the way when he put the rabbit in the hat." In other words, the purpose of models isn't to explore the kinds of surprising outcomes that might emerge out of some situation, but something else altogether. All things equal, surprises aren't welcome.

But that's just it. The rabbits that we don't know are in the hat matter most, because they surprise us. They can hurt us. This is where we can learn a lot by building simple, plausible models to capture the nub of this or that situation. This is a relatively new game for those studying the financial markets, but already we've seen some stunning things.

6

Ecologies of Belief

Far better an approximate answer to the right question,
which is often vague, than an exact answer to the wrong question,
which can always be made precise.

—John Tukey

If economists wished to study the horse, they wouldn't go
and look at the horses. They'd sit in their studies and say to
themselves, "What would I do if I were a horse?"

—Ely Devons

AS A GRADUATE STUDENT IN PHYSICS, I once got a job working three days over the Fourth of July holiday. I needed extra money to pay the rent. I earned $270 in three long days shoveling and spreading gravel under a hot Virginia sun, and it would have made a big difference, except that on the final afternoon, I skipped back to the lab at lunch to do some calculations. The speeding ticket I got on my way back came to $271. Net gain from the three days: -$1, some exercise, and a chuckle—even I had to appreciate the irony.

The world is unpredictable. Often it bites back.

Of course, unpredictability can be far more serious, and the American economist Frank Knight made a big deal of it. The intellectual founder of the famous Chicago school of economics, Knight distinguished "risk" from "uncertainty." Risk, in his view, is what we face when we know what's possible, and the various probabilities for different things to happen. Risk describes a game of roulette at the casino. In contrast, "uncertainty" is a more serious form of unknowing, the situation of an individual confronting risk untamed and unconstrained, the dangers of living in a world of true surprises, unimagined twists, and "unknown unknowns."

Knight based his view of economics on an appreciation of this deep uncertainty, as much as it may seem an obstacle to theoretical science. Indeed, he did not even see the core task of economics as technical theorizing, but as the "discovery and definition of values—a moral, not to say religious, problem." Knight doubted, as one economic history describes,

> that there could be any possibility of the scientific management of society, through the manipulation of self-interest in the market, or otherwise. Human reason was a frail instrument, often corrupted by the baser elements in human nature . . . he [also] did not believe that individuals could exist independent of a grounding in some culture or society—human beings, he thought, were social by nature.[1]

But Knight was an old-school economist, and he began to establish his worldview in the days before the cult of rationality. What Knight took as the starting point for human behavior, other economists have pushed to the side.

One thing that makes social science and economics different from physics is that peoples' expectations matter. What will happen in a market tomorrow or next week depends strongly on what people think or expect is likely to happen. Hence, any attempt to build models of markets or economies has to face up to the difficult question of how to model peoples' expectations. A theory of markets immediately comes face-to-face with the infinite complexity of human psychology. In 1961, however, economist John Muth suggested that theorists could get around this problem if they assumed that people have "rational expectations," a minor variation of the idea of human rationality, as explored in chapter 5. The idea is that people—while they don't know the future, and may well be totally mistaken about it—will at least be unbiased about the likelihood of different possible outcomes.

This assumption achieves the neat trick of wiping away uncertainty about the future and human perceptions of it, and lets economists build tidy theories without having to worry about psychology. It turns consideration of Knight's wild "uncertainty" into tamer "risk," which can be analyzed with probabilities, and for forty years this idea has been the primary driver of economic theory, especially of markets or whole economies. As we've seen, it bears a less than desirable relationship to reality. But just as importantly, theories that make this assumption, at least the ones we've been working with for these past few decades, have another failing: they offer little or no insight into some of the markets' most important events. Events like the recent financial crisis and the deep recession following it, the dot-com boom and bust of the late 1990s, or the "black Monday" crash of 1987. Rational expectations theories don't even really try to make numerical sense of these events, in fact, instead setting them aside as the consequence of hypothetical but unmeasurable "economic shocks"—the appearance of new technologies, for example. In the world of rational expectations, there can be no excessive accumulation of debt driven by, for example, irrational confidence in the future of housing prices. Every market event is assumed, by definition, to reflect the optimal outcome of a market of rational actors.

The British economist and writer John Kay makes an apt analogy. In Bertolt Brecht's play *Life of Galileo*, Kay notes, there's a moment when the grand inquisitors of the Catholic Church refuse to look through Galileo's telescope. Why? Because the church has already deduced the motion of the planets from a set of axioms. They refused to look, as Kay puts it, "on the grounds that the Church has decreed that he sees cannot be there. This makes me think of the way some of the economists who believe in Rational Expectations have reacted to events of the past few years. [They're like the inquisitors with Galileo] . . . They refuse to look through the telescope because they know on a priori grounds that what he saw wasn't actually there."

With much of the economic mainstream locked into this view,[2] it has taken the determined effort of a small group of renegades and scientists from other fields to begin making meaningful adjustments to the theory of markets. Their approach has been to turn away from the rational expectations fantasy, and to demote rationality and human calculation. If you listen to psychologists, people don't really think rationally, at least not very often. What people do is act, err, observe, and learn—and we're generally pretty good at that.

Thinking about Thinking

As a young man in his twenties, Adriaan de Groot played chess for the Dutch national team, then turned his interests to psychology, especially the psychology of thinking about complex problems—problems like chess. De Groot wrote a Ph.D. dissertation—it later became a book, *Thought and Choice in Chess*—that is today still considered a classic. How do chess champions play chess, and what is it that makes an expert so much better than an ordinary player? It's not, as common fascination would have it, that Garry Kasparov has superhuman mental abilities and can see how move and countermove will play out thirty or fifty moves in advance. The difference, as De Groot discovered—and presumably knew from his own personal experience—lies elsewhere.

Chess is an enormously complicated game. No two matches ever play out exactly alike, and even if both players have lost half their pieces, the number of possible five-move sequences from any position is typically in the thousands. There's no way to figure out the "best way" to play a game of chess, and a good player has to invent strategy on the fly, in response to the actions of his opponent. Indeed, De Groot found in experiments that chess experts don't actually think forward a larger number of moves, or consider more possible moves, than do amateurs. Instead, experts are more like good shoppers: rather than looking at every single shirt on the rack, they know how to quickly narrow it down to two or three promising ones, while the beginners are busy sorting through the first three they see.

De Groot also found that grand masters have an almost photographic memory for chess positions. He let both chess masters and ordinary good players look for between two and fifteen seconds at an arrangement of chess pieces on a board, and found that grand masters and masters were able to recall the location of 93 percent of the pieces, while ordinary players remembered closer to 50 percent.

Why does this happen? Do grand masters simply have better memories than the rest of us? Actually, no, they don't.

Decades later, a follow-up study by William Chase and Herbert Simon showed that what chess masters have is a very specific, special-purpose kind of memory.[3] Chase and Simon repeated De Groot's experiments, but studied the recall of both piece arrangements taken from real games as well as totally random arrangements. The chess masters did much better than nonexperts if the board arrangements came from real chess

games, but did no better than the others with truly random arrangements. In the latter case, both typically remembered the positions of about
seven pieces, which seems to be around the limit of human short-term
memory. Most of us can remember a list of about seven numbers read
out to us, but not much more.[4]

Hence, chess masters' memories seem to be attuned to their subject.
It's a plausible conjecture that this is so because they've trained themselves through long experience to recognize a wide range of patterns that
often appear in games. As a result, they can quickly see a board not as a
handful of pieces with specific positions, but as a construct of three or
four common patterns or "chunks," each comprising a few chess pieces,
thereby greatly reducing the burden on memory. This is the same memory trick that allows a reader to easily remember a pithy sentence like
"these are the times that try men's souls" but could never recall a detailed
sequence of a random string of letters of the same length. As Chase and
Simon put it, "Behind [the chess master's] perceptual analysis, as with all
skills, lies an extensive cognitive apparatus amassed through years of
constant practice. What was once accomplished by slow, conscious, de-
ductive reasoning is now arrived at by fast unconscious perceptual pro-
cessing. It is no mistake of language for the chess master to say that he
'sees' the right move."

With this greater insight and ability to penetrate into common patterns,
experts naturally build better strategies. They're tuned in to patterns
known from past experience to have "weight" and importance because
they carry predictive value, reflecting core features on which strategy can
be built. Grand masters don't have to just calculate their way to the best
move—a task that is, mathematically, quite impossible. They use pattern
recognition, developed through long practice, to build theories about what
works best—or at least reasonably well—in different situations, and they
revise those theories throughout their careers.

This research, with its emphasis on learning at the core of human behavior, was well established by the 1970s, when the rational expectations
frenzy took over economics. But few economists took much note of it. For
forty years since, most mainstream economists have paid mere lip service to the process of human learning and its potential importance in
economics, seeming to regard it only as a way to justify using their preferred assumptions of rationality. Maybe, they suggest (unconvincingly),[5]
there is good reason to treat people as having rational expectations be-

cause this is how good learners should end up acting in the long run. But it doesn't work that way. Many studies have shown that people learning in even mildly complex environments end up behaving in ways that fall well short of the perfectly rational ideal. The more people feel they have lost control, for example, the more they become desperate and begin seeing patterns even in completely random noise.[6]

A move to put some of the insights of cognitive psychology at the foundations of market theory only came in the 1990s, when Stanford economist Brian Arthur began playing around with a seemingly frivolous intellectual game. Arthur wondered how people might make decisions when—in situations at least as complex as a game of chess, or more so—strictly rational planning is just not possible. His game has launched a minor revolution in market modeling, and this movement has one big advantage over rational expectations: its theories actually look like reality. Arthur's game offers a promising path to models of markets that respect their rich internal dynamics—their character as close cousins of the weather.

Recipes for Imbalance

What chess masters do in chess, Arthur reasoned, ordinary people do, too, in those parts of their lives where they are experts—at work, or in planning their daily actions. As in chess, people typically cannot work out an "optimal" plan for action in any situation; overwhelming complexity demands more flexible ways for planning actions. What might this lead to in a setting where many people face the same situation together? To explore this question, Arthur devised a seductively simple example— the puzzle of El Farol bar.

Suppose there's a college bar, El Farol, with music and cheap drinks every Thursday night. Naturally, lots of students want to go. Trouble is it's a tiny place, and they will enjoy it only if 60 percent or fewer of them go. They will, otherwise, suffer miserably in the cramped heat. Hence, each week, every student faces the tricky decision of how to do what most other people will not do. In the world of this game, there's no cheating, calling up others to find out about plans, etc. Everyone has to decide at the same time.

Now, if an economist were trying to predict the behavior of these students, he would traditionally employ game theory. Theories cascading from John Nash's landmark work from the 1950s (see chapter 5) argue that every person will think hard about his best strategy, while remaining well aware that others will do the same. Everyone will decide with full knowledge that everyone else will also play the very best strategy they can. But here, rational thinking leads you to a dead end. If everyone is rational, then everyone will make the same rational decision, thereby arriving at the bar on the same night, and thus failing at their objective of being in a small crowd. It's even worse than chess: a solution is not just hard to find, but simply cannot exist. Strict reasoning collapses on itself.

With rational thinking off the table, Arthur wanted to find a way to describe how people would really react to this situation. Thinking about the practical learning and theorizing of chess masters, Arthur argued that people would most likely make decisions in a practical way—using simple theories or hypotheses.

For example, a person might think, "If the bar was crowded last week, it should be less crowded this week," and choose to go to El Farol. Another might think, "If the bar was crowded two weeks in a row, then it is likely to be crowded again," and stay at home. Psychologists have shown that people often make decisions by holding a handful of such theories in their minds, and using whichever one seems recently to be working best.

Looking at the bar puzzle this way, Arthur used a computer to simulate a group of people using various theories about whether to go to the bar, and learning by trial and error. The weekly attendance quickly settled at an average of about 60 percent. But—and this is the significant point—the number didn't hold at exactly 60 percent. Rather, it kept fluctuating above and below in a random way, as people changed their tactics from week to week, responding to others who were also changing theirs. There's no "equilibrium" here of the kind that economists typically like and expect, no state of unchanging balance into which things settle. Endless changes and surprises emerge from a completely static situation: people just trying to solve the same problem week after week.[7]

Okay, cute puzzle. So what? Arthur's game is a toy model, but also much more than a toy. It actually illuminates a path to building better models of markets.[8] Suppose we replace "go" with "buy" and "stay at home" with "sell," and suppose the difference in the number of people buying and selling drives a price change up or down, as it does in real markets. Suddenly the bar game isn't a bar game at all, but a direct step toward John Maynard Keynes's vision of the market as a beauty contest, with everyone guessing what others will think. (Of course, it is only one step, as investors don't necessarily want to buy when most others sell or vice versa; the market is more complicated.)

In the 1990s, Arthur, along with economist Blake LeBaron and others, developed this early idea into a more detailed market model that simulated traders buying or selling a stock, or instead putting their money into a safe interest-bearing bond, and using a wide range of predictive strategies to guide their actions. Arthur and his colleagues, working at the famed Santa Fe Institute in New Mexico, ran experiments to see if the traders would come over time to hold a rational, unbiased view of the market whose performance their own behaviors determined. In general, the experiments suggested no; the traders went on switching between a wide variety of predictive ideas and holding different views about the market, without any convergence to a rational equilibrium. Out of their behavior came a largely unpredictable record of prices prone to violent sporadic fluctuations including large rallies and crashes.[9]

Compared to any equilibrium theory, the bar game and the Santa Fe model take quantum leaps toward realism. Both models, while crude, show how it is possible to include thinking and perpetual learning in a model of markets—and how unpredictable market "weather" is the immediate result. By adding details, physicists, computer scientists, and economists over two decades have transformed Arthur's game into what are now arguably the most realistic models of markets. Blake LeBaron, in particular, has steadily improved and elaborated models of this kind that can now create simulated price fluctuations that are virtually indistinguishable from those of real markets.[10]

But the lessons to be learned from a good theory often depend on simple aspects of its structure rather than on the complications and details. The big picture sometimes matters more. If these models capture the essence of markets in at least a rough first approximation, we can ask if this picture holds any surprising predictions—things we should expect to be true about markets, but are by no means obvious to casual observation. It does—as becomes clear from an even simpler, stripped-down version of Arthur's game, which focuses with laser precision on the abstract idea of strategies in competition.

The Atomic Structure of Markets

In 1997, inspired by Arthur's lead, two physicists, Yi-Cheng Zhang and Damien Challet, tried to strip down Arthur's El Farol game to its essential core, creating the simplest possible example of a game in which intelligent play requires perpetual adaptation and learning. They called it the "minority game." Physicists often use the phrase "the hydrogen atom" as a metaphor for the simplest model that captures the essence of some situation, much in the way the hydrogen atom, with just one electron orbiting a single proton, is the simplest of all atoms. Understanding the hydrogen atom gives enormous insight into all atoms, even those with dozens of electrons in complex arrangements. The minority game, we might say, is the hydrogen atom for how markets work.[11]

As with the bar game, you start with a bunch of people who, on every play of the game, make a simple choice between two alternatives, say, A or B. Their goal is to be in the minority—to do what most other people don't do. That's it. In the game, following Arthur, Zhang and Challet let their agents work with theories or hypotheses, while having the capacity to learn. Each agent works with a random sample of, say, fifteen or twenty "strategies," which you can think of as their intellectual inheritance, a collection of different "ways to think" about how to predict the world. The agents use these strategies to play and keep track of which ones work well. On each play, the agents look into their bag of ideas and play whichever strategy has worked best in the past.

That's it—logically, just like the bar game. A collection of agents uses simple trial and error learning to try to predict the future based on the past, choosing at each moment what most others will not choose. No one strategy can emerge as the winner, because if it did, and everyone started using it, then they would all be in the majority, and all be losers. As many quantitative hedge funds saw in 2007, successful strategies sow the seeds of their own demise. As with Arthur's bar game, the minority game becomes a simple model of a financial market if we think of those choosing A or B as the "buyers" or "sellers" of some stock.

Only one thing—the mathematical simplicity of the minority game— brings a profound advantage. It is so simple that it can be solved completely—with pencil and paper alone.

What makes Arthur's El Farol or the minority games tricky is "frustration"—the awkward setup that makes it impossible for every agent to be right at the same time. By coincidence, Zhang and Challet knew that physicists in the 1980s had encountered similar frustration in a class of weird materials known as spin glasses. In these materials, atoms interact like tiny magnets with north and south poles. Ordinarily, the forces acting between magnets tend to make them line up parallel, but in a spin glass, this is only true for some pairs. For others the forces instead tend to make them line up "antiparallel," meaning they point in opposite directions (one north, the other south, for example). Now, consider what could happen as a result. If atoms A and B prefer to align parallel, and atoms B and C want to align parallel, but A and C prefer to point oppositely, you have automatic "frustration": no matter what, one pair of atoms will be left in a state of tension. In physics, the result is materials that have a hard time finding a unique state of lowest energy. In most materials—a piece of copper or silicon, or a chunk of salt—the atoms fall naturally into a preferred arrangement with a nice geometric order, each atom cozying up to others in a satisfying way. In a spin glass, that's just not possible. The atoms instead settle into any one of millions of different configurations, all with some degree of frustration.

Using techniques developed in physics for understanding frustrated systems, Zhang and Challet found they could solve the minority game exactly. Their solution tells us something profound—that we should expect markets to be a little like a physical substance. Specifically, markets in general should have two very distinct phases or regimes of behavior, as different as liquid water and solid ice. And they should be able to flip from one to the other quite unexpectedly.

Over the years, Zhang and Challet, and many others in their field, have done simulations of the minority game under a variety of different conditions. The goal of these "experiments"—which are really just computer simulations—was to look for patterns in minority game markets. They found, as the mathematics of frustrated systems predicted, the market does indeed have two different types of behavior, as well as a tendency to flip suddenly between them.

This abrupt transition shows up in the way the "predictability" of prices—the ability to make future projections based on past results—depends on the number of people in the market. When the number of people is smaller than a certain threshold, it turns out, the market always has some predictability in its movements. The degree of predictability gradually falls as the number of people grows, until finally it vanishes, then staying at zero if more people enter (see figure below).

Curiously, this regime of random movement looks rather like the economist's ideal of an "efficient" unpredictable market in which, in Samuelson's words, "properly anticipated prices fluctuate randomly." The predictable region looks rather different; here there are patterns that market participants can learn and exploit.

This transition to unpredictability really matters. As we'll see in chapter 8, there's good reason to think it may lie behind recent changes in the dynamics of markets at high frequencies, in particular the increasing frequency in such markets of sudden spiking events like the flash crash.

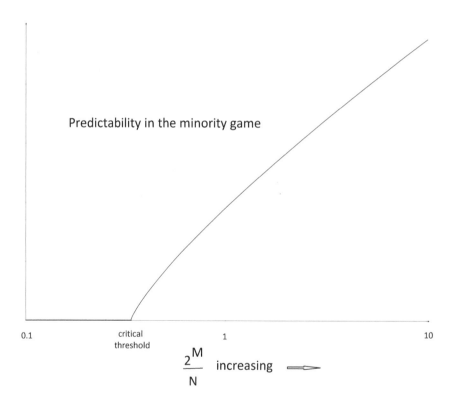

The figure shows a measure of the predictability of the minority game market as it depends on the number of market participants, which decreases moving to the right. When the number of participants is sufficiently high, the market is fully unpredictable. It becomes predictable in a sharp transition with less people in the market. (Figure courtesy of Tobias Galla)

But before we get to that, we need some deeper understanding. What causes this fundamental change? The answer, it appears, is fairly simple.

In their studies, Zhang and Challet had their agents look to the past to predict the future. Specifically, each took into account the last m moves (up or down) of the market, m being some number like 2, 4, 7, or what have you. Any move is either up or down, so 2^m expresses the number of total possible "market histories," e.g., up, then down, then up, then up, etc. If there are five moves, then your number of market histories would be 2^5, which means thirty-two different possible histories.

Now here's the kicker: the transition point—the edge where the market goes from being predictable to being unpredictable—turns out to be when the number of people is equal to this key number 2^m.[12] (Returning to our example of five total moves, we have thirty-two possible market histories. So, in this case, as long as there are thirty-two or fewer investors in the market, it remains predictable.) This is surprising, but it makes sense.

Here's how it works. The full collection of market histories—those thirty-two possible sequences—represents the full spectrum of possible market behaviors, for people looking five moves into the past. Players are sensitive to a few of these sequences and trade actively when a sequence appears. These are their preferred patterns and they are indifferent to others. The lower the number of players in the market, the higher the chance that the market will follow a pattern to which everyone is indifferent. Such a pattern can persist because no one will trade and profit and thereby wipe it out. Loosely speaking, the strategies in use by the players don't cover the space of possibilities; they remain blind to some patterns. In contrast, once you cross that threshold of thirty-two, the space of strategies becomes effectively covered or crowded; it becomes very likely that any predictable pattern will suit some agent's bag of strategies. That agent, by jumping on it and profiting, will act to destroy that pattern. What was the best strategy will then cease to be best. Once more we are plunged into the unpredictability of markets.

In other words, the fundamental transition in our hydrogen atom of a financial market is a transition based on "crowdedness," not of a physical kind, but intellectual and strategic. Following the tumultuous losses by hedge funds in the first week of August 2007, Cliff Asness of AQR Capital Management put the episode down to "a strategy getting too crowded." He probably knew what he was talking about.

Spiraling Toward . . . Reality

Let's go back to the weak form of the efficient market hypothesis, namely, that markets are fundamentally unpredictable. It can't possibly be true, at least not strictly speaking, because an army of traders and investors like Asness make a good living by predicting it. Asness's strategies include a general "managed futures" strategy that, as he has described it,

> boils down to some type of trend-following strategy, which is also known as momentum investing. Simply put, momentum investing is buying securities that are improving and selling securities that are deteriorating. There has been a mountain of research since the early 1990s showing that momentum "works"—meaning that price momentum has significant predictive power . . . We look at trends over two different time horizons and try to determine when things have gone too far. We look over 1. short-term trends, 2. long-term trends, and 3. at whether or not a trend has become overextended.[13]

Indeed, it is by pursuing such successful predictive strategies that traders are supposed to drive the market back toward the "efficient" and fully unpredictable ideal. But it'd be bad news if they ever succeeded. In fact, analysis shows it's actually impossible. As economists Sanford Grossman and Joseph Stiglitz pointed out in 1981, markets really should be just slightly predictable. Predictability gives investors an incentive to gather information and study markets—because they can profit from it. The hydrogen atom version of the minority game lends a new perspective to this idea, and suggests a clear picture of why markets should generally be slightly predictable, but not strongly so.

Here's what it looks like. If a market is in the crowded phase, it is strictly unpredictable, and traders cannot make systematic profits. As investors realize through painful experience they can't make money by investing in this market, they tend to leave. At least more should have that experience than should, by luck, make profits. Hence, the flow of people, on balance, should be out of the market. But people leaving the market in turn makes it uncrowded, and thus predictable. Now it becomes easier to profit, and investors and traders should be tempted to come back in.[14] Just around the transition point looks to be the most likely place for the market to hover, although it may well fluctuate to the right and left. The efficient market hypothesis (weak form) is a crude approximation of the tendency of markets to evolve toward the very edge of this transition—to a condition where the predictability of prices is low but not zero, making it hard but not impossible to find patterns in the market. This is pretty much where markets often seem to be.

It's possible to go on adding details and tweaking the minority game, pushing it step by step toward reality. The hydrogen atom version insists that every agent trades exactly once at each moment, so the volume of trading is fixed. In this formulation, it's simply impossible to have a crazy manic day of buying and selling, or another of unearthly quiet—which of course are things that happen all the time. If a market lurches through a stomach-churning series of ups and downs over half a day, an investor might well decide he or she has absolutely no clue what's coming next, shut down the computer, and go golfing. Indeed, experienced traders say that a crucial component of trading success is having the discipline to wait for a good opportunity, while otherwise remaining inactive.

It is easy to fix the minority game by making it a little more flexible. Tweak the model so that agents enter into a trade only if their best strategy has recently done sufficiently well. This simple idea captures the notion of investor confidence: people don't risk their money unless they think they have a valuable insight—a way to beat the market. This minor change to the minority game gives us a market model that not only has a naturally fluctuating volume, but also reproduces most of the rich statistics of real markets, including the notorious fat tails of market returns and long memory. This model does far better than traditional economics in reproducing the real behavior of markets, right down to the subtlest features of their statistics.[15]

Indeed, simulations of this kind of game show a typical pattern of fluctuations in both price and trading volume that bounce around haphazardly and have a mind of their own, just like real markets. Sudden large movements in price well up out of nowhere, yet they aren't caused by anything dramatic from the outside—just the internal mechanics of the system. At one moment the market may fall almost silent, as most traders become wary and lose confidence in the strategies they had been using. At others, it's just the opposite; trading volume soars and prices gyrate rapidly as many traders think they have real insight into what will come next. Tumultuous events can arise from nothing more than a chance momentary concentration of investors' strategies—a crowdlike similarity in thinking and behavior.

Since Zhang and Challet invented the minority game, thousands of other studies have extended it in different directions. Obviously, markets do get knocked about by outside shocks—policy announcements, for example, and corporate news—and it's easy to include this.[16] Others have extended the model to include gossip and exchange of ideas between different traders, another obviously real market phenomenon: information and rumors about the latest successful strategies fly about wildly between different investors, leading some to copy the strategies of others. Zhang himself has generalized the simplest minority game to include the usual agents who try to profit by predicting—playing the role of market traders and investors—plus another class who buy and sell without working too hard to profit. This, too, reflects a real market truth—that some actors buy and sell stocks, bonds, and other instruments not for speculation but just as a part of carrying out other kinds of business. Versions of the minority game don't even have to stick to the principle of the minority; it's been extended to much more general situations in which those in the majority do well, or some more complicated mixture of the two.[17]

You might say that the minority game isn't really a model at all, but a class of models. Or there's a better way to put it. It's the basis of a whole new way to look at markets: markets as ecologies of interacting strategies.

The Ecological Perspective

Wall Street professionals and smart investors take pride in their ability to see the likely consequences of events. If a cruise ship sinks off the coast of Italy, what does this mean for the stock of the company owning it—or their direct competitors? If the European Central Bank opens discussions with Greek authorities about a possible bailout, how will this affect the price of gold, or the values of Italian, French, or Portuguese bonds? Some people have real skills in such matters, the ability, like chess grand masters, to pick up on subtle clues learned through long experience and study. Even so, the possibility of calculating the ultimate consequences of one or several events is probably vastly overestimated; the number of pathways along which influences can travel is too great.

Two decades ago, ecologist Peter Yodzis made a profound argument to this effect in the context of ecological food webs. Seals eat cod. So, if there were fewer seals—perhaps the result of a cull designed to help the fish-ing industry—there should be more cod. Or so you'd think. But seals also eat hake, for example, another fish species, and a direct competitor of cod. Hence, fewer seals should also mean more hake, and more competition for cod. Both effects need to be counted, and, as Yodzis showed, this is only the beginning. Looking at the structure of real food webs, and including "paths" (little chains of cause and effect like the one described here) involving four species or less, Yodzis found more than 225 million different interfering influences. A simple and convincing story of how A will affect B, causing C and in turn D, really presents a profoundly incomplete view. This one causal pathway actually counts for little in the face of a profusion of similar causal pathways that could be just as influential.

It is the comparable complexity of such networks of interdependence in finance and economics that will almost certainly demand the use of computer models as experimental tools to study feedbacks within complex ecologies of interactions. The minority game, both the simplest version and its many extensions, illustrate what's possible when looking at markets from a systems perspective. It already reveals the existence of a profound phase transition—between predictable and unpredictable, or "liquid" and "frozen"—that has never before been anticipated by equilibrium theories. But similar models treating markets as ecologies of interacting beliefs and strategies can also be put to practical use.

About fifteen years ago, executives at the NASDAQ stock exchange had plans to drop its historical use of fractional prices and to change to a modern decimal format. They expected that changing the "tick size" of prices from 1/16th to 0.01 would lower the bid-ask spread, and encourage more business to the exchange. Before going ahead, however, the company hired scientists to test the idea in a market model inspired by the minority game—a variant closely styled after the NASDAQ exchange details. The model included market makers as well as traders of many sorts, operating on different timescales in different markets, and let all these traders learn on their own, hence being able to discover new effective strategies never known before in the real market. NASDAQ sensibly tested the model first to make sure it reproduced the market's normal behavior—fluctuations of volume, prices, behavior of the market makers, and so on. Then, satisfied that it was working, they used it to test their plans.

The model confirmed that the move to decimalization could help, in principle. However, it revealed a potential problem as well, as the lower price increment would enable the market makers to manipulate trading to their own advantage, profiting even while increasing the overall volatility of the market. Having been warned, NASDAQ took further steps in their market design to avoid the problem when actually going to decimals in 2001.[18]

Andrew Lo (among many others) has put much of the failure of financial economics down to economists' "physics envy"—a desire to produce theories couched in elegant mathematics and striving for the universal validity of general relativity or quantum mechanics. This assessment is accurate, or at least partly so. Modern theories of macroeconomics employ some of the same mathematics one finds in fundamental field theories of physics, in quantum electrodynamics, for example. But as I argued earlier, the idea that physics is mostly about fundamental theories of this kind is profoundly misleading. Most physics research—in anything from the formation of galaxies or black holes to the propagation of fractures through a metal—cannot be wrapped up in a few equations, and demands the understanding of myriad instabilities and feedbacks. This generally implies lots of different mathematical models, and—unavoidably—large-scale computer simulations. If economists have suffered from physics envy, it's because they have envied a false image of physics.

They ought to envy the right kind of physics—indeed, the right kind of science. Facing up to a disequilibrium world means giving up any hope for a "theory of everything." Physicists and other scientists have learned this the hard way. Even really simple problems can easily foil our desire to give clever and elegant equilibrium solutions.

Like Herding Cats

The house cat is the most intransigent creature ever to walk the earth. It will not do what it is told. The American phrase—"like herding cats"—draws on the mulish obstinacy of the cat to express the difficulty of trying to control any collection of unruly things—a gaggle of schoolchildren within line of sight of an ice-cream truck, for example. Similar headaches can arise even in efforts to control some of the world's simplest things.

At some point in your high school science education, you probably learned that there are four states of matter: solid, liquid, gas, and one lesser known state, plasma. Plasma is a gas—say, simple hydrogen gas—heated to the point at which the atoms come apart. At high enough temperature, the energy binding an electron to the nucleus of an atom is overwhelmed by powerful collisions between different atoms. Thus atoms get ripped apart and the result is a hot gas of charged electrons and protons, in which the particles, being charged, interact over extended distances, rather than only when colliding.

This is what makes plasmas totally unlike ordinary gases, whether the plasma in question is in the sun or the earth's upper atmosphere, or in a nuclear reactor. The basic properties of plasma in equilibrium—say, held at a fixed temperature in a glass tube—were roughly determined long ago. Take plasma a little out of equilibrium, however, and things get infinitely more complicated.

A good example comes from the ongoing project to harness energy from nuclear fusion. The recipe seems simple: heat hydrogen gas to enormously high temperatures and you create conditions in which colliding hydrogen nuclei can fuse together to form heavier nuclei,[19] giving off energy in the process. The reaction can be self-sustaining, too. Fusion requires nothing but high temperature (so the collisions are very energetic) and high density (so there are lots of collisions). You put some hydrogen into a container, heat it up and compress it, and there you go—cheap, virtually inexhaustible energy.

The only problem—a very big problem—is making the plasma behave as you try to do this. It is like herding cats, maybe even worse.

At Lawrence Livermore National Laboratory in California, physicists and engineers for about half a century have been trying to achieve fusion using so-called inertial confinement of the plasma. The idea is to blast a tiny pellet containing hydrogen with high-intensity X-rays coming from all directions. The blast vaporizes the pellet, produces a ball of hydrogen plasma, and crushes that ball inward, heating it in the process. Get enough compression and you get temperatures hotter than the sun and nuclear fusion.[20] In effect, you make a miniature star in the laboratory, at least in principle. Yet what starts out a nice, symmetric, imploding sphere of plasma doesn't stay that way.

A natural instability of physics creates ripples on the surface of the plasma ball and these tend to grow.[21] As the ripples get bigger, this first instability causes secondary instabilities of other kinds, and the initially nice symmetry gets hopelessly ruined. The result is that different parts of the plasma get mixed together; cold stuff from outside penetrates into the inside, spoiling the process. Temperatures don't get so high.[22] The

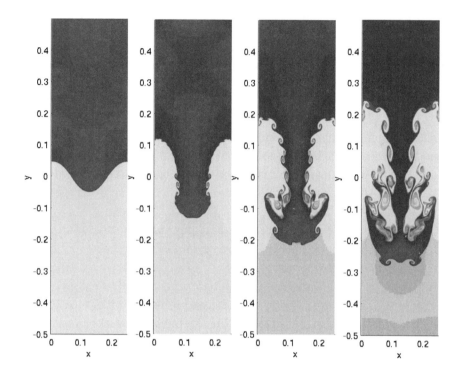

The ripples that grow into jets through the Rayleigh-Taylor instability lead to a cascade of further chaos. As this figure from a computer simulation shows, positive feedbacks destroy the initial simplicity and create a turbulent sea of complexity. (Figure courtesy of Shengtai Li, Los Alamos National Laboratory)

figure above shows how one wave growing from this natural instability soon creates a cascade of other instabilities, and the situation soon becomes hopelessly complex.

Imagine how hard it is to try to predict or control the location of any of these waves and particles. Remember—all this mess comes out of nothing but the compression of a simple gas of charged particles. The situation is naturally unstable. Because of this and other instabilities, almost nothing is simple in plasma physics. Send a beam of charged particles racing around the circular ring of a particle accelerator and that beam can go from uniform to unstable in a hundred ways—bunching together, wobbling about, and so on. A massive *Handbook on Plasma Instabilities* in three volumes, each like a small phone book, lists and describes all the known ways that positive feedbacks will make plasma in different situations do surprising and unexpected things. Every entry testifies to some situation in the past in which physicists or engineers had tried to do something with plasma, only to find that it refused to go along. The names refer to what happened, why it happened, or who first explained what happened. There's the bump-in-tail instability and the Cerenkov instability, the filamentation and firehose instabilities, the oscillating two-stream instability, the Weibel instability, and the Z-pinch instability. I could easily list hundreds.[23]

All of which should, I think, teach us a lesson in expected humility when it comes to finance and economics. Proving infallible theorems probably isn't the basis for a lot of progress, though it's what economists have been trying to do for a century or so.

And think—plasma is dead simple when compared to the nearly infinite complexity of any real financial system or economy, with millions of people driven by thoughts and emotions and unpredictable interactions with others. We know the laws of physics for atoms and molecules with enormous precision, yet we understand human behavior in only the crudest qualitative way, with few sound rules to guide us. Compressing some hydrogen plasma is *nothing* compared to pushing around millions of humans with other humans. At least electrons or protons can't randomly decide to move in another direction by their own free will. This is why markets and economies are among the most complex things in the universe.

The Physics of Finance

Economic history itself might be taken as one long colorful illustration of this basic point, decorated as it is with weird events and crises of a hundred kinds. Most, in one way or another, involve collective human movements in which thousands and millions end up herding together toward one illusory end or another, coming to believe for a time that the prices of tulips, Internet stocks, or houses always go up and never down. These movements get created only by positive feedbacks—an initial spark creating conditions that make for yet more of the same.

That's why it's such a problem that economics and finance still center so much on the study of equilibrium systems, with positive feedbacks generally ignored. As Erik Reinert says, economics through history "occasionally goes bonkers," and this seems a fair description of much research over the past fifty years that has tried so hard to fit everything into the equilibrium framework. We are, perhaps, now nearly at the tail end of this period.

If one were to make a list of economic and financial instabilities it would certainly be much longer than the list in plasma physics. It would have to span feedbacks operating on timescales from milliseconds to years, even decades and longer. Some feedbacks likely act through fairly mechanical processes such as contracts, laws, and powerful social norms that more or less compel certain behaviors. Others may work on the basis of natural psychological and decision-making tendencies—our habitual modes of learning, speculation, and so forth. Some may take off through the triggering actions of only a few parties—a small subclass of hedge funds during the quant meltdown of August 2007, for example—and others through large-scale network effects, the cause effectively spread out over individuals and firms on a global scale.

In the next chapter, I'm going to begin looking at some of the basic instabilities affecting financial systems, and also at how a disequilibrium view helps to illuminate how they work. I have no intention of even beginning an outline of a *Handbook of Financial and Economic Instabilities*. My goal is only to illustrate some of the possible categories of events that might enter such a book. I'm only trying to demonstrate beyond any doubt that we need to think in terms of disequilibrium, rather than equilibrium, if we're to understand the kinds of situations in which serious instabilities should be expected.

No theory of markets will ever come to a final set of elegant equations, like one sometimes (but only sometimes) finds in physics. Understanding markets, like understanding evolution or the weather, means dealing in approximations, in decent but flawed models, and exploring any scheme that helps make sense of a very chaotic and changeable reality—even if it does start off as a silly game about a bar.

7

Perils of Efficiency

Our fundamental risks will thus be insured against, hedged, diversified, making for a safer world. By lightening the burden of risk, a new democratic finance will encourage all of us to be more venturesome, more inspired in our activities.

—Robert J. Shiller, economist, Yale University (2003)

The greatest threat to our markets comes not from our adversaries but from ourselves . . . banks are so bent at using expanded balance sheets, using derivatives, using off balance sheet, confusing the net with the gross, pretending that risk is in the net when it's really in the gross, pretending that risk is a linear function of scale when it's an exponential function of scale . . . and other such blinders which may destroy the markets before science is able to fix it.

—James Rickards, financial security analyst, senior managing director, Tangent Capital Partners

IN 1768, AN ENGLISH LAWYER NAMED George Hadley died in the village of Flitton, northwest of London. His biographer noted that Hadley, despite working for decades as a lawyer in London, possessed notably little wealth: "it did not exceed the patrimony which his father had left him; it may therefore be fairly argued that the practice of his profession had not been lucrative to him." Neither had he much enjoyed legal practice. Instead, Hadley had spent most of his energies pursuing projects as an amateur scientist, perfecting a number of early telescopes and helping his elder brother John to create an early version of the sextant—a device for measuring latitudes at sea that became widely used in navigation.[1]

More impressively, in May 1735, Hadley delivered a short paper to the Royal Society—"concerning the cause of the general trade winds"—in which he proposed the first modern explanation for the global movements of air in the earth's atmosphere.

With a warmer equator and colder poles, Hadley suggested, warm air ought to rise skyward near the equator, flow toward both poles in the upper atmosphere, and then descend and cool near the poles. This colder air should then flow back toward the equator at the surface. This looping flow would carry heat from the hot tropics toward the colder poles. Hadley went further, arguing that the spinning of the earth should cause high-altitude air (already moving toward the poles) to flow to the east, creating strong winds well above the earth's surface. Meanwhile, the same effect near the surface should create persistent *westerly* winds near the equator.[2] In a stroke, Hadley explained the "trade winds"—the steady winds that European explorers had depended on for centuries in sailing to the Americas.

Hadley envisioned the atmosphere more or less in equilibrium, with smooth stable airflow held in overall balance. It was a natural first step,[3] yet also wrong, or at least seriously incomplete, because in reality the looping flow Hadley described only stretches from the equator to about 30 degrees latitude—the position of Florida in the Northern Hemisphere, and South Africa in the Southern Hemisphere. Further away, in the midlatitude regions, Hadley's picture doesn't hold at all. There's no stable balance, but instead ceaseless change, storms, and weather fronts, meandering cyclones and anticyclones—a global maelstrom of persistent chaos.

What most of us call the weather—the atmosphere's unpredictable behavior at midlatitudes—was only understood conceptually beginning in the 1950s. Around that time, researchers came to what may seem like an obvious realization: that no steady equilibrium-like pattern can possibly account for the chaos of the weather. Instead, weather emerges from perpetual instability and turbulence.[4] The primary culprit, in scientific terms, is something called the "baroclinic instability"—a close cousin of the plasma instabilities of the last chapter. The famous high-altitude jet streams that circulate around the planet in the midlatitudes won't stay in a tidy ringlike pattern. Positive feedbacks make any deviation of the circular path grow, turning the jet streams into wiggling snakes. The wavy pattern often becomes so pronounced that large eddies or swirls break off and take on a life of their own, drifting through the midlatitudes and causing our unpredictable weather.

What this means is that storms and weather fronts are absolutely central to the way the sun's energy flows about the planet. You cannot have a spinning planet like ours, warmed by a sun like ours, without also having thunderstorms and hurricanes and tornadoes. Our atmosphere is a perfect example of a system living not in equilibrium, but in perpetual imbalance.

There's one more interesting element to this history. Because the movement of atmospheric air is too complex for our mathematical brains, we didn't arrive at our modern understanding of weather patterns until 1956. At that time a scientist named Norman Phillips used an early computer to simulate a virtual atmosphere based on a crude approximation of the equations of atmospheric fluid dynamics. In the computer, Phillips did an experiment—starting the air at rest and letting it gradually speed up as the earth's turning dragged it into motion, and as temperature differences made air rise and fall. It took twelve hours to run, but the simulations showed that the simple baroclinic instability really does account for the fundamental character of atmospheric flows—how the stable flows always fall apart, creating cyclonic storms and weather fronts just as we see.[5]

It is ironic that in the midfifties, just as meteorology was being set free by an appreciation of instability and its role in creating complexity, economics was busy binding itself into a rigid framework of equilibrium thinking. Arrow and Debreu's 1954 proofs of the "theorems of welfare economics" led several generations of economists to interpret economic reality through equilibrium concepts, despite later studies—primarily the works of Sonnenschein, Debreu, and Mantel, but also of others—casting doubt on their relevance to any real economy. Since then many if not most economists have gone right on as if those negative results were never published. Milton Friedman once remarked that he didn't worry about the results because "the study of the stability of general equilibrium is unimportant ... because it is obvious that the economy is stable."[6]

Because of this attitude, economics today stands where atmospheric science was in around 1920 or so—trying to force disequilibrium puzzles into the ill-shaped framework of equilibrium thinking.

Over the past few chapters we've seen what taking even a few small steps away from equilibrium can do. Market models as simple as the minority game reproduce the basic stylized facts of real markets—the fat tails reflecting their tendency to unpredictable upheavals. These "ecologies" of interacting strategies also naturally reproduce the delicate long memory of real markets—the fact that what the market does today provides real information about what it will do ten years or more in the future. The ability of these simple "agent-based models" to capture complex market dynamics already distinguishes them from the equilibrium models of traditional economics. They *act* like real markets—presenting a natural internal "weather" that equilibrium thinking cannot even begin to explore.

The serious study of such models has only begun in the past fifteen years or so. Some of the simpler and less surprising results demonstrate how easy it is for quite ordinary market feedbacks to generate speculative bubbles and crashes, whether in stocks, houses, or pretty much anything else. It's clear from many surveys[7] that individual investors tend to fall into two broad types—what you might call "fundamentalists" and "chartists." Fundamentalists try to judge the "true" values of the things they buy or sell, which basically means stock values reflecting the realistic long-term potential of a company. As a result, they tend to act in ways that stabilize markets. (In the weather analogy, very loosely these folks act a little like winds that transport air and so reduce pressure differences, keeping the atmosphere more in balance.) In contrast, chartists look to profit from speculative trends and so tend to reinforce them, often destabilizing markets. (The speculative energy of these folks is crudely akin to the sun's energy, heating air that rises and creates all the eddies that spin off the edges of the jet stream.) An insight from many studies is that just a slight tendency for fundamentalists to act more like chartists during market surges—not wanting to be left behind by everyone they see profiting—can lead to sustained bubbles. But that also a weak tendency for chartists to grow more cautious during downturns, to turn into temporary fundamentalists, creates the energy of sustained crashes.[8]

Again, these results aren't so surprising for anyone who watches markets, although they make a satisfying step toward bringing bubbles within scientific study. But other early lessons emerging from disequilibrium models should be more alarming for efficient market diehards. After all, the received wisdom holds that markets should generally work better when credit is easy to obtain, as smart investors seeing profit opportunities can leverage up their bets, erasing mispricings and market efficiencies more quickly. They should also work more efficiently as they become more "complete"; hence, derivatives should bring benefits by helping investors jump on any kind of information and bring it into the market. These assertions of equilibrium thinking spurred two decades of policies to encourage unbridled innovation and market deregulation.

To the contrary, however, studies probing the dynamics of markets out of equilibrium suggest that these celebrated routes to efficiency are boobytrapped; they actually stir up fundamental instabilities and increase the potential for market collapse or disruption. The very pursuit of efficiency creates instability.

"Let Me Be Technical: It All Sucked"

That was how Cliff Asness later described the darker moments of the four-day quant meltdown in 2007, during which AQR Capital Management, the fund he cofounded and manages, lost close to $1 billion. In the same period, a handful of similar funds lost an estimated $100 billion, all using strategies that had worked fabulously for a decade. What made it happen? Could it happen again? Were there early warning signs that nobody had seen?

Soon after the event, some clues and partial answers to these questions emerged from a postmortem investigation carried out by MIT finance professor Andrew Lo and graduate student Amir Khandani. Owing to the secrecy of the hedge fund industry, they had to work like forensic scientists, reconstructing the crime from scraps of evidence. The first question was how had these funds consistently made profits for the past decade.

Lo and Khandani knew that these funds generally use so-called long/short equity strategies. For example, a fund might buy ("go long") a range of stocks it sees as undervalued, while selling short others it sees as overpriced, aiming to reverse the trade and profit when the values revert. Not having access to the specific strategies the funds used, nor the stocks they bought or sold, Lo and Khandani tried something else. They used past data to test a simple strategy of the same general kind to see how it would have performed over the same period of time. If it worked, they reasoned, they could be relatively confident that the funds had probably followed a fairly similar strategy.

For the test, they chose a "contrarian" strategy: buy stocks today if they fell in value yesterday, and sell those that went up yesterday. Bet on ups being followed by downs and vice versa. It's hard to imagine anything simpler, yet the data shows that this strategy would indeed have made consistent profits of about 1 percent per day on average between 1995 and 2007. That works out to roughly 250 percent per year—a huge profit, although this number is unrealistic. The strategy, after all, demands buying or selling some of every single stock on the market and doing that in practice would incur massive transactions costs. As a probing tool, however, it was perfectly useful; it suggested that the basic long/short strategy was indeed consistently profitable over the ten years. There's no need to think the funds were doing anything particularly exotic.

The next question was how the test strategy would have fared during the fateful period August 6–9. Again, the data gave a direct answer—terrible. The simple contrarian strategy would have suffered extreme losses quite comparable to what happened to the hedge funds themselves. Hence, a second conclusion: whatever happened to the funds in August probably wasn't due to any sudden change in their behavior. Their preferred long/short equity strategies would have led them straight into the disaster.

So far, this only confirms that the funds stumbled unwittingly into some strange cataclysm. A more telling clue emerged from the probe strategy's performance over time. In 1995, the average daily return of Lo and Khandani's contrarian strategy was 1.38 percent. By 2000 it had fallen to 0.44 percent, and it was only 0.13 percent in the seven months of 2007 prior to the quant meltdown. Over the twelve years, that is, the hedge funds' core strategies had grown much less effective. Yet in the same period this sector of the hedge fund market had grown explosively—from $10 billion under management to $160 billion, and from one hundred funds to roughly one thousand. Strange, and for Lo and Khandani, significant. "It may seem counter-intuitive," they noted, that investors were shoveling money into these funds even as their performance deteriorated. But this paradox reveals something not evident in the raw returns. "Recall that the average daily returns reported [here] . . . are based on unleveraged returns. As these strategies begin to decay, hedge-fund managers have typically employed more leverage so as to maintain the level of returns that investors have come to expect."[9]

The most urgent task for a fund manager, after all, is to attract investors, and that means reporting high returns. If increasing competition reduces a strategy's raw returns, the simplest option is to use higher leverage to boost returns and maintain the appearance that all is fine. It is, however, the strategy of the drug user injecting ever higher doses to achieve the same high.

This race into excess leverage, Lo and Khandani finally argued, set the stage for the catastrophe, which then played out as a classic "run for the exits." In the second week of August, one fund had to sell some assets to raise cash—quite possibly to meet a margin call, i.e., make a mandatory payment to a bank to keep the fund's total borrowing less than an allowed fraction of their total capital. The sale, driving down the value of the asset, would have reduced the overall wealth of other funds holding it, possibly triggering additional margin calls for other highly leveraged funds. As these in turn sold assets to raise cash, values fell further, triggering more margin calls and so on.

The key thing was that once it started, no one had a choice. The funds may have filtered into the theater of high leverage quite willingly and slowly, over a decade; but once the fire started, they had no choice but to flee in a fierce stampede, each fund trampling others on the way out.

It's a clever analysis backed by convincing if indirect evidence. And the run-for-the-exits scenario is well understood.[10] Yet the sudden violence of the event still seems puzzling. The funds had been leveraged like this for a year at least, and nothing happened. Why did the trouble strike so suddenly, in a matter of hours, while things had been so apparently stable for a decade?

The American physicist Richard Feynman counseled students studying the strange laws of quantum theory not to waste time pondering, "How can it be like that?" To do so is like falling into a black hole of impossible nonsense, for what happens at that level just doesn't make sense in terms of the concepts we find familiar. But finance isn't quantum physics. "How can it be like that?" Here there has to be an answer.

Invisible Boundaries

The earliest computer models of the atmosphere captured only the most basic physics—conservation of energy and angular momentum in the air and solar heating that grows stronger from pole to equator. Clouds? The effects of mountains and oceans? There was none of that. Even so, the model made it possible to explore the logical interplay of uneven heating of air held close to a spinning sphere by gravity. That was enough, even with a computer less powerful than the simplest of today's cell phones, to answer the elemental question, "How can it be like that?" This roughest of theories showed how a few simple factors could interact to create the ever-shifting weather we have on earth.

A half century further on, we can begin doing the same for systems involving people, including markets. Set up a simple virtual market with hedge funds and investors and banks, let them act much as these firms do in the real world, and it is possible to do experiments, as Phillips did, to see the kinds of outcomes one might expect. In 2009, some economists and physicists did just that—and found that the quant meltdown doesn't look like a puzzling event at all. It looks more like a thunderstorm emerging quite predictably out of a hot moist summer atmosphere.[11]

In their virtual market, Stefan Thurner, Doyne Farmer, and John Geanakoplos could explore the delicate interplay of three simple factors. First, they had a handful of hedge funds compete to attract investors, with those investors doing what they do in reality—pushing their money toward the recent best performers. Second, they gave funds the opportunity to borrow from banks and boost their returns with leverage. Third, they included banks, who restrict the funds' leverage—the ratio of money they borrowed relative to the actual money they have on hand, either in cash or in stocks—to remain below some specified ratio, which might be, say 5, 10, 12, 20, or what have you. As discussed earlier in this chapter, banks enforce this rule by demanding margin calls or repayments from the funds when necessary to keep this ratio small enough.

What the researchers had assembled was a skeletal market, including all of its most important features—not unlike many standard models of equilibrium economics. But there was a key difference: in standard economic models, a balanced equilibrium is the only outcome allowed, presupposed at the start. In this simulation, there were no such restrictions.

With the model, the researchers could run hundreds of experiments, letting the hedge fund market evolve many times. While every run was slightly different in detail—different funds leading the field in profits, prices following a novel erratic path—a consistent story line also emerged. As some funds outperformed others, those doing slightly better attracted more investors, luring money away from competitors. To stay in the game, those funds increased their leverage to get higher returns. The result was a natural arms race for higher leverage, as happens in reality. This was no surprise: everything in the model was set up on purpose to mimic just this process.

It was also not surprising—at least for anyone believing in the power of arbitrage to keep markets in line—that the trend toward higher leverage made the markets more efficient. In the experiments, the competition between funds led to a steady decrease in price volatility; in other words, the stocks zeroed in on their "true" values as time went on. It's understandable. With high leverage, funds could jump all the more vigorously on any momentary mispricings, thereby keeping prices closer to their realistic or fundamental values. The funds' main goal may be to make obscene profits, but they also provide a service for the market.

But the simulations also showed something else: this increasing stability is actually a temporary and highly fragile illusion.

In economic circles, "volatility" is a dangerous word, easily misinterpreted. It sensibly refers to the true inherent wildness of a market—its tendency to fluctuate and do surprising things in any of a million ways. But the same word also refers to one specific, conventional, and extremely crude measure of that wildness—the mean square price fluctuations averaged over a time. The latter is simple to understand and easy to calculate, but it captures nothing of a market's susceptibility to rare cataclysms or black swan events. In fact, a market's conventional mean square volatility can easily decrease even as that same market becomes more prone to extreme events.

In the simulations, this is precisely what happens when investors increase their leverage. As the market gets more efficient, and prices zero in on their realistic values, the market's conventional volatility decreases. But its volatility in the larger sense increases. Running hundreds of long simulations to study the likelihood of extreme movements, Thurner and colleagues found that increasing leverage gradually but inexorably pushes the market into an unstable condition in which explosive catastrophes become much more likely. Suppose you measure the likelihood of finding large market returns exceeding a value r—1 percent, 5 percent, 10 percent, and so on. When leverage is low, the probability to see really big market movements is extremely small and fully consistent Gaussian, normal statistics. Large movements really are rare. But as hedge funds start using higher leverage, the market moves over a threshold and the probability of extreme movements becomes far larger. Now the pattern of price movements has fat tails; the market becomes prone to disaster.

In other words, the calmness and efficiency in the market is a sham; it is purchased at the expense of more frequent catastrophes. If the market were a race car, leverage might be your foot on the accelerator, allowing your car to go faster. But the market is like a race car that begins to shudder and vibrate at higher speeds, becoming ever more likely to break down.

This is a first lesson, but there's another. Once leverage passes this instability threshold, market collapse becomes only a question of time and specific detail, of names and dates. In a typical simulation history the funds sail along comfortably until one day, without warning, everything explodes, just like the quant meltdown. It is no accident, no twist of fate involving a conspiracy of rare factors, no episode of twenty-five standard deviation events three days in a row, but a predictable consequence of the way leverage ties the funds and banks together into a tight and dangerous loop. Of course, for the funds themselves, the final cataclysm does arrive like a bolt from the blue. It's a sudden run-for-the-exits scenario, just like Lo and Khandani described, with a feedback of margin calls and forced deleveraging, but the day it strikes is no different from the day before, or the week before that.

And that's the most important point: the cause of the final meltdown really has nothing to do with events on the day in question, but with the generally unstable condition of the market. It's no one's fault—and everyone's fault. As competition and leverage lead to less "volatility," financial theorists marvel at the beauty of the apparent market efficiency. But it's an illusion, and disaster waits in the wings, the certain product of this very efficiency—and apparently reasonable behavior on the part of everyone. What this model so clearly reveals is an inexorable dynamic that some perceptive market watchers speculated about even just a few weeks after the quant meltdown. Former investment banker and hedge fund manager Rick Bookstaber wrote in August 2007:

As more capital flows into the market and as leverage increases, there is more money chasing opportunities . . . A hedge fund now has to leverage up more in order to try to generate its target returns. And so the cycle goes—more leverage leads to more liquidity and lower volatility and narrower opportunities, which then leads to still higher leverage . . .

This relationship between liquidity, volatility versus risk is hard to observe, because there is nothing in the day-to-day markets to suggest anything is wrong. In fact, with volatility low, everything looks just great. We don't know that leverage has increased, because nobody has those numbers . . . On the surface, the water may be smooth as glass, but we cannot fathom what is happening in the depths.[12]

Of course, this is hardly surprising; it's in the nature of positive feedbacks. The danger lies not in the parts of the system themselves, but in how they're linked together, how they interact.

Traffic

In my earlier book *The Social Atom*, I argued that social scientists often make a mistake in attributing the complexity of social outcomes to the complexity of the individual human being. We see roads snarled in traffic, riots, persistent poverty, as well as crazy fashions and social transformations. Confused and lacking a good explanation, it's easy to suspect that things are so difficult to understand because people as individuals are just so complicated.

This thinking is not always wrong, but it does contain a logical error: the conclusion does not follow from the premise. A confusing collective reality does not necessarily have to originate in the character of the individual parts that produce it. Instead, as we've seen on numerous occasions in this book, much of the complexity of social reality may originate in the interactions of groups.

In these and many other cases, understanding means thinking about patterns, not people.

Seen from the wrong perspective, it can seem counterintuitive, but this isn't a radical idea, indeed we experience it every day. Millions of people spend hours idling in traffic jams every day—and in those hours they experience a huge range of thoughts and emotions. We tend to think that someone or something is responsible. Yet no one aims to start a traffic jam, and in many cases you cannot point to a single car or driver who caused the jam through their own behavior. Many traffic jams are the inevitable result of too many cars, as smooth distributed flow becomes unstable above a certain density of traffic. Traffic jams then emerge all on their own, and the real cause is the high density, not the particular person whose accidental touching of brakes triggered its initial growth. Indeed, these jams are so lawlike and predictable that they can be modeled accurately with simple equations: they travel back upstream in the direction of traffic at about five miles per hour.[13]

At the root of all this is interactions—one element exerting a direct or indirect influence on others. On the road, interaction is obvious. Cars can't occupy the same space at the same time, and so my preferred path has to take your position into account. We should expect interactions between people or firms or other social agents to create similar surprising collective outcomes elsewhere, including in economics and finance. Yet economists have curiously tried to keep the notion of interactions out of their thinking—again, mostly for the simplicity of mathematics—using a trick known as the "representative agent."

The idea is to suppose that the behavior of a group simply reflects the sum of the behaviors of the people making it up. Interview a bunch of people. You might find that if banks offered another 3 percent interest in a savings account, people on average say they will save 5 percent more of their income. From this information, you can extrapolate that if all banks in America were to offer a 3 percent interest spike, Americans collectively would save 5 percent more. Each person in this view responds independently and the group acts much like a giant agent—the "representative agent." It sounds plausible enough, right? But it is a radical oversimplification.

If groups represented only the interests of the individuals within them, we'd never get traffic jams; no one ever decides they would like to create one. Interactions matter, often far more than intentions and desires.

Traffic is a reminder that collective social outcomes need not reflect in any obvious way the desires or intentions, even the specific actions, of any individual at all. Sudden dramatic outcomes can arise from collective processes and webs of feedback operating in a way that is mostly invisible to any human brain, even those participating (and perhaps especially them). Who hasn't been irritated and baffled as traffic around you suddenly and unexpectedly grinds to a halt? Yet you see no road work, no broken-down vehicles, no accidents, no obvious cause at all. The cause just isn't there to be read out of the local details, but exists elsewhere—at the global level, in considerations of traffic density.

The Thurner-Farmer-Geanakoplos experiment is different from traffic, but it demonstrates, in the context of finance, a very similar point.

Less Risk = More Risk?

A clear lesson of the study of Thurner and colleagues is that mechanisms making markets more efficient can also make them less stable. Scientists and engineers, of course, routinely confront similar trade-offs between stability and efficiency. To save fuel, engineers build the engines of cars, buses, trains, jets, and anything else to be as light as possible, and, in principle, could make them ever more efficient by using progressively thinner, lighter materials. But there are limits. It's no good having a superefficient lightweight engine that melts when it heats up, or clatters into pieces on a bumpy road.

For any technology, too much efficiency will compromise stability. After all, efficiency means doing more with less, while stability implies having some extra breathing room, extra strength, and capacity. Yet in economics, efficiency has been proclaimed as an unqualified good, and something we should expect as the inevitable result of financial innovation in all its forms. Merton and Bodie wrote in 2005:

New financial product and market designs, improved computer and telecommunications technology, and advances in the theory of finance over the last generation have led to dramatic and rapid changes in the structure of global financial markets and institutions . . . Surely the prime exemplifying case is the development, refinement, and broadbased adoption of derivative securities such as futures, options, swaps, and other contractual agreements. Practitioner innovations in financial-contracting technology have improved efficiency by expanding opportunities for risk sharing, lowering transaction costs, and reducing information and agency costs.[14]

Oddly, the paper never mentions the concept of market stability. A report giving the combined view of the OECD, World Bank, and International Monetary Fund from May 2007 echoed the same view that derivatives reduce risk and make markets more efficient by giving investors more options to fine-tune their positions:

> Derivative instruments contribute to overall market efficiency and liquidity. These benefits include the ability for market participants to hedge positions effectively, the ability to trade in and out of markets at any time, continuous price updates and market intelligence through trading in the derivative asset class . . . In turn, these factors can contribute directly to lower funding costs for the government, with more competitive participation in auctions (by investors and intermediaries) and better market-making in the secondary market.[15]

As economists' glowing words attest, equilibrium theory sees multiple pathways leading to the golden city of market efficiency, and one of the most promising is paved with derivatives. But again—what about stability?

It was in his 2002 letter to investors that legendary financier Warren Buffett famously asserted that "derivatives are weapons of mass destruction." He said more, too:

> Many people argue that derivatives reduce systemic problems, in that participants who can't bear certain risks are able to transfer them to stronger hands. These people believe that derivatives act to stabilize the economy, facilitate trade, and eliminate bumps for individual participants . . . On a micro level, what they say is often true. I believe, however, that the macro picture is dangerous and getting more so. Large amounts of risk, particularly credit risk, have become concentrated in the hands of relatively few derivatives dealers, who in addition trade extensively with one another. The troubles of one could quickly infect the others . . . The derivatives genie is now well out of the bottle, and these instruments will almost certainly multiply in variety and number until some event makes their toxicity clear.

He was right—and how. On September 16, 2008, the U.S. Federal Reserve Bank had to step in with an $85 billion credit line to prevent the collapse of insurance giant American International Group, Inc. Ignoring the looming trouble with subprime mortgages, AIG had blithely sold credit default swaps—essentially contracts insuring increasingly dubious mortgage-backed securities—to Goldman Sachs, Société Générale, Deutsche Bank, and other firms. Suddenly, AIG was potentially on the hook for almost half a trillion dollars in payments. Through these derivatives, AIG's failure would have spread distress throughout the entire global financial system.

But Buffett's intuition goes beyond one firm and one emergency, and indeed beyond any one kind of derivative. Derivatives offer a mechanism for spreading risks, and standard thinking in equilibrium economics holds that "risk sharing" of this kind should make both individual institutions and the entire financial system more stable and efficient. Once again, this isn't the case, at least not completely.

Two years ago, physicist Stefano Battiston led a team of physicists and economists, including the Nobel Prize winner Joseph Stiglitz of Columbia University in New York, in exploring the stability of a financial network in which lots of banks or other financial firms are linked together by derivatives and other financial contracts. Suppose that bank A makes a big loan to bank B, thus exposing itself to the risk that B might not be able to pay it back. Bank A can reduce this risk by selling an interest in that loan on to other institutions. Bank A is then linked not only to bank B, but also to these other institutions. It is commonly believed in economics that risk sharing of this kind—associated with a dense proliferation of links between institutions—should not only make individual banks safer, but should also make the entire system more stable.

But as Battiston and colleagues found, this broad assumption is unjustified.[16] In their study, they modeled a banking system as a network of interacting institutions, and studied the network's stability—its ability to hang together following a shock. Specifically, they supposed that each institution in the network has its own independent operations that may be sometimes profitable and sometimes less so. Each institution, in other words, is subject to random shocks. In this setting, the financial resilience of any institution depends on two things: its own local conditions, good or bad; and the resilience of its financial partners, because if a partner's financial health fails, its distress will cause immediate trouble for others from whom it borrowed.

The researchers then used this basic picture of a network of financially interdependent institutions to probe the likely consequences of the sudden bankruptcy of one specific institution. What happens, they found, depends strongly on the overall connectivity in the network (see figure below). If this is relatively low, then if one bank makes bad decisions and suddenly goes bankrupt, the repercussions are not so serious; the trouble causes problems for a few other institutions but does not generally propagate too far. The benefits of risk sharing in this case work just as the textbooks say.

However, with rising connectivity, things change dramatically. Beyond a certain connectivity threshold, risk sharing paradoxically has the opposite effect. Because there are so many pathways along which trouble can

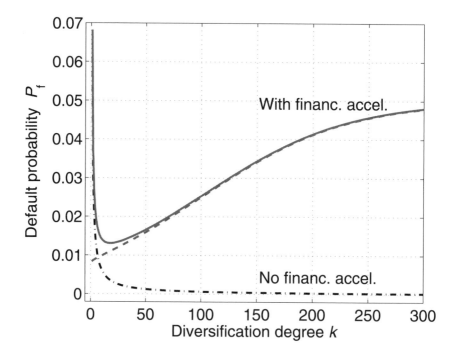

The probability of bank failure as it depends on the density of links between banks (k is the average number of deals linking a typical bank to others). The classical result (dashed line) suggests that failure probability always decreases with more risk sharing. In contrast, the reality of "financial acceleration" or feedback—being in financial distress often makes it harder to borrow, making the distress even worse—means that too much risk sharing can increase system wide instability. (Reprinted with permission from S. Battiston, D. D. Gatti, M. Gallegati, B. C. N. Greenwald, and J. E. Stiglitz: "Liaisons Dangereuses: Increasing Connectivity, Risk Sharing, and Systemic Risk," *Journal of Economic Dynamics and Control* (2012))

spread, system-wide collapse actually becomes more likely. So although risk sharing does indeed lower the risk to individual banks, the dense web of links makes the entire system unstable. This discovery directly contradicts earlier economic analyses, which suggested that risk sharing could only have positive consequences in reducing systemic risk.

What these analyses missed is the dynamics—not part of the equilibrium analysis—by which financial trouble can ripple through a network along many independent routes. The increasing number of paths for spreading, along with "financial acceleration" or feedback—the fact that individual financial fragility can amplify itself, as a distressed bank may suddenly have to pay more to borrow, for example—can actually boost the effect of the initial shock and lead to a serious systemic crisis.

Here again we see the individual versus collective problem. The troubles of derivatives come not from the weakening of individual institutions but of the group as a whole.

Of course, this doesn't mean that derivatives never have any uses. Companies that sell credit-default swaps argue, for example, that they do reduce risks, and many of their arguments are convincing. International banks making loans to banks or corporations in a particular country may buy swaps on sovereign debt to protect themselves from systemic economic turmoil in that country. The possibility of protection encourages lending. But there are limits. What reduces risk for individual institutions in small quantities spells trouble for the larger banking system when pushed too far. This rather undermines the naïve belief that we can follow the road of derivatives to the perfectly efficient nirvana of complete markets.[17]

There is considerably more to say on this issue. Indeed, two other recent studies reinforce this idea that derivatives often tend to erode market stability. Obviously, if you can hedge some of your investment risks, one consequence is that you can take bigger risks with other investments. Economists William Brock, Cars Hommes, and Florian Wagener have shown that this effect can easily lead to investors chasing after the latest, best investments, shifting money from one investment to another very quickly, with the market becoming increasingly unstable as a result. A second effect, identified by physicists Fabio Caccioli and Matteo Marsili, is closely related, though a little different. With more derivatives, financial firms hedge their risks more effectively, and the market gets more efficient—as prevailing theory suggests. But the hedging balance also becomes increasingly precarious, as firms have to readjust their holdings perpetually in response to small market shocks so as to remain fully hedged. The market remains stable, but just barely, like a pencil balanced upright on your fingertip. Each new derivatives makes the balance more precarious.

So, from what we've seen so far, two of the pathways to greater efficiency—leverage and derivatives—don't work quite as advertised.

Rethinking Cause and Effect

Historians have thought as much as anyone about the tricky nature of cause and effect—and the difficulty of explanation in a world where potential causes often compete and interfere in intricate webs of interaction. History has a chaotic element, as tiny events can intervene, pushing the fate of entire nations down peculiar pathways. In 1920, the king of Greece died after being bitten by a pet monkey; this was a small part of a chain of events ultimately leading Greece and Turkey to war. Future British prime minister Winston Churchill commented at the time that "a quarter of a million persons died of this monkey's bite."

Explaining events in economics and finance is just as confusing. Clever people can propose multiple explanations for almost any event. When the investment bank Lehman Brothers filed for bankruptcy on September 15, 2008, it was the largest bankruptcy ever—and had immediate devastating effects. In the next month, global markets seized up and more than $10 trillion evaporated from global equity markets, the biggest decline ever. The explanation? It was not exactly a matter of consensus.

According to University of Chicago economist John Cochrane, it was all a matter of expectations—and a run on investor confidence caused by the government. Derivatives? Subprime mortgages? The housing bubble? They had nothing to do with it, suggests Cochrane. "The signature event," he wrote just over a year later,

> was the "run," "panic," "flight to quality," or whatever you choose to call it, that started in late September of 2008 and receded over the winter. Short-term credit dried up, including the normally straightforward repurchase agreement, inter-bank lending, and commercial papermarkets. If that panic had not occurred, it is likely that any economic con-

traction following the housing bust would have been no worse than the mild 2001 recession that followed the dot-com bust.[18]

In this view, prior to the Lehman event, investors believed that the "too big to fail" banks would always be bailed out. When the government let Lehman collapse, everyone had to think again. What if Citigroup or Goldman Sachs go down, too? "Suddenly," as Cochrane put it, "it made perfect sense to run like mad." Banks and other institutions hoarded their cash, and lending shut down instantaneously.

For a contrasting view, consider the blog *Economics of Contempt*, written by a finance lawyer in New York, who suggested that Cochrane's perspective was "mind-boggling nonsense." If Cochrane claimed that Lehman's failure caused no secondary bankruptcies, the blog pointed out, it did immediately wipe out plenty of hedge funds. More importantly, it observed, when the administrator overseeing the bankruptcy of Lehman's European subsidiary froze $40 billion in clients' funds, "that's $40 billion that was suddenly and unexpectedly unavailable to hedge funds . . . hundreds of billions in liquidity suddenly vanished from the markets." Finally, it noted, Lehman's biggest counterparties—big banks like Bank of America, Citigroup, and Deutsche Bank—would have collapsed, but were all bailed out by governments.[19]

One explanation sees all expectations and human intentions, with government mismanagement at fault. Another sees a mechanical process kicked off by the quite understandable collapse of a hugely indebted and highly central institution with important links to others all over the world. Which is true?

The British historian Edward Hallett Carr suggested one way to cut through such confusion. When confronted with myriad conflicting causes, we should, he suggested, seek "generalizable" causes, by which he meant those that teach lessons for the future. On May 6, 1937, the German airship the *Hindenburg* caught fire while mooring at the Lakehurst Naval Air Station in New Jersey, killing thirty-six people. The major part of the disaster ensued from the ignition of the hydrogen gas used to make the ship float in the air. It was ignited—according to one theory—by an electrostatic spark created by the design of the ship's metallic skin, which allowed it to accumulate electrical charge while passing through clouds en route. If so, then obviously the spark ignited the hydrogen, causing the disaster that followed. Okay, so the lesson is to avoid sparks in the future. Right?

Big metallic objects traveling through the atmosphere generate sparks all the time, as do big metal objects attempting to dock with steel-framed docking stations. Yet it's not generally true that such sparks create explosions. In contrast, filling great balloons with explosive hydrogen gas is part of a general recipe for big explosions; it is a generalizable cause. Send up lots of hydrogen-filled airships and you should expect to get quite a few disasters, even though each one might be triggered by something different.

Getting at generalizable causes often means going beyond narrative stories of how A led to B led to C, which is precisely where models prove so instructive, whether it is a model for atmospheric circulation, or leveraged markets, or networks of interdependent financial institutions. The latter model instructs us that building extremely dense webs of interdependence between large numbers of financial institutions will make collective disaster increasingly likely, although how the trouble will unfold, where it will start, and how it will travel are hard to predict.

Seen from this perspective, Cochrane's explanation seems like blaming the *Hindenburg* disaster on the electrostatic spark, while ignoring the presence of the hydrogen. Of course sudden changes in expectations can cause runs. Even a healthy bank can go under from one. But Lehman Brothers in September 2008 wasn't a healthy institution of any sort. Lehman had increased their use of leveraged assets from around 24:1 in 2003 to 31:1 by 2007. This implied that the bank would be bankrupt if its assets fell by only 3–4 percent. Through July 2008, Lehman stock lost 73 percent of its value.

To make matters worse, Lehman was connected by derivatives to seemingly everyone. Around eight thousand different firms had paid billions in collateral to Lehman through derivatives deals. Three years after the collapse, Lehman Brothers Holdings Inc. was still negotiating over unresolved derivatives trades with more than a dozen of its largest counterparties. The website of Lehman Brothers International (Europe) says bankruptcy administrators have identified more than six thousand counterparties to whom Lehman still owes money.

So it seems rather more sensible to me to see the trouble ensuing from the Lehman collapse as a fairly predictable event caused by positive feedbacks and a network linking Lehman to other institutions. It's certainly true that a bank run created a spark, but a spark was coming from somewhere eventually, and the air was already filled with hydrogen.

These simple models also help explain, perhaps, why we always seem surprised by financial and economic crises. There is obviously a psychological effect—the "this time is different" factor—that makes disaster inconceivable to many people until it is upon them. But there is a deeper reason, too: the phenomenon slips outside the box of our traditional ways of thinking. The truest cause looks like a collective march over an invisible threshold of danger. I have no doubt that many economists and bankers really did believe that the world they had created was more efficient and more stable than ever before. But their models—and thinking based on them—were fundamentally flawed.

Beware the "Efficient" Frontier

There is nothing new in the idea that pushing something too far brings trouble; it's as old as the ancient story of Icarus and his wings. Theoretical economics largely seems to have forgotten this piece of timeless wisdom, intoxicated by its visions of welfare theorems and perfect market efficiency.

In finance, the theory of investing has a core concept known as the "efficient frontier," introduced long ago by economist Harry Markowitz. The core principle is that it is not wise to put all your eggs in one basket. In a slightly more refined way, it asserts that the careful selection of items in a portfolio of investments can reduce the portfolio's overall risk for any given level of expected return. You might spread your money over ten different beer manufacturers; that would be a start. But that mix will be prone to larger random fluctuations than will a portfolio of stocks in three beer companies, two pharmaceutical producers, plus Google, Apple, General Motors, Nike, and Toys"R"Us. Random changes in the economy should tend to affect those stocks differently, causing a smaller shock to the overall combination.

Considering the thousands of stocks out there, there is, mathematically, an efficient frontier of optimal portfolios for a desired return and level of accepted risk.

Conceptually, the efficient frontier is very much in the spirit of the standard economic view of the unregulated market—as a machine that becomes naturally more efficient with the addition of more derivatives, easy credit, and opportunities to conduct any trade, anywhere and anytime. As I've argued in this chapter, the vision is mostly advertising, not science. There is little evidence that efficiency can be achieved without stirring up other problems, no matter how you approach it. Two models I've explored here explicitly show that high leverage linked to easier credit and more derivatives can act through very simple mechanisms to make markets less stable, not more. Perfectly efficient markets begin to look like perfectly unstable markets.

This emerges clearly out of these disequilibrium studies, but these really only make more precise an idea that others have worried about on many occasions. As economist Robert Nelson noted a decade ago,[20] much of equilibrium economics' conventional wisdom has come from the vast influence of books like Paul Samuelson's *Economics*, a college textbook used by generations of students. They have absorbed its proclamations, without noting the reservations:

> The problem is that this image of the market mechanism of Economics is more poetry than science. It is best understood as a compelling metaphor for its time designed to attract converts to a new understanding of the progressive gospel of efficiency. None of the claims Samuelson made for the market mechanism rest on any strong scientific foundation, as leading economists over the next 50 years would increasingly conclude.

That message, obviously, hasn't spread as widely as it should.

But to be clear, I don't mean to imply—as it might seem—that every insight coming from equilibrium economics is wrong, or that disequilibrium models make it easier to settle every question in economics. In the early 1970s, economist James Tobin suggested that a small tax on financial transactions—he was originally thinking of foreign exchange transactions—might act to deter unnecessary speculation and make markets more stable. Those acting speculatively tend to act on short times, making many trades, and so would pay more than long-term investors less driven by speculation. Speculation would be deterred. Since then economists have argued over the merits of the idea without coming to any conclusion; the idea resurfaces and creates controversy after every momentary crisis.

From the disequilibrium perspective, German economist Frank Wester-hoff has recently run experiments[21] to test how the idea works in plausi-ble models of markets that include natural feedbacks and show all the stylized facts of real markets. His results show just how tricky we should expect the answers to such questions to be. At low tax rates—below 0.1 percent—the tax works very well, reducing market volatility and keep-ing prices closer to their realistic, fundamental values. Increase it to 0.3 percent, however, and mispricings again grow—along with some weird, unexpected effects. Taxes that are too high can drive investors who act as fundamentalists to leave the market, and when they do, prices stray fur-ther from their realistic values, creating big bubbles that make specula-tion profitable again, even despite the transaction tax. That's in just one market. In a model of two markets, with a transaction tax in only one, Westerhoff found more stability in the taxed market, with more wild fluc-tuations in the other created as speculators migrate there. In contrast, a uniform transaction tax in both markets decreased market volatility in each.

So the answer to whether to tax transactions is clear and definitive: it depends. But at least these models make it possible to explore the answer in the context of a scientific means for including the various effects and influences we know work in markets, without any preconceptions about what might come out.

Of course, it's important to remember that the lessons emerging from all the models of this chapter might well never have occurred to anyone exploring without the modern digital computer. Through history, great philosophers and theorists have played fascinating games of what if. Yet they have had limited means to really experience and see what might come out when assumptions A, B, and C collide on intricate webs of feed-back. This is no longer true—at least not always. And computation is changing both markets and the science of markets faster than any single human brain can comprehend.

Trading at the Speed of Light

High-frequency trading has improved the overall quality of markets.
Trading costs are lower, markets are deeper and more liquid,
discrepancies in prices across related markets are reduced, and prices
better reflect information about the value of stocks and commodities.

—Jim Overdahl, former chief economist, SEC

Fast is good . . . "dumb and fast" is dangerous.

—Quote from a high-frequency trading blog

MIKE MCCARTHY WAS MUGGED BY the flash crash. It attacked him in broad daylight on an ordinary afternoon and stole at least $15,000. And there's no way he can get it back.

Over the past few years, McCarthy has had a rough time of it. In 2006, after twenty-three years, he finally left a job in a struggling division of the financial wing of General Motors, and found a new one at a thriving mortgage firm, Countrywide Financial. The company was then originating about 20 percent of all U.S. mortgages. Unfortunately, McCarthy didn't know that Countrywide was about to be buried under a pile of subprime mortgages gone bad; he left within a year as the firm imploded. At age forty-nine, McCarthy was unemployed.

In 2009, he was saddened by the sudden death of his mother. She left him a trust, including a portfolio of shares, and he managed to make ends meet for his family from interest and dividends. In May 2010, convinced the markets were about to plunge, McCarthy decided to sell. He called his broker at Smith Barney on the afternoon of the sixth and said, as he later recalled, "I'm concerned about the market and I'd like to sell my positions in P&G and DirecTV. And on second thought, liquidate the other ten, too."

He was a moment too late. And also a moment too early. McCarthy's broker hit the button to sell his Procter and Gamble shares at roughly two forty-six P.M., about one minute after the flash crash had hit rock bottom, yet minutes before it managed much of its meteoric rise back to normality. The sale happened at $39.37, the lowest price for Procter and Gamble in about seven years, and only two thirds of the $60–$63 the shares traded at a few minutes before and after. The difference amounted to more than $15,000.

"That's like six to eight months of my mortgage payments right there," McCarthy later said. "I'm looking at P&G, it's at, like, sixty-two now. I can't even believe this happened; it's like I'm in the twilight zone."[1]

In 1926, British physicist Lewis Fry Richardson, a pioneer in weather forecasting, published a paper in which he posed a peculiar question. "Does the wind possess a velocity?" This seemingly foolish question, he pointed out, doesn't have an obvious answer. Sure, you may see the clouds in the sky passing at about twenty m.p.h., but their drift only reflects a crude average over a large volume of air. Try to pin down the air speed more precisely at specific positions, and things get messy. Winds generate swirling vortices that break up into smaller vortices; currents writhe and twist like smoke rising from a cigarette. Look closely, and the speed and direction of the air from point to point change wildly and erratically. The wind doesn't really have an obvious speed.

As McCarthy discovered, something like this is true in markets. Procter and Gamble may look like it's at $62, but a microgust of financial wind may take it to $37 before you can sell it. This is the reality of markets driven by algorithms trading at the speed of light.

A New York company called Inforeach sells an algorithmic trading platform called HiFreq that can execute more than twenty thousand trades per second over a single computer link. This is just one of hundreds of companies fueling a race toward "zero latency"—the ideal in which zero time passes between a button being pushed and a trade being completed. The fastest trades now execute in the time it takes light to travel a football field or so; that's one millionth of a second. This is so fast that the principles of Einstein's theory of relativity now determine the laws of finance. To shave five milliseconds off transatlantic communication times between U.S. and U.K. traders, a company called Hibernia Atlantic is laying down the first new transatlantic cable in ten years[2] along a path that is 310 miles shorter than other cables.

There is no sign of anything slowing this technological arms race, and trading times will soon dwindle down toward single nanoseconds and below, at which point a couple of feet of extra cable leading to a computer could determine whether one firm's trade beats another's. Exotic islands in the Pacific may soon become trading hubs ideally suited for "relativistic arbitrage," a term created to describe the stock advantages afforded to firms that are better at navigating the laws of Einstein's relativity. If you aim to profit from small price differences for stocks on exchanges in Japan and Los Angeles, then Einstein's theory implies you should set up trading precisely halfway between the two—on a platform somewhere in the Pacific Ocean—where you'll get price signals from both places before anyone else in the universe possibly can.[3]

When it comes to trading, nothing is hotter than speed and intelligence, now embodied by raw computational power. But as the speed of business literally approaches the speed of light, you might start to wonder, is this really a good idea?

In July 2009, Paul Wilmott, a veteran expert in quantitative finance, wrote an op-ed in the *New York Times* asking whether this might not be a little dangerous. "On top of an already dangerously influential and morally suspect financial minefield," Wilmott noted, we're adding "the unthinking power of the machine."[4] Sensibly, and thinking of the distant origins of stock markets, he wondered how any of this superfast trading really helps raise money for worthwhile enterprises. More specifically, Wilmott worried about feedbacks among high-frequency algorithms that might lead to dangerous surprises. In 2003, for instance—back when things were slow by today's standards—a U.S. trading firm went bankrupt in sixteen seconds when someone at the firm switched on a trading algorithm.[5] It took the company nearly an hour to realize it had gone bust. Could something similar happen to a big investment bank, to an entire exchange, or even a nation's entire financial system?

To the high-frequency traders, and to many economists, Wilmott's concerns seem ridiculous—akin to late nineteenth-century fears that incessant horse traffic would sooner or later clog up the roadways with horse poop. After all, trading in equilibrium economics can never be bad, and faster trading should let markets find their efficient state more quickly. If trading brings information into the market, then it should make prices more accurate; the obliteration of any barrier to trade, including time, can only be a good thing. More and faster trading should only lubricate the gears of the market. What could be better?

Wilmott sounded his warning that high-frequency trading "may increasingly destabilize the market" just over a year before the flash crash. Two years further on, what do we really know? Is high-frequency trading helping or hurting markets? It's a tricky question.

Market Liquidity—Breathing Easily

As human beings, we need to both inhale and exhale, preferably with as little friction or impediment as possible. Generally we can, and it's the liquidity of the air around us—its readiness to flow through rooms and nostrils to our lungs—that makes it so useful as a supplier of oxygen. A cubic meter of sand, which is mostly silicon dioxide (SiO_2), holds as much oxygen as a volume of air about three thousand times as large, but because sand is solid, not liquid, its oxygen is trapped and unavailable.

In a sense, trading is like breathing, and markets work best when their working substances—money and assets—flow easily. If trades flow through a market without getting hung up on the activity of many buyers and sellers, traders copy physics and say a market is "liquid." Anyone wanting to buy or sell a stock, bond, future, or house readily finds someone else willing to take the trade, and at a reasonable price. In contrast, in an illiquid or "thin" market, with a relative scarcity of willing buyers and sellers, it is harder to find someone to take the other side of a trade. Now you can't sell an asset without dropping the price, or buy without paying in excess.

A trader in an illiquid market is like a man with a malfunctioning and unreliable air supply. Sometimes it has no air to offer, and at others it readily offers, but won't let him exhale. The result in either case is predictable—anxiety, if not panic.

Metaphors are nice, but they're even more useful if the qualities they describe can be measured. With liquidity, finance theorists have worked out how to do it. Looking at market liquidity offers a window into whether high-frequency trading has helped markets—or perhaps made things worse.

If you want to buy or sell some stock, your broker will send an order to a firm acting as a so-called market maker—it might be GETCO or Tradebot—whose algorithms stand ready in the market to buy or sell at any moment for stated prices. For any asset they deal in, a market-making firm advertises "bid" and "ask" prices at which they agree to buy or sell it. These market makers aren't charities, of course, and the differences between the bid and ask prices reflect their view of how much they need to charge to make a profit in this role. GETCO is not in the speculation business, so if they buy a stock from you, they want to turn around and sell it on to someone else, quickly, in case the stock's value falls. The more liquid a market, the easier the market maker finds buyers or sellers, and the lower their "bid-ask spread."

So, high liquidity generally means low bid-ask spreads. Hence, one obvious way to judge the effect of this near-light-speed trading on the markets is to see what their activities have done to the spreads: if the bid-ask spreads have gotten lower, then the market is likely more liquid. On this measure, everything looks good; high-frequency trading really does seem to make markets breathe more easily. Spreads for equities in the United States and the U.K., for example, have fallen by roughly a factor of ten over the decade in which high-frequency algorithmic trading has become so influential.[6] In the year 2010, HFTs (high-frequency trades) made up less than 2 percent of the twenty thousand firms actively trading, yet accounted for 73 percent of the total volume of trading. Their trading is a blurred chaos of orders and counterorders and cancellations, flitting through wires at the speed of light down fiber optic cables, but it clearly has improved liquidity.

This may seem like an "obvious" outcome, hardly even worth testing. Put more traders into the market, trading on either side and at warp speed, and how could the market not be more liquid? But the opposite effect is possible, at least in principle. Market makers aren't the only ones using algorithms. Their algorithms work passively, waiting to buy or sell on demand at specific prices, but lots of other traders use algorithms actively: like predators, they seek out the market makers' offers and try to "pick them off." Armed with better information, for example, a predatory algorithm might see that a market maker is selling IBM too cheaply. It can buy the stock, and sell it elsewhere for a profit. If there are too many sharp predators profiting at the market makers' expense, the cost of market making rises, and with it the bid-ask spread. This of course makes the market less liquid, not more.

So there's no simple equation: more high-frequency trading = more liquidity. Flood the market with algorithms, and the market makers and predators might just battle in an arms race of increasing speed and sophistication, with the spread going up or down. Fortunately, it seems from the data that the good generally prevails; high-frequency trading has made trading overall cheaper. And with information finding its way into the market easier, prices should be more accurate. "Algorithmic trading improves liquidity and enhances the informativeness of quotes," as one study of the market concludes.[7]

It's a happy story of technology and profit seeking making the world a better place—a poster-style illustration of the invisible hand in action. Except that it is really only a partial story. By now it's an old refrain. What about stability?

Kicked off at 14:32:00 by Wadell and Reed's big sale of E-mini futures, the downward plunge of the flash crash of May 6, 2010, ran for thirteen minutes and twenty-seven seconds. At 14:45:27, a cascade of orders caused the price of the E-mini to drop by another 1.3 percent in a single second. This tripped a circuit breaker on an electronic trading platform run by CME Globex, which halted the execution of all further transactions for five seconds. At 14:45:33, when trading resumed, E-mini prices fluctuated for five seconds, and then started back upward from 14:45:38. This was a matter of seconds before Mike McCarthy's broker initiated his fateful trade. Twenty-one minutes later, at 15:06:00, the market was practically back to where it had been before the crash.[8]

No one knows what might have happened had the circuit breaker not been in place. Nor does anyone know the real "cause" of the flash crash. The final government report on the matter found no evidence of fat fingers, the diabolical actions of "rogue algos," or conspiracies to manipulate markets. Nor were there any significant breakdowns of order routing systems or data systems or any other elements of the stock trading infrastructure. It was business as usual for the system's basic plumbing.

But it's also clear that something strange did happen during the crash: all that wonderful liquidity provided by the high-frequency traders abruptly vanished. According to the final report[9] of the Commodity Futures

Trading Commission and the Securities and Exchange Commission (CFTC-SEC) data from the flash crash suggests that "some HFT firms [were] reducing or pausing trading during that time . . . between 2:41 and 2:44 P.M., HFTs aggressively sold about 2,000 E-Mini contracts in order to reduce their temporary long positions." In other words, the market makers had stopped taking either side of a trade, and were instead dumping stocks they had accumulated up to that point.

"For both futures and equities," an executive from trading firm TD Ameritrade later commented, "there was a complete evaporation of liquidity in the marketplace."[10]

So the liquidity high-frequency trading provides isn't quite what it seems. At least it wasn't in the flash crash. It was like motor oil in a car's engine that evaporated just when the engine got hot and needed cooling and lubrication the most. As it turns out, this "disappearing act" isn't just an oddity of the flash crash, but a more general phenomenon, and the heartening story of high-frequency trading greasing the wheels of finance needs some amending. The grease often vanishes, and this is actually just what we should expect.

Of Rivers and Risks

In 1906, a young English civil servant named Harold Edwin Hurst traveled to Cairo, Egypt, then under British rule. Hurst's task was to improve predictions of the notoriously hard to predict size of Nile floods from year to year. Despite records of floods going back some eight hundred years, it seemed that dams built by engineers were suddenly overwhelmed within decades by floods bigger than anyone expected. Hurst found out why: flow in rivers, and in the Nile in particular, have a long-term memory. Flood years tend to cluster together rather than arriving randomly through time.

Hurst hit on a clever idea for analyzing the data in a new way. First, calculate the average flow and make a graph of the fluctuations around it. You get an erratic line, wandering up and down. Next, place a window on this pattern, which you can make horizontally larger or smaller, stretching or shrinking to contain more or less of it. For every value of the window's width, T, look inside the window and measure the difference between the highest and lowest values found within. Call this the range R: it represents

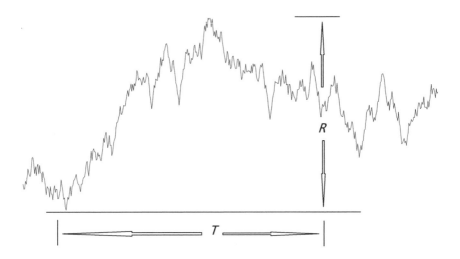

As introduced by the British hydrologist Harold Edwin Hurst, the rescaled range is a statistical technique to characterize how wildly a time series fluctuates or wanders about. The technique considers how quickly the range of values (*R*) increases as one looks over longer intervals of time (*T*). Compared to the standard random walk, a time series can wander about either faster or more slowly than the standard random walk, for which *R* grows as the square root of *T*.

the biggest change in river flow in the window of time you've chosen. Do this repeatedly for lots of values of *T*, and you can see how the size of fluctuations grows as you look over longer and longer intervals of time.

Hurst's idea can be used to judge the wildness or tendency to wander of any fluctuating signal, whether it measures rainfall or temperature or humidity or any number of other measurable things. In cases in which these fluctuations are strictly random, it turns out that *R* grows as the square root of *T*, or as $T^{1/2}$. For the Nile, Hurst found that the wanderings seem to be stronger, *r* grows not as the square root of *T*, but as $T^{0.7}$, which is faster. (We'll use the letter *H* to refer to this exponent, which describes the relationship between range and time. The Nile has an *H* of 0.7.) What this means is that fluctuations up or down tend to be followed by further fluctuations in the same direction, so the signal wanders away from zero faster than you'd otherwise expect. This turns out to be illuminating also for trends in markets on short times.

In 2010, physicist Reginald Smith found that stock movements over short times since around 2005 have begun showing wilder behavior with

H above 0.5.[11] His data shows the value of h rising gradually over the period 2002–2009 from 0.5 to around 0.6, with some fluctuation, of course, on top of this trend. This rise means that the market on short times has increasingly violent excursions.

This isn't surprising. It just means that markets now show the same patterns over short periods (a few minutes) as they have long shown over hours, days, and weeks, with intermittent bursts of volatility that cluster together. Given this increasing wildness, and the speed at which they operate, it's natural to suspect that high-frequency market makers have grown more skittish as they gradually lose control in an increasingly hazardous world.

Recall that the bid-ask spread reflects how much market makers think they need to charge to make a profit. You can think of it as an insurance premium they charge to cover the natural risks of being a market maker. Insurance payments obviously grow as risks grow, and those risks do grow as large price movements over short time intervals become more likely, as they have. GETCO and other market makers don't want to get whacked like Mike McCarthy. The higher price volatility, the more likely a stock's value may plummet before they can sell it on to someone else. In volatile periods, high-frequency market makers have to charge more; they get burned more often by unexpected chaos.

Hence, it's quite natural for a market maker to widen its bid-ask spreads in a crazy market, sometimes drastically. HFT is a risky business, and the trades coming at market makers in a turbulent market can rightly be called "toxic"—very likely to be poisonous. It makes sense for algorithm designers to train their programs to be skittish and even to jump ship entirely if things get too dangerous, withdrawing liquidity by refusing to trade. Algorithms, of course, can bail out in a microsecond.

The ultimate point here is that HFT may well reduce bid-ask spreads in calmer times, but they do just the opposite in stormy times. As Andrew Haldane, executive director for Financial Stability at the Bank of England, put it in a speech in 2011:

> Far from mitigating market stress, HFT appears to have amplified it. HFT liquidity, evident in sharply lower peacetime bid-ask spreads, may be illusory . . . Bid-ask spreads [during the flash crash] did not just widen, they ballooned. Liquidity entered a void. Algorithms were running on autopilot . . . Prices were not just information inefficient; they

were dislocated to the point where they had no information content whatsoever.[12]

If Haldane's interpretation is correct, then right at the heart of today's markets lies a potentially explosive positive feedback acting on very short timescales. Markets depend on liquidity to run smoothly, especially in times of stress. But stress, even over milliseconds, can drive market-making algorithms to flee the market. More volatility means less liquidity, which creates more volatility and again less liquidity and so on. In principle, such a feedback could kick in at any moment.

Indeed, something very much like this does seem to be happening—currently about ten times a day.

Spikes and Fractures

It's one thing to undertake postmortem examinations of big events in any dynamic system, seeking clues and evidence to explain what happened and why. There is much we can learn from it, but it's also only a part of the story. It's often more illuminating to scour data in the absence of any obvious big event, searching for telling details that may easily slip by unseen, but could point to a deeper understanding of the basic dynamics out of which crises emerge. If we only ever studied plate movements after an earthquake, we might think that the earth beneath our feet is always still—except when buildings fall and cracks open in the sidewalk. Only with sensitive seismic detectors did geophysicists eventually discover that the earth's crust is subject to a continual stream of tiny earthquakes, or microfractures, too weak to be noticed to by the unaided human senses.

Intrigued by the persisting mystery of the flash crash—and many subsequent events on a smaller scale, affecting just one stock or another—physicist Neil Johnson decided to look at markets with the same goals as those geophysicists. Exploiting a database collected by the market data company Nanex, he and others, including Nanex CEO Eric Hunsader, scoured the records of stock movements on multiple exchanges over five years looking for odd events.[13] It was worth it. On short timescales, they found more than eighteen thousand instances in which prices of individual stocks, in a second and a half or less, ticked either up or down at least ten times in a row, making prices rise or fall in that span by more than 0.8 percent. That may not sound like much, but many of these minicrashes and minibooms—the researchers called them "fractures" and "spikes"—took place in well under a tenth of a second, effectively instantaneous from a human perspective. A stock dropping at that rate for only ten seconds or so would be wiped out completely.

These events, the data show, have been happening roughly ten times per day. A typical spike and fracture are shown in the figures below, which illustrate just how fast and violent these events are. It's as if the markets are throwing off sparks.

You can of course "explain" each of these by giving a narrative account of the specific sequence of trades that made it happen, as the SEC ultimately did for the flash crash. But any episode in the market, strange or normal, has some set of trades behind it. That's true by definition. The deeper question is what has changed in the market to make it prone to such events.

Seeking some leads, Johnson and his colleagues decided to take things apart by time. These spikes and fractures represent sudden large market movements over very short times—much less than a second. You might assume that these minicrashes look just like full-size crashes, only smaller. But you'd be mistaken. Looking at the data for large market movements taking place over a range of times, they found that events lasting one second or longer show the familiar fat-tailed distribution—the norm for markets, as we've seen. In contrast, the distribution for events lasting less than one second is very different. It is actually "fatter than fat," and

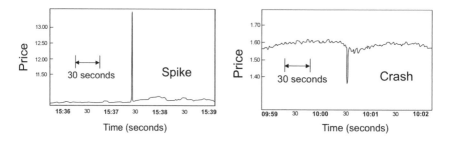

Two examples of ultrafast "black swan" events in the market. The spike (left) hit the stock of Super Micro Computer, Inc. on October 1, 2010. In this case the stock ticked upwards thirty-one times in a row, going up by 26 percent, again in just 25ms. The crash (right) hit the stock of the Ambac Financial Group on November 4, 2009. The stock value ticked down twenty times in a row, dropping by 14 percent in just 25ms (0.025 seconds). (Figure courtesy of Neil Johnson)

reflects an even greater than normal tendency for black swan–type up-heavals.

The dividing line is at one second. Something changes profoundly here, with crashes or spikes on either side of the divide looking very different. What's so special about one second? Well, for human beings, it holds a special place in the spectrum of time intervals.

Studies with automobile drivers, for example, show that their brains process visual or sound stimuli and "recognize" these stimuli in two hundred milliseconds or so. But it takes up to a second to process and respond to the detected reality: "That !!%&!&% is about to slam into me!!" How fast can you hit your brakes when surprised by a puppy crossing the road? Again, it's about one second. Experts acting in their areas of expertise face a similar limit. Chess grand masters can assess a complex chess situation and identify a threat of checkmate in about two thirds of a second, no faster.

In other words, no one can respond well to things happening much quicker than about one second, especially when making decisions of any reasonable complexity.[14] Coincidence? Probably not. Put this together with the tendency of liquidity to evaporate in dangerous times, and it starts to look like what happens on subsecond times may reflect a fundamental transition as markets break free of human control. Any random fluctuation large enough to make high-frequency algorithms withdraw liquidity, perhaps, has a chance to create a spike or fracture—a sharp burst of trading with prices moving strongly in one direction.

This final idea remains speculative, but Johnson and colleagues have shown with further evidence that this transition into a "machine dominated phase" really does seem to be happening at very short times. As I explored in chapter 6, mathematical studies of simple market models based on the minority game show that one of the most fundamental factors influencing their basic dynamics is how "crowded" the market is— again, crowded in an intellectual and strategic sense, measuring the number of available choices versus the number of investors making them. If participants in a market use a diverse range of trading strategies, the market is uncrowded. It's like a world with relatively plentiful food where all creatures can find a distinct niche and thrive. Participants earn profits in different ways—thinking and acting on different timescales, taking different views on the future, and so on.

As Johnson points out, real markets look a lot like this uncrowded phase, with highly irregular market fluctuations and fat tails.

In contrast, if a market becomes overcrowded—that is, if many traders chase few opportunities and use very similar strategies to do so—then the continuity of the market tends to break down. In this regime, the market becomes prone to what might be called "glitches" or "fractures," sudden moves up or down much like those now observed in the sub-one-second trading regime. The figure below shows market behavior in the crowded regime (left) and in the smoother uncrowded regime (right).

There are good reasons to think that market dynamics on subsecond times have indeed entered such a crowded phase. High-frequency algorithms by their nature compete on speed, have to be relatively simple, and can't waste time analyzing too much information. You might pack sophisticated mathematics into an algorithm to predict price movements, and be able to use it to trade after only fifty milliseconds of calculation. But someone else may write a less accurate "quick and dirty" algorithm using simple mathematics and able to work with only five milliseconds of calculation. They'll be able to trade ten times before you can even go once.

What this means is that the winning strategy is very easy to identify, generally speaking, faster is better. And as you'll recall from chapter 6, an obviously good strategy can quickly become a very bad one if it gets too popular. Given the number of traders chasing these opportunities,

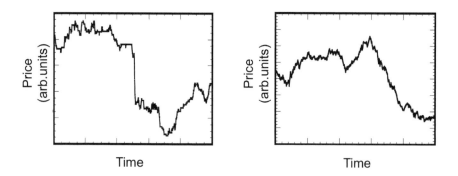

Crowded to uncrowded transition in a market based on the minority game. The figure shows typical price dynamics in the crowded (left) and uncrowded (right) regimes. The variable η represents the ratio of market participants (N) to the number of strategies in play. Hence, $\eta < 1$ implies many agents per strategy, meaning crowding in strategy space. The result is frequent, abrupt price changes as on the left. $\eta > 1$ implies very few agents per strategy, hence no crowding. Large abrupt changes here are rare. (Figure courtesy of Neil Johnson)

overcrowding is quite likely—as are the fractured market dynamics arising from it.

This is a beautiful example of how nonobvious insights can come from simple adaptive models of markets. Nothing in the efficient equilibrium view of markets offers anything similar. As trading moves to inhumanly short timescales, we should fully expect to see increasingly frequent black swan events over microscopic times. It is the natural consequence it seems of trading becoming uncoupled from the influence of conscious human decision making. Perhaps these tiny sparks will always fizzle out, never triggering any larger trouble. Or perhaps not, we really don't know. Everything depends on delicate details of how algorithms and human traders in the market are likely to respond, a matter about which we know very little.

Behind the Flash Crash: Fractious Finance

From this perspective, the flash crash no longer looks like such a puzzling event. It was a massive and shocking surprise, yes, and in full detail still a mystery, but quite plausibly a consequence of the ongoing rapid evolution of market "microstructure"—the actual mechanics of how trading happens. Forget images of well-dressed traders for the big investment banks doing battle on some big central exchange. Now the "market" is a complex ecosystem of banks, hedge funds, and individuals, with its dynamics accelerated by computer firms providing hardware trading platforms and software algorithms. Trading is computers crunching data and sending orders over wires to servers to a host of electronic exchanges in direct competition with one another, plus many other smaller trading forums.

And if the older markets were already charged with positive feedbacks, high-frequency trading has perhaps helped make them even more explosive. Single-day share-price changes as big as 3–4 percent are now more likely than at any other time in recent stock market history. Since 2000, single-day price fluctuations of 4 percent or more have occurred almost six times more frequently than they did in the four decades before.[15]

When the CFTC-SEC final report on the flash crash attributed it to the big trade in E-mini futures by Waddell and Reed, many newspapers and magazines reported in the manner of "crime solved, case closed." At

Nanex, swimming in the market data his firm specializes in handling, Eric Hunsader thought he smelled a rat. The Waddell and Reed trade, after all, represented little more than 1 percent of the E-mini's daily volume. Could such a small amount of trading really cause such an upheaval? Getting a direct look at Waddell and Reed's own data of their trade-by-trade activity on the day, Hunsader argued that the CFTC-SEC story has gaping holes. It may be comforting to attribute the crash to a shock from outside the market—thereby preserving belief in the market's own inherently stable and self-regulating equilibrium—but the data, he suggests, doesn't back it up.

He points to two basic inconsistencies. First, Waddell and Reed executed their trade in a cautious way, precisely so as to minimize its impact on the market. They fed into the market purely passive "limit orders" to sell, steadily throughout the day, offering to sell at a fixed price, and then waiting for buyers to come along. This way of trading adds liquidity to the market, and should, he argued, have little effect on the market price; indeed, it is designed specifically to minimize how much selling reduces prices and loses a seller money. Second, the real violence of the flash crash kicked in at precisely 14:42:44, when the trading data shows a sharp discontinuity and the E-mini prices really fall off a cliff. Waddell and Reed's background trading goes on mildly through this period with no abrupt changes. But at this point, some other trader did suddenly and aggressively begin selling—and they did it with no regard for the effect on prices. These trades weren't passive limit orders waiting for buyers to come along, but so-called market orders commanding the sale of thousands of contracts at whatever price could be found.

This second agent appears to have been a high-frequency trader, most likely a market maker, who bailed out of their normal trading at this point. Someone's algorithm kicked in at the critical moment, and created a high-speed sell-off. In Hunsader's view, this then led to a chain reaction among other high-frequency traders. Market-making algorithms then bought beyond their set limits, abandoned their own bids, and just sold to anyone they could, mostly other HFT algorithms, who then did the same. Firms then fled the market altogether, furthering the crash. Between 2:45:13 and 2:45:27, HFTs traded over twenty-seven thousand contracts; that made up nearly half the total trading volume. Meanwhile, Waddell and Reed—the supposed cause of the event—sold fewer contracts during the flash crash than in any similar interval during the entire day.

As Hunsader reads the data, the cause of the flash crash was something else entirely:

> The Waddell & Reed trades were not the cause, nor the trigger. [Their] algorithm was very well behaved; it was careful not to impact the market . . . The buyer of those contracts, however, was not so careful when it came to selling what they had accumulated. Rather than making sure the sale would not impact the market, they did quite the opposite: they slammed the market with 2,000 or more contracts as fast as they could . . .
>
> The first large e-Mini sale slammed the market at approximately 14:42:44.075, which caused an explosion of quotes and trades . . . all occurring about 20 milliseconds later (about the time it takes information to travel from Chicago to New York). This surge in activity almost immediately saturated or slowed down every system that processes this information; some more than others. Two more sell events began just 4 seconds later (14:42:48:250 and 14:42:50:475), which was not enough time for many systems to recover from the shock of the first event. This was the beginning of the freak sell-off which became known as the flash crash.[16]

I'm not sure that Hunsader is totally right and the CFTC-SEC totally wrong. As others have pointed out, even passive limit orders, if they're large enough, can exert pressure on prices; algorithms in the market sense their presence and respond. In any event, the Waddell and Reed trade wasn't an exceptional outlier in terms of its size, and the worst of the crash clearly emerged more directly from the actions of others in the market. What happened looks like an infrequent but perfectly normal event for the market as it currently exists. Panic set in quickly in this tight network of high-frequency traders, who en masse decided to bail out of the market in a time of stress, creating a powerful feedback effect. Like the *Hindenburg* disaster, it may have begun with some specific spark, but it was really a consequence of very volatile conditions. And in the same way it's very much the kind of thing we should expect to happen again.

And, of course, it could have been much worse. As computer scientists David Cliff and Linda Northrop noted in report for the U.K. government[17] analyzing risks from high-frequency trading, we were in this case actually rather lucky:

The true nightmare scenario would have been if the crash's 600-point down-spike, the trillion-dollar write-off, had occurred immediately before market close: that is, if the markets had closed just after the steep drop, before the equally fast recovery had a chance to start. Faced with New York showing its biggest ever one-day drop in the final 15 minutes before close of business on May 6th . . . traders in Tokyo would have had only one rational reaction: sell. The likelihood is that Tokyo would have seen one of its biggest ever one-day losses. Following this, as the mainland European bourses and the London markets opened on the morning of May 7th, seeing the unprecedented sell-offs that had afflicted first New York and then Tokyo, European markets would have followed into precipitous free-fall . . . The only reason that this sequence of events was not triggered was down to mere lucky timing. Put simply, on the afternoon of May 6th 2010, the world's financial system dodged a bullet.

We can be thankful that the circuit breaker worked as designed. Those five seconds were enough time to give all the algorithms time to regather their collective heads. But we should clearly expect that similar things could happen again. The flash crash really only directly involved two markets—futures and equities. Since then, high-frequency traders have been working hard to extend their business into markets of every kind, creating webs of interconnection with far greater reach.

Global Chaos Inc.

On June 8, 2011, a rogue algorithm caused a weird several-minute oscillation of the prices of natural gas futures.[18] Look at this peculiar rising and falling time series, leading up to an abrupt crash, and it's easy to suspect some kind of market manipulation. Criminality, cheating, and exploitation take place in any system of adaptive interacting agents, even if the agents are not human. Even colonies of bacteria face problems with cheaters—mutants who gain an unfair advantage by using the resources produced by the community without contributing to their production.

But most of our disasters aren't the result of anyone's malign intent. We bring them on ourselves, step by step, as small and apparently well-intended changes set up the conditions for disaster, but behind the scenes and out of view. Listen to computer scientist John Bates, chief technology officer for Progress Software, a large supplier of financial trading software, and you get an insider's vision of what the problems may be next. We've had the flash crash, and the markets now rest uneasily under a barrage of mysterious and alarming microfracture events. Too afraid to look under the hood of the market, we're driving onward in the vain hope the banging and grinding sounds will miraculously go away on their own. More likely, Bates suggests, there will be something worse and more pervasive than the flash crash.

As he points out, aside from ever-higher speeds and more sophisticated technology, the most aggressive trend in high-frequency finance is to extend its reach beyond stocks and futures and into derivatives, commodities, foreign exchange, energy, and other asset classes. As a consequence, he suggests, when the next big flash crash hits it won't be a simple flash crash but a "cross asset" event—a "splash crash" or "domino effect where the crashes 'splash' across asset classes, possibly wreaking havoc for market participants and regulators."[19]

It's all too easy to imagine. After all, the stock of an oil company such as Exxon depends on U.S. interest rates and the value of the U.S. dollar, as well as of currencies in countries where Exxon operates. It depends on oil prices and political events. Automated traders have already begun to use artificially intelligent algorithms able to trade on such information. An algorithm running for a big bank or hedge fund, doing something somewhat unusual, might easily trigger an event much as the high-frequency market makers did on May 6, 2010, although the consequences could spread further, triggering massive automated sell orders for everything from oil shares and derivatives to energy futures. The result wouldn't be pretty. "It would be pandemonium. Trading systems could clog up, limited bandwidth could choke orders, exchanges could freeze up—splashing across all of the affected asset classes . . . I think there is an extreme risk of seeing this because we're not serious about putting measures in place to police against it."

Bates's fear resonates with principles of network engineering. As we saw in the last chapter, more interconnections, useful in normal times, can make matters worse in times of trouble. Again, it's a matter of efficiency versus stability. The electrical grid, for example, is built as a "distributed network," a decentralized structure that improves efficiency because generators everywhere can be smaller. (Try to imagine the presumed alternative—some massive compound in the geographic middle of the country that stored and sent out all the electricity for everyone in America.) In our system energy can flow to where it is currently needed most, and away from places with current low demand. The direct corollary, however, is that trouble and breakdown can spread just as easily as energy, with longer-lasting consequences. In 2003, overgrown trees in Ohio took out a single power line and the resulting cascade of failures and power surges took more than five hundred generators offline, affected 50 million people, and blacked out the entire northeastern United States for nearly a day.

It turns out that the trouble grows worse—or at least more likely to spread—if networked systems of different kinds link together in networks of networks. In a study last year, for example, physicist Gene Stanley and colleagues looked at how breakdowns travel through combined or interlinked "networks of networks," systems mingling different kinds of elements such as electrical grids, communications systems, financial firms, and so on, versus how they spread through simpler networks of more or less similar elements. It turns out that the diversity of elements and relations between elements provides additional avenues for trouble to spread quickly. For such interlinked networks, they concluded,

> a failure of a very small fraction of nodes in one network may lead to the complete fragmentation of a system of several interdependent networks. A dramatic real-world example of a cascade of failures ("concurrent malfunction") is the electrical blackout that affected much of Italy on 28 September 2003: the shutdown of power stations directly led to the failure of nodes in the Internet communication network, which in turn caused further breakdown of power stations.[20]

This is all a little abstract, but think of these system breakdowns like viruses: the more contact between different entities, the more opportunity there is for the bad news to spread. And what Bates is describing is ever more likely, because the global world has never been more interdependent. A failure in markets could rapidly bring down enterprises and industries in all corners of the globe, interfering with energy and food supplies—and communications—from which further disruption would feed back into finance.

Clearly, equilibrium thinking of any kind is of little use in examining the positive feedbacks and chains of amplification in scenarios of this kind, or in providing counsel on how markets might be adjusted or monitored to avoid them. To gain insight, we need to understand the possible positive feedbacks in detail, as well as how they can interact with one another. As I'll explore in chapter 10, this almost certainly means building and using very large computational simulations able to represent and explore the dynamics of the entire system.

Currently, nothing like this exists, and the high-frequency industry, thrilled by technology and comforted by the rhetoric of equilibrium economics, pursues the race to zero as never before. This is not to say, I should emphasize, that high-frequency trading is a bad thing, or that markets were better in the "good old days" before computers came along. Back then, traditional market makers, facing little competition, charged clients huge fees for trading. The benefits of reduced bid-ask spreads are very real, and technology can be a very good thing. But its wise use has to be based on more than blind faith in the invisible hand to make things work out.

The Technological Predicament

In 1986, Saroo Brierley, then five years old, lost track of his older brother, with whom he had been sweeping trains in rural India. Exhausted, Saroo fell asleep; when he awoke, not finding his brother and disoriented, he got on a train that took him for fourteen hours to the slums of Calcutta. Saroo became a wandering homeless beggar in some of the most desperate slums on earth.

He finally ended up in an orphanage. An Australian couple adopted him, he moved to Tasmania, and grew up there.

Saroo could not even recall the name of the village where his family lived. In 2011, however, he discovered Google Earth and began using it to search India systematically. He multiplied the time he had traveled, about fourteen hours, by the typical speed of Indian trains and came up with a rough distance of twelve hundred kilometers. He drew a circle with radius twelve hundred kilometers on a map, its center in Calcutta, and soon discovered what he was looking for: Khandwa. "When I found it," he said, "I zoomed down and bang, it just came up. I navigated it all the way from the waterfall where I used to play."

Within a year, Saroo had been reunited with his mother, twenty-five years after their separation.[21]

Modern technology is an amazing thing, and its ever-expanding power convinces many people that humanity can always innovate its way out of any problem. It is easy to look at the story of Saroo Brierley and see that without Google, he'd never have found his mother. But technology can cause problems as well as solve them, and some anthropologists question whether we have a realistic picture of our own affect on the world around us. Anthropologist Sander van der Leeuw of the University of Arizona argues that there's a fundamental mismatch between our mental models of how we influence the world around us, and the actual changes we induce in that world, especially through technology:

> No matter how careful one is in designing human interventions in the environment, the outcome is never what it was intended to be. It seems to me that this phenomenon is due to the fact that every human action upon the environment modifies the latter in many more ways than its human actors perceive, simply because the dimensionality of the environment is much higher than can be captured by the human mind . . . We transform the environment in ways that affect not only the short-term, but also the long-term dynamics involved in unknown ways . . . the unknown longer-term challenges that are introduced accumulate.[22]

The result, he suggests, is that unknown, long-term risks accumulate, leading to "time-bombs."

This is equally true for the influence of technology and innovation over our economic and financial environment, including the functioning of markets. The metaphors of equilibrium economics have long contributed to a certain complacency and belief that the market will sort itself out. Yet this is an act of pure faith.

By pushing questions of stability aside, the equilibrium theory of markets is only a fragment of a theory. Imagine a theory of nuclear reactor operation that proved the existence of an equilibrium, self-sustaining nuclear reaction that would generate energy in the most fuel-efficient way possible. Imagine that physicists argued that real reactors could be brought closer to this ideal in a variety of ways—by using a "complete" mixture of fuels, for example—but really had no idea if the reactor would remain stable and safe, or whether it might instead become prone to explosions. Nuclear energy use would be a case of "build it and hope."

This is the situation with financial economics today. And it seems that hope isn't enough. The quant meltdown illustrated dramatically how excess leverage, even as it pushes markets toward efficiency—lowering apparent volatility along the way—also makes markets increasingly prone to violent collapse. Likewise, too many derivatives—creating dense networks of interdependence—can also push markets past a threshold of instability. In the decade before the crisis, trading in derivatives exploded. Credit default swaps, virtually nonexistent in 1998, had over $3 trillion in market value by 2008 and played a huge role in inflating the housing bubble. It is really no wonder that the financial world collapsed.

Now we see technology for high-frequency trading taking us down another road to nirvana, this time efficiency through speed and ease of trading, through market liquidity. Yet the liquidity created turns out, at least sometimes, to be an illusion and markets become less stable than before. Traveling down this road, we know next to nothing about what to expect, partly due to the fundamental mismatch Van der Leeuw talks about, but also because we've made almost no serious effort to understand the origins of this instability, and the positive feedbacks driving it.

Technology is great, but not if it creates more problems than it solves. Finance isn't just a game. Paul Wilmott certainly had a point. "Buying stocks used to be about long-term value, doing your research and finding the company that you thought had good prospects. Maybe it had a product that you liked the look of, or perhaps a solid management team. Increasingly such real value is becoming irrelevant. The contest is now between the machines—and they're playing games with real businesses and real people."[23]

The alternative, of course, is not to play games, not to just hope for good outcomes, but to work hard to understand all the various ways technology might lead to unpleasant surprises. If high-frequency trading suffers from basic instabilities, learning how to control them may be a problem in engineering—of crafting the rules of the game to ensure or encourage stability, so liquidity doesn't vanish when it is most needed. Economists, as Jean-Philippe Bouchaud points out, aren't used to thinking this way. "They tend to think that markets don't need to be stabilized, because they ARE stable."

Twilight of the Idols

*The typical graduate macroeconomics and monetary economics
training received at Anglo-American universities during the past 30
years or so may have set back by decades serious investigations of
aggregate economic behaviour and economic policy-relevant
understanding. It was a privately and socially costly waste of time
and other resources . . . Most mainstream macroeconomic theoretical
innovations since the 1970s . . . have turned out to be self-referential,
inward-looking distractions at best.*

—William Buiter, chief economist, Citigroup

*We are trying to prove ourselves wrong as quickly as possible,
because only in that way can we make progress.*

—Richard Feynman

THEORY IS THE CREATIVE ENGINE OF science. It thrives on new possibilities and speculation, on visions of what might be. Yet theory, in any practical science, has to be tempered by experimental test. Theory unchecked
by reality leads too easily to wishful thinking and to beautiful ideas of no
practical import. Unfortunately, a certain reality aversion has been common among leading figures of neoclassical economics.

Over several decades, Gary Becker of the University of Chicago has
applied the idea of rational optimization to everything from crime to
physical addiction to drugs or alcohol. For most of us, a shivering junkie

in an alleyway is trapped in a destructive behavioral feedback, caused by addictive physical substances interacting with brain chemistry, emotions, and so on. Becker sees something else. The addict is making a series of rational choices that maximize his or her expected utility. Economist Gordon Winston described how such "rational addicts" behave: "[The addict] . . . sits down at (the first) period, surveys future income, production technologies, investment/addiction functions and consumption preferences over his lifetime to period T, maximizes the discounted value of his expected utility and decides to be an alcoholic. That's the way he will get the greatest satisfaction out of life."[1]

In other words, rational addicts have chosen a life of substance dependency because, after careful consideration, they have decided that it is the best life available to them. Incredibly, this theory has actually become influential. The number of annual citations of Becker's original 1988 work has steadily increased to about fifty each year, with nearly half coming from fields such as substance abuse, psychiatry, law, and psychology. Given this influence, most of us would expect there to be lots of empirical evidence backing up Becker's theory. But not really.

Last year, economists Ole Røgeberg and Hans Melberg undertook a survey of researchers who had authored or coauthored a research paper with the term "rational addiction" in the title, abstract, or keywords, probing their views both on the status of the theory and the evidence supporting it. A majority of their respondents, they found, took the original theory and its subsequent development as a "success story that demonstrates the power of economic reasoning," yet at the same time expressed belief that the empirical evidence for the theory is weak. They even disagreed on the kind of evidence that could be used to test the theory, as well as its policy implications.[2]

In any area of science, of course, people disagree over the evidence that really matters. For two decades, physicists working to explain the puzzling phenomenon of high-temperature superconductivity—electricity flowing through a material with absolutely zero resistance at temperatures as high as 150K, this temperature being far above what would ordinarily be expected—have reported experimental evidence they say gives "definitive" proof of how it works. Every such paper has been immediately countered by another arguing that the evidence is actually anything but definitive, and may even suggest it works another way entirely. This kind of disagreement is normal in science, and even the most confident physicists studying superconductivity don't believe they've solved the riddle; at best, they are gaining only a fragmentary understanding of it.

Attitudes seem different in economics. As Røgeberg and Melberg point out, the main thrust of rational addiction research is that people become addicts because they face certain kinds of choices and act rationally in making them. This means they're making a claim about what goes on in the addict's brain. That's a pretty bold thing to claim, particularly if you haven't done any testing to prove it. Economists in this field, as they put it,

> show no interest in empirically examining the actual choice problem— the preferences, beliefs, and choice processes—of the people whose behavior they claim to be explaining . . . The claim of causal insight, then, involves the claim that a choice problem people neither face nor would be able to solve prescribes an optimal consumption plan no one is aware of having. The gradual implementation of this unknown plan is then claimed to be the actual explanation for why people over time smoke more than they should according to the plans they actually thought they had. To quote Bertrand Russell out of context, this "is one of those views which are so absurd that only very learned men could possibly adopt them."[3]

Russell's comment seems to apply equally well in other areas of economics. The efficient market idea that markets always "get things right" rather obviously took a beating in the recent financial crisis, but afterward, Eugene Fama didn't hesitate to claim in an interview with the writer John Cassidy that the theory "did quite well in this episode." The most spectacular rise in housing prices in half a century may have spurred a frenzy of borrowing and speculative gambling, ending with a crash back to reality and a massive government bailout to preserve the entire financial system, but to Fama, the bubble actually had nothing to do with it. Bubble? What bubble? As he exclaimed, "I don't even know what a bubble means. These words have become popular. I don't think they have any meaning . . . They have to be predictable phenomena. I don't think any of this was particularly predictable."

Fama's argument seems to be that there's no sense talking about a bubble unless you can describe a clear recipe for recognizing one and predicting when it will burst. Otherwise, such talk is superstition, not hardheaded economic science. Loose arguments like this often seem superficially plausible, but what does this really mean for the science of economics? If we're having a difficult time describing a phenomenon, is it more appropriate to try to define it better, or just pretend it's not there? Try to imagine Fama at a geophysics conference arguing that earthquakes, on account of being unpredictable, do not exist.

This effort to pretend bubbles don't exist is near tantamount to a denial of the existence of time. After all, market efficiency, in Fama's view, follows from the supposition that all new information flows into the market "instantaneously," so that for the purposes of investment strategy, the element of time can effectively be ignored. The dynamics of how it flows can be ignored, too; all that matters is the "long run," and the market is supposed to get to that point very quickly. Assuming equilibrium means assuming that there is no real role for time, or for dynamics. Indeed, as the writer of one graduate economics textbook proudly put it, "We don't do dynamics." Rather, time and dynamics get swept under the rug by assuming that individuals plan their future behavior now, and all at once, by solving an optimization problem over the entire future. As Røgeberg and Melberg describe it in the context of rational addiction theory, addicts are people whose

> addictions are nothing more than the gradual implementation of a certain class of forward-looking, time-consistent, well-informed consumption plans satisfying certain properties. For instance, a beginning heroin user in the model knows that injecting or smoking heroin has immediate effects (enjoyment or relief of some kind) and lagged effects (on health, future tastes, labor market opportunities, etc.). The heroin user maps out a plan for future consumption that takes all of this into account, adjusting the consumption plan to exploit all trade-offs across and between different points in time. The result is an intricately structured plan accounting for the pains of withdrawal, the effects of learning to enjoy the heroin daze, effects on wage earning potential, expected changes in heroin prices, etc.

This is of course a fantasy. Does anyone really imagine that heroin addicts think this way, that they are making a calculated and fully planned decision to risk financial, physical, and emotional devastation in exchange for few-hour episodes of psychological relief? The real world emerges not from well-laid plans brought to fruition but from action and learning, in time, through adjustment and adaptation. Think seriously about what comes out of a world populated by adaptive, learning, adjusting agents and you get models more like the minority game, where the dynamics never stop or settle down. Or you get a model like that of Stefan Thurner and colleagues exploring how leveraged competition can create explosive instability quite naturally, leading to crashes that arrive sporadically and unpredictably. We need to think in time, as reality exists in time, and models like this are important tools for thinking. They help us learn about what is possible and why.

It is hard to imagine how anyone familiar with these conceptual examples could fail, like Fama, even to imagine "what a bubble could be." That's a spectacular failure of imagination, but this failure has been inserted systematically at the very foundation of today's theories of economics, especially theories of whole economies or "macroeconomics."

Macroeconomics and Microconfusion

"The data analysis presented in the paper is mildly interesting," the referee's report read, "and the study offers a somewhat novel perspective on industrial growth." That was the positive part. "However, the theoretical argument is unconvincing. While it appears to account adequately for the statistical patterns observed in the data, the model lacks microfoundations. This makes the paper wholly unsuitable for publication."

This was a portion of the report of an economist to whom I had sent a paper when acting as an editor for the science journal *Nature* in the mid-1990s. The other two referees had been glowingly positive in their reviews of the paper, which reported an interesting statistical regularity in the growth rates of business firms, and also offered a simple explanation. In his report, this economist reiterated the charge "lacks microfoundations" several times. The paper presented what I thought was a convincing, logically coherent, and well-founded argument, and the other referees agreed. So I was puzzled. Why was our economist colleague seeing this matter so differently?

What I didn't understand then is that due to recent economic history, "microfoundations" is for economists a loaded word.

The idea of modeling the entire economy and making useful forecasts of things like inflation, GDP, and the like got started in the 1960s, when most economists called themselves Keynesians. That is, following the ideas of the British economist John Maynard Keynes, they saw the economy as a system that could occasionally stagnate and suffer from maladjustments like high unemployment merely from a temporary lack of demand, perhaps linked to a lack of confidence, cash shortages, and the like. In 1970, the Federal Reserve Board began using an early version of a Keynesian model for the U.S. economy, based on about sixty crude equations capturing the historical relationships among economic variables. In spirit, the model aimed to do for the economy what meteorologists had recently begun doing for the weather—to forecast likely future changes, and give some guidance on useful policies.

But this project came to a crashing failure in the mid-1970s when the model failed spectacularly to forecast the high inflation and persistent unemployment—"stagflation"—of the era. So economists went back to the drawing board, and one of them, Robert Lucas, offered a seemingly visionary analysis of what must have gone wrong and how to fix it.

In a paper in 1976, in which he put forth what has come to be known as the Lucas critique, Lucas argued that the model then in use had failed largely because it hadn't taken account of how individuals' expectations matter to the economy, or how they might change. "When people make decisions, especially in times of uncertainty," Lucas argued, "they often get drawn into guessing about what policy makers will do. Their expectations of what is likely to come may influence their behavior, altering the historical patterns on which the forecasting model was based." Any prior regularity that might have existed in a set of data had been present only in the context of the policies prevailing in the past. Change the policies and those changes, by influencing the way people act and anticipate the future, may well strongly change or destroy the regularity on which you had based your plans.

Lucas's argument[4] is in a way similar to the famous problem of Schrödinger's cat, which he imagined had been put into a box along with a special device that might or might not kill it. If you take very seriously the basic mathematics of quantum theory, Schrödinger argued, you have to conclude that the cat becomes definitely alive or definitely dead only when the box is opened and someone looks in. Before that moment, quantum theory implies that the cat is in a peculiar state in which it is both alive *and* dead at the same time. The act of looking in the box ultimately changed the outcome one way or the other for the cat. Lucas's point was much the same, though without the metaphysical weirdness of quantum theory: the mere act of drawing attention to a pattern in the market has the effect of changing that pattern.

This view had a transforming effect on theoretical economics, and it explains why that economist didn't like the paper I'd sent him to review: it articulated a pattern, but it didn't try to explain it by looking in detail at human beings and how they form expectations about the future. A way out of this puzzle, Lucas suggested, would be to build models of the economy in terms of people and their behavior, looking explicitly to their expectations and taking those into account. The only thing to be assumed as fixed in the model would be so-called deep structural facts that remain unchanged by any policy—basic human preferences, for example. Pursuit of this program soon led to the so-called rational expectations revolution in economics, linked to Lucas and other economists such as Edward Prescott and Thomas Sargent, who began building such theories. Henceforth, a good theory of any large economic system, to be respectable, had to base itself on the behavior of the individual agents in an economy, people and firms, looking to their choices and actions. Such a theory would have "microfoundations," take shifts in peoples' expectations into account, and therefore be trustworthy as a guide to policy.

There is obviously some good sense in Lucas's idea. To make an analogy to physics, think of the air in a balloon. You might do some experiments in summertime, measuring how the volume changes as you blow up the balloon and increase the pressure inside. Come wintertime, you might do the experiments again and find that everything had changed, the air now being colder and therefore denser. To build a trustworthy theory, you need microfoundations, a theory that derives the relationship between pressure and volume by looking at the behavior of the micro-level dynamics: the individual atoms and molecules flying around the inside of the balloon and banging into each other. You'd get a relationship between pressure and volume that depends explicitly on temperature and thus would work in wintertime or summertime. (There is, incidentally, such a theory in physics. It's known as the kinetic theory of gases.) Theories with microfoundations, by examining the dynamics of the smallest players on the stage, can give a plausible account of how large-scale macroreality emerges out of microreality.

It's the Lucas critique that has made the charge "lacks microfoundations" so powerful in economics.

But this story isn't quite complete, because economists don't actually use microfoundations in the way I've suggested, to refer to sensible assumptions about human behavior and their expectations. In later developments, Lucas not only demanded microfoundations, but decreed their only acceptable form as well. To qualify, a theory actually has to model the behavior of people (and firms) as being determined by fully rational planning over a long span of time, as the drug addicts do in Becker's theory, and most economic agents do in most economic theories. It was actually the failure to do this that my economist referee didn't like. The authors of the paper in question[5] did indeed make plausible assumptions about human behavior, in particular about how managerial directives might flow from one level in an organization to another, but they didn't have individuals maximizing anything, a mortal sin.

Of course, when you get down to it, the need for microfoundations in an economic theory has little to do with making that theory realistic. On this point, a commenter on the blog of economist Simon Wren-Lewis expressed the matter quite clearly:

> Microfoundations would be important if there were clear evidence that they represented the truth. For example, if there had been a series of experiments demonstrating that individuals are rational and make decisions so as to maximize some measurable quantity called utility, it would be important that macro models were consistent with this and the most direct way of ensuring that would be to incorporate rational utility-maximizing households into the model . . . The fact is that there is no such evidence. Microeconomics is not based on empirical evidence, and the approach used in microeconomics has no special claim to the truth.[6]

In other words, microfoundations don't actually give foundations to anything. Indeed, they are almost certainly inconsistent with real human behavior. To be considered scientific and state of the art, weirdly enough, theories in macroeconomics have to be founded on things we know to be untrue. This is Milton Friedman's perverse F-twist revisited.

Economists even readily admit this is the case, and that those developing theories with microfoundations often don't care if the models fit reality. As economists Andrea Pescatori and Saeed Zaman put it in an essay on the state of macroeconomics:

> Structural models are built using the fundamental principles of economic theory, often at the expense of the model's ability to predict key macroeconomic variables like GDP, prices, or employment. In other words, economists who build structural models believe that they learn more about economic processes from exploring the intricacies of economic theory than from closely matching incoming data.[7]

The leading figures in this field even go so far as to demote empirical evidence as a standard for judging a theory; its consistency with rational expectations is more important. In a 2005 interview, Thomas Sargent recalled the reaction Robert Lucas and Edward Prescott had when empirical tests showed their models didn't fit. "I recall Bob Lucas and Ed Prescott both telling me that those tests were rejecting too many good models."[8] This is still the attitude today, and it comes with the reverse attitude that rejects theories that do fit the data if they don't fit the theoretical orthodoxy of microfoundations.

After discussion with other editors at *Nature*, I eventually ignored the critical economist and published the paper, which I'm pleased to say was well received. It's received nearly three hundred citations since then.

Autistic Economics?

Ten years ago, French graduate students in economics staged a minor and short-lived rebellion against their professors. Fed up with the extreme unrealistic assumptions in most economic theory, they refused to attend class and wrote a manifesto charging their professors with teaching an economic theory wholly disconnected from reality. The professors, naturally, mounted a defense, and the students ultimately backed down. But out of the tumult eventually arose a new journal that was called, for a time, the *Journal of Post-Autistic Economics* (since renamed the *Real World Economics Review*). The journal aimed to publish economic research that aspired to more than useless mathematical gymnastics.

Poking around in the details of the rational expectations models currently used by many central banks to forecast economic changes, it's easy to understand the students' objections. The model currently used by the European Central Bank to forecast and understand the European economy is of a class currently considered by many economists to be the "state of the art." Devised by economists Frank Smets and Raf Wouters and known as a dynamic stochastic general equilibrium (DSGE) model, its equations take full note of the demand for rational expectations microfoundations. The DSGE model has one equation capturing the behavior of "households," people who work, earn an income, and spend. And they have another equation for firms, which sell things, hire, and invest. These equations define their behavior as resulting from a complex optimization of their utility over the future.

In the United States, the Federal Reserve Bank currently uses a fairly similar model known as FRB/US (normally read as "firbus"), which also puts an emphasis on modeling expectations. From the Fed's own description of the model,[9] it makes "extensive use of dynamic optimization theory to characterize responses of households and firms to shocks," and bases its equations for households, firms, and financial markets "on economic theories of optimizing behavior." Like the Smets-Wouters model, this model also assumes that people and firms have expectations that are perfectly rational and consistent with whatever their models predict. In such a model, it's just not possible for most of the country to be buying up properties in the full expectation of rising prices and huge profits even as the economy, in reality, nears the point of certain implosion. They're not allowed to be that wrong.

Unfortunately, microfoundations in the economists' sense haven't led to any significant degree of predictive success. Predictions one year in advance for U.S. GDP growth have failed to anticipate any of the recessions over the past few decades. They've generally overestimated growth during economic recessions while underestimating it during recoveries; in other words, they tend to predict we'll see more of what just happened, and so they miss any change. Similarly, predictions of the U.K. Treasury over the twenty-five years up to 1996 had an average prediction error of 1.45 percent of GDP, a number that looks especially huge when compared to how much the GDP fluctuates every year: 2.10 percent. The same is roughly true across Europe. In general, the error is large compared to the actual data, and most of the accurate forecasts were made when economic conditions were relatively stable, meaning that in general, these economic models are bad at predicting any kind of change.[10]

As economist Paul Ormerod concluded in a review of forecasting success, "By scientific standards, the accuracy of short-term economic forecasts has been poor, and shows no sign of improving over time."

None of this changes if we look at the biggest events either, the historic crashes and recessions. For the great recession of 2008, none of the models even came close. They were predicting more sunny weather even as the great storm welled up before them.[11]

But none of this is actually too surprising, because the models really don't try to explain much—rather, they explain away.

The most dramatic claim DSGE modelers make is that the models reproduce certain statistical features of the way GDP fluctuates—in particular, its long memory, with changes now giving information on likely changes to come. This is nothing to sneer at, of course, because the detailed statistics give the best way to test models of highly irregular processes. But this claim should be taken with a grain of salt—or maybe a whole pile of it. It's one thing to put simple and plausible assumptions into a model, and find that out of it emerges something complex and realistic; this approach may lead us to underlying causes of real-world events. Put the right ingredients into an oven, and out comes a cake.

But the DSGE models do something very different. To explain the complex statistics of GDP and other economic time series, they suppose agents do all their optimizing of utility and so on, and then also assume that the economy gets hit by a string of shocks to things like technology, individual preferences, and policies. And to get a good fit with the outputs, they have to assume that incoming shocks arrive with the very same complexity, the same long memory. This is more like putting a cake in the oven, and then removing the same cake. Voilà!

In 2009, at a meeting of economists at the London School of Economics, the Queen of England famously asked why economists hadn't seen the financial crisis coming, or at least hadn't warned about the possibility. This is obviously a fair and sensible question, and the apparent answer is that economists' favorite models are so fixated on their microfoundations that they neglect other factors equally relevant to human behavior. Financial innovation and credit out of control? An enormous bubble in housing? These don't exist in the rational expectations world of DSGE. To "explain" the crisis (after the fact, of course), DSGE modelers have had to resort to crazy assumptions that even they find hard to swallow. As DSGE economist Narayana Kocherlakota admitted in 2010:

Most models in macroeconomics rely on some form of large quarterly movements in the technological frontier (usually advances, but sometimes not). Some models have collective shocks to workers' willingness to work. Other models have large quarterly shocks to the depreciation rate in the capital stock (in order to generate high asset price volatilities). To my mind, these collective shocks to preferences and technology are problematic. Why should everyone want to work less in the fourth quarter of 2009?[12]

In order to generate real-world outcomes, these economists had to make increasingly implausible assumptions about the behavior of their rational actors. What good is a system that forces you to think this way? How can we take unrecognizable actors and put them into improbable situations, and then expect reality to emerge from their behavior? It might be better to wipe the slate clean, forget the rational expectations revolution, and start over. The idea of microfoundations is a little like waterboarding; sounds good until you find out what the term refers to. Authentic and plausible microfoundations really would be a good idea.

Humans are actually not great or even decent optimizers. But we are social creatures. Our expectations matter a lot, but they often come not from careful deliberation about what policy makers may do but from what we see others expecting. Today's rational expectations contain a thousand embarrassments, but perhaps worst of all is that everyone in these models decides and acts on their own, without any influence of others. If everyone else is buying and flipping houses, this makes it no more likely that you will, too. There is no social influence at all. In this regard, it is no surprise at all that these models could not predict even the possibility of the crisis.

Animal Spirits

In the early 2000s, professor Alex Pentland served on the board of an MIT initiative to create spin-off laboratories overseas, especially in India. It didn't go quite as planned. "We had some of the most brilliant and powerful people in the world," he recalls, "but our work was a disaster, just an incredible disaster. People were making decisions that were, on the face of it, ridiculous. Two days later you'd think, 'How in the world did I go along with that?' It was as if your brain had been turned off."

Pentland is a computer scientist by training and, like most scientists, is oriented toward rational thinking and decision making. But this experience left him unsettled. Pondering what had happened, he came to the conclusion that the leading directors, all extremely charismatic and certain of themselves, had pulled others along with nonrational, or at least nonverbal forces, and he soon began doing experiments to pin down such effects more clearly.

In one experiment at a major call center, for example, he set up electronic devices that analyzed the speech patterns of the operators on the call center floor. The devices captured neither the specific words that the operators used nor the logic of their conversations, but only the physical voice signal: the measured variations in tone and pitch. Even so, Pentland could predict accurately, after only a few seconds of listening, the ultimate success or failure of almost every call. Successful operators, it turned out, speak little and listen much. When they do speak, their voices fluctuate strongly in amplitude and pitch, suggesting interest and responsiveness to the customer's needs. Operators who speak with little variation come across as too determined and authoritative, but by speaking invitingly, being responsive but not pushy, a skilled operator can let callers find their own way to a sale. The company was able to use this insight to improve telephone sales performance by 20 percent or more.

From an anthropological point of view, it's not surprising that a lot of human influence takes place nonverbally. Apes, chimpanzees, and other primates—our close evolutionary cousins—lack anything like our facility for language, yet they still lead sophisticated social lives. They organize groups for hunting, collective defense, and child rearing. All this takes place through nonlinguistic means, by displays of power, meaningful noises, and facial expressions. Instincts for this kind of communication enabled humans' ancestors to form strong, cohesive groups, and human beings still possess those instincts, alongside more recently evolved talents for language and reason.

Some of the most famous social psychology research of the last century documented the extent of group influence on individuals. In a 1951 experiment, for example, psychologist Solomon Asch asked experimental subjects to say which of three lines on a paper matched the length of another line, using lengths so different that the correct answer was obvious. If they heard a number of people give the same wrong answer, many people followed along with the crowd, completely ignoring the clear input of their senses. People in group situations don't consciously weigh the options and then deliberately (or timidly) choose to conform. Instead, the conforming happens automatically and unconsciously.

In economics, Keynes had seen similar forces at the root of financial instability, working through their influence over things like optimism and pessimism and their effect on spending and savings. He referred to "animal spirits." Keynes worked on the basis of experience and insight, but modern research documents these effects even more clearly.

The idea of expectations invokes having some clear view of the past. Having expectations means having some experience of what to expect based on past experience. But our memory isn't so clear and unambiguous, nor free from social influence. A few years ago, psychologist Micah Edelson and colleagues in Israel had volunteers watch an eyewitness documentary, and then several days later tested their ability to recall facts without any interference, or after being presented with memories as recounted by some other individuals. They found that volunteers often had memories conforming to the erroneous recollections of others, producing both long-lasting and temporary errors, even when their initial memory was strong and accurate. More profoundly, the study went on, using functional brain imaging, to look at the sites in the brain where these memory changes took place. The volunteers weren't merely reporting something they didn't actually remember just to fit in; their brains actually changed under social pressure, so they remembered something different.

This is similar to other experiments by Gregory Berns and colleagues, who reexamined the famous Asch experiments on social conformity. Berns and colleagues did the experiment in such a way that they could tell that conforming volunteers—who were effectively discarding their own observations in favor of those reported by others—weren't just trying to fit in. Social pressure actually made them *see* the world differently, and specific mechanisms in the brain made it happen.

What's true in the lab in controlled conditions is also likely true more broadly. Our memories and views of the past, as well as our views of the present, conform to social pressure. "Housing values never go down," a British friend of mine told me in 2005, having just taken out a mortgage to purchase a third speculative property. This friend is a smart, levelheaded, and intelligent person, but his opinion wasn't the result of independent research. Newspapers then were full of stories of people becoming instantly rich by flipping houses. "There is nothing so disturbing to one's well-being and judgement," the economic historian Charles Kindleberger once said, "as to see a friend get rich." My friend's mind, like that of many people, had absorbed the prevailing atmosphere of ideas, and his brain had probably been physically altered as a result.

None of this thinking, or any thinking like it, enters into today's macroeconomic models, DSGE or otherwise. Mainstream economists have attempted a few very cautious steps away from the rational expectations straitjacket, but nothing very serious. Of course, it seems like a risky step, as the world of realistic psychology looks wild and unfathomable, infinite in variability; one who enters may well become hopelessly confused and lost. But it is possible to take measured steps into this forest without attempting to handle all that detail at once. The minority game, for example, made significant progress just by taking seriously the idea that people learn and adapt, act in the future based on what they've seen in the past. Other obvious factors that demand exploration include real differences between people, and the social factors that often make human behavior contagious. A few models in disequilibrium economics have already begun exploring how these basic features feed into economic dynamics, and they suggest that none of this is a recipe likely to guarantee a safe and stable equilibrium. Therein may lie an explanation of the continued resistance of the economic mainstream to research of this kind. Thinking has many uses, and trying to find the truth is just one. "How convenient it is to be a reasonable creature," Benjamin Franklin once said, "since it enables one to make or find a reason for whatever one has a mind to do."

Physicists and Failed Philosophers

Physicists come in all types. There are, of course, the string theorists for whom mathematical beauty is an end in itself, and who, like the great British physicist Paul Dirac, see physics research as "a search for pretty mathematics." Other physicists take a very different view and look to the data to see if it might speak to them through patterns.

Last year, in this spirit, German physicist Tobias Preis and colleagues looked at price movements in markets on times ranging from ten milliseconds (high-frequency trading in futures markets) up to around 10 billion

milliseconds, or several decades (the S&P 500 Index over a forty-year period). Market participants talk a lot about bull and bear markets, and
about moods leading to sustained ups and downs. Momentum, as many
studies have shown, is real. As Preis found, there also seems to be a universal pattern in the way it switches from one direction to another.

Their analysis focuses on what they refer to as "switching events"—an
upward trend that breaks off into a negative one, or vice versa. These can
be identified (or defined) in a mathematically unambiguous way. They
find essentially the same mathematical pattern across all timescales,
even when moving between the futures market and the stock market—in
effect, a signature of switching points that shows up in the volume of
trades and predicts approaching changes. The basic pattern can be expressed in simple formulae, but the idea comes across even better in the
diagram below. It shows how the volume of individual trades increases as
the moment of a switching point approaches. Remember, this isn't just at
one timescale, but is averaged over many timescales.

The middle of the diagram is the moment of a switching, where the
volume per trade becomes very large. That is, people start trading in
larger amounts as the switching moment approaches. Their behavior is,
in effect, an early warning sign of the coming event.[13]

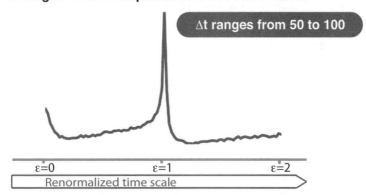

Averaged volume sequence for FDAX time series

Δt ranges from 50 to 100

$\varepsilon=0$ $\varepsilon=1$ $\varepsilon=2$

Renormalized time scale

The universal pattern of switching as averaged over many time scales. The figure shows
how the volume of trading rises and peaks at the moment of switching from an upward
to downward trend, or vice versa. This pattern shows up whether looking at price
movements over months or over seconds. (Reprinted with permission from Tobias
Preis, Johannes Schneider, and H. Eugene Stanley, "Switching Processes in Financial
Markets," *PNAS* 108, 7674–7678 (2012).)

What this pattern seems to suggest is a universal mechanism of amplified switching from one kind of collective behavior to another, not unlike a flock of birds abruptly changing direction. In fact, biologists know that such abrupt shifts take place not because all the birds have made the same rationally optimal calculation and simultaneously changed their minds—the rational expectations view of bird navigation—but because each bird responds to its neighbors, and avalanches of change travel through the flock. Experiments with starlings a few years ago even suggested that flocks, by design, maintain a collective state of flight that is maximally sensitive to the actions of any one bird, thereby making best use of information that may come from any source. The pattern Preis and his colleagues found suggests something similar in the markets. Many people follow a trend for a time. Then, a few become wary of a potential reversal and act accordingly. Others, sensing those peoples' actions, follow suit. A growing avalanche of behavior reverses the trend—and may well set one off in the opposite direction.

In specific mathematical form, this insight reflects some of the gut feelings of the most experienced traders and financiers. Legendary financier George Soros is a kind of Leonardo da Vinci of investing—a talent so profound he stands out even among a collection of the world's experts. Over four decades, Soros has with rare exception seen every major crisis coming in advance. Even in the current economic disaster, he has come out a winner again, earning a healthy profit even as storied investment banks around the globe have gone under.

How does he do it? Soros has tried to explain the source of his insight in a number of books; he's written, in a highly intuitive language, about his theory of "reflexivity," which aims to capture the subtle interplay between belief and behavior, how human theories of markets change human behavior and so also influence how markets work. By his own admission, Soros's theories have never met with anything like the success of his investing. He now sees himself as a "bad communicator" and a "failed philosopher."[14]

Soros's ideas have been criticized by economic academics in both fair and unfair terms. It's fair to say that he has described his theory of markets mostly in qualitative and quite abstract philosophical terms, and his perspective lacks the explicit detail of a predictive science. His way of arguing fits more comfortably with the premathematical age of economics, now long past. Unfairly, however, Soros's ideas have been ignored simply because they don't fit tightly with economic orthodoxy, and actually threaten the seemingly impressive edifice on which modern economics—and the social status of many economists—has been built. But George Soros may yet have the last laugh, as (in addition to the billions of dollars he's made) his view of markets resonates quite strongly with the simple dynamics seen here. When Soros writes that "every bubble consists of a trend and a misconception that interact in a reflexive manner," what he means isn't necessarily obvious. But from everything he has written, he seems to be trying to describe positive feedbacks between real-world events and human thinking and reaction to such events.

His first principle isn't human rationality and knowledge, but fallibility and lack of knowledge. The market is made of people trying their best to see what's true and false and to understand the coming future, but they always do so imperfectly, in some approximation, which may be relatively close to reality, or may be very far from it. Participants, insofar as they begin to understand, also want to use that understanding to guide their actions more effectively, following what Soros calls the mind's "manipulative function." This, to my mind, gets a little too philosophical, but the basic ideas seem sound. And in this respect, Soros is in good company with other renegade economists.

A Theory of Economic Weather

Four decades ago, in his midtwenties, Charles Gray wasn't always happy working under his Ph.D. adviser, American economist Hyman Minsky. At Washington University in St. Louis in the 1970s, he was, like other young economists, swept off his feet by the excitement of the rational expectations revolution and its exuberant call for financial deregulation in pursuit of optimal equilibrium outcomes. But Gray, now a professor at the University of St. Thomas in St. Paul, Minnesota, got stuck working under an economist who didn't buy into the mathematical enthusiasm of equilibrium theory. "He pretty much just harped on the fragility of the financial system and the economy," Gray later recalled. "Here was this guy harping on this thing nobody believed. I had to labor under his tutelage, and I wasn't sure I believed it either."[15]

Influenced by the ideas of Keynes and other historically minded economists, Minsky asserted that economic systems, like the weather, cannot possibly be understood with equilibrium thinking alone. Fundamental elements of human psychology, he argued, along with inventions and new investments that sporadically arise, create a natural breeding ground for positive market feedbacks capable of bringing storms out of economic blue skies.

The story he told, consistent with many historical episodes, is compelling. In prosperous and stable times, people naturally grow optimistic. Investors borrow and take on risk—buying houses, opening factories, starting new companies—in the expectation of gain. The longer times stay good, the more risk they take on. But investors, who typically borrow and use leverage to multiply their potential payoffs, have to make loan repayments; they need to pour into increasingly risky investments to keep things ticking over. Eventually, things reach a point where the cash generated by their assets no longer is sufficient to pay off the mountains of debt they took on to acquire them. A trigger of some sort may then cause a reversal. The failure of a prominent company, a report of a major accounting scandal or some similar event causes loss in broad confidence of continued expansion, and decline then ensues with violence. Losses on speculative assets prompt lenders to call in their loans, and when that happens, things unwind quickly as the values of assets collapse. The economy enters a downward spiral akin to the quant meltdown, but possibly on a vastly larger scale.

The crisis of 2008 fits this pattern perfectly. Low interest rates from 2002 onward encouraged people to buy houses, and at first it was old-fashioned buying—taking out traditional mortgage loans with the full intention of paying them back completely, both principal and interest. But easy credit led to higher house prices and this soon drew in a more speculative element—first borrowers taking on "interest-only" loans, and then "ponzi" borrowers taking out mortgages with payments so low they don't even cover the interest, so what is owed actually increases with time. The bubble at this point became a self-supporting wave of optimism: lenders only provided funds to ponzi borrowers because of belief that housing values would continue to increase, which they of course, could not, precipitating the massive spiral downward.

This brings in the second element in Minsky's picture—the essential role of financial institutions in inflating such bubbles. Ponzi borrowers need ponzi lenders, and the principal achievement of the rapidly expanding shadow banking system was to devise mechanisms to make lending ever more speculative, riskier, and fueled with higher leverage. This helped drive the housing bubble, as the availability of credit encouraged higher home prices. The bubble inevitably burst, and now we are seeing the progression in reverse, as businesses deleverage, lending standards are raised, and the share of borrowers in the three stages shifts back toward the hedge borrower.

In his 1984 book *Stabilizing an Unstable Economy*,[16] Minsky described this mechanism and its repeated occurrence in history, from the South Sea bubble of 1720 to the U.S. stock market bubble of 1928–29. But he was on the wrong side of the rational expectations revolution, which conquered academic economics "as completely as the Holy Inquisition conquered Spain," to use a phrase of Keynes. For the rational expectations mainstream, nothing can be more anathema than the notion of perpetual sources of instability at the heart of the market economy. But times change. Minsky never took the step that Norman Phillips did when he mapped the world's wind patterns, putting his model into a computer to simulate its dynamics and explore the interaction of factors in more detail than the human mind can. But some adventurous economists have begun to do so.

Last year, for example, economist Blake LeBaron set up a beginning model every bit as crude as Phillips's was, but also equally valuable. It showed the promise of such models in establishing the natural processes that routinely get economies—and economists—in trouble. In rough outline, LeBaron's model involves traders that try to predict market prices, as in the other adaptive models we've seen. In interaction, these agents generate a financial market that works much like real markets. In particular, movements are unpredictable—just as the EMH and observation suggests. It also shows fat tails and long memory in statistics, also corresponding closely to those seen in real markets. In this, LeBaron's virtual market is like others. But it takes one step further.

One of Minsky's insights is that some people are naturally more speculative than others. In his model, LeBaron tried to reflect this, setting it up to explore what might happen if some people or firms think more cautiously, trying to scrutinize "fundamentals" and investing for the long term, while others are more speculative and jump more aggressively on what they believe to be profitable trends. The world really isn't made of identical automatons. This difference turns out to have a huge effect.

In simulations of this virtual world, he found that the most speculative types in the long run typically controlled about 40 percent of the overall wealth, compared to only about 10 percent for the fundamentalist investors. This explains why the adaptive, speculative sector of the market had a dominant effect on its overall dynamics, momentum being a force to be reckoned with. The market repeatedly went through periods of slow, long bubblelike climbs as the assets rose in value, followed by a precipitous crash of just the kind Minsky had described. And the model points out some things that aren't necessarily obvious from Minsky's description.

First, the very trait that makes speculators speculative—their attention to short trends—makes them oblivious to the risks of the crash as it builds. Even as the market reaches a peak, they think the risks are still low—and can point to the sound performance of their strategies to that point as proof. Second, the fundamentalists who remain in the market, while they are well aware of the coming crash, can do nothing to stabilize the market, as Friedman and other neoclassical economists would argue they should. Their inability to profit from the rapid rise in prices means they end up with less wealth and don't control enough of the market to stabilize it.

It's also illuminating that these waves of rising and then falling prices can occur even in the absence of firms increasing their leverage, a practice Minsky felt was a key factor, but was a little too complex, for now, for LeBaron to put into his model. Even without leverage, it seems that simple psychological factors and appetite for risk create such speculative instability. Of course, leverage would almost certainly make the model more unstable still, especially on the way back down due to the amplifying spiral of deleveraging.

As with any such computational model, this is meant to be a tool for thinking and exploring what might possibly come out of a few simple behavioral rules in interaction. Of course, LeBaron's work is only a first attempt, an examination of what might be possible, and a demonstration of how apparently puzzling events might not be puzzling at all if we take off the blinkers of rational expectations and equilibrium. Why is it, as historians have noted, that many financial bubbles pass through a period of "financial distress," just after the peak of the bubble, and before the crash, during which the market rests uneasily, often for quite a long time? This subtle detail also appears to emerge naturally from fairly simple disequilibrium models, and again depends on the existence of investors with different ways of thinking.[17] It certainly looks as if Minsky's basic insight was spot on.

People aren't perfectly rational. We're all different. Markets aren't in equilibrium. It's all a recipe for a messy world, but take these things seriously and you can make progress in understanding it.

Lament: How It Might Have Been

Rational expectations. Perhaps nothing in economics so clearly illustrates a compulsive desire to push economic phenomena into the conceptual box of equilibrium, rejecting all other possibilities on ideological grounds alone. This desire appears wholly bizarre from any scientific point of view, but less bizarre from the point of view of sociology and human behavior. The economics profession is hardly the first to get itself locked into an intellectual dead end. If the pressure of social conformity can make people actually perceive shorter lines as longer, as they did in the Asch experiments, then it's easy to conceive of them making economists see empirically unfounded rational expectations models as reflecting the real economy in some way.

And economists do experience a considerable degree of social pressure and conceptual indoctrination in their graduate education. As one economist told me, referring to the profession's apparent dislike for new methods, "Much of this goes deep into Friedman's old paper on economic methodology which is drilled into all economists as they get started. I think people have a hard time detaching from this."

The result is more than a minor intellectual crisis for the field. As economist David Colander and colleagues put it in their postcrisis critique of current economic thinking:

> The global financial crisis has revealed the need to rethink fundamentally how financial systems are regulated. It has also made clear a systemic failure of the economics profession. Over the past three decades, economists have largely developed and come to rely on models that disregard key factors—including heterogeneity of decision rules, revisions of forecasting strategies, and changes in the social context—that drive outcomes in asset and other markets. It is obvious, even to the casual observer that these models fail to account for the actual evolution of the real-world economy. Moreover, the current academic agenda has largely crowded out research on the inherent causes of financial

crises. There has also been little exploration of early indicators of system crisis and potential ways to prevent this malady from developing. In fact, if one browses through the academic macroeconomics and finance literature, "systemic crisis" appears like an otherworldly event that is absent from economic models. Most models, by design, offer no immediate handle on how to think about or deal with this recurring phenomenon. In our hour of greatest need, societies around the world are left to grope in the dark without a theory. That, to us, is a systemic failure of the economics profession.[18]

It's as if the profession did, as Paul Krugman put it, mistake "beauty, clad in impressive-looking mathematics, for truth."

The mathematics of economics, to be honest, isn't really all that beautiful. Look into the seminal paper on rational expectations by Lucas, and you find the following equation:[19]

$$U'\left(\sum_j Y_j\right) p_i(y) = \beta \int U'\left(\sum_j Y_j'\right)(y_i' + p_i(y'))dF(y',y),$$

Gorgeous, isn't it? Like a sunset over Rome. This decidedly unspectacular vista is an Euler equation, named after the German mathematician Leonhard Euler. Here it purports to describe how an individual in the economy chooses optimally between consuming wealth now and investing it for the future. This decision depends on the current state of the market and the individual's rational (of course) estimation of its likely future path. As mathematics, the equation is indeed alluring; its has lots of symbols and looks deep and impenetrable, and Euler equations do represent an elegant bit of mathematics, used frequently in physics and engineering mathematics.

But this equation, as economics, is really not worth penetrating. It's an intellectual game having little if anything to do with real economic behavior—a "parlor game of logical quibbles," to borrow a phrase that Evelyn Waugh used to describe much of modern philosophy. This is the kind of thing that caused the economist Robert Clower to confess that "much of economics is so far removed from anything remotely resembling the real world that it is often difficult for economists to take their own subject seriously."

Indeed, this isn't modeling at all, but an almost psychotic fantasy and certainly a dishonest application of mathematics that removes from economics all the important feedbacks and nonlinearities. The intent is solely to transform a problem of inherent richness and complexity into one of great simplicity, even triviality. As William Buiter, chief economist of Citigroup, notes, it's the systematic obliteration of real complexity in economic theory that has been the major "achievement" of rational expectations macro models:

> Those of us who have marvelled at the non-linear feedback loops between asset prices in illiquid markets and the funding illiquidity of financial institutions exposed to these asset prices through mark-to-market accounting, margin requirements, calls for additional collateral, etc. will appreciate what is lost by this castration of the macroeconomic models. Threshold effects, critical mass, tipping points, non-linear accelerators—they are all out of the window . . . The practice of removing all non-linearities and most of the interesting aspects of uncertainty from the models that were then let loose on actual numerical policy analysis, was a major step backwards.[20]

In other words, dynamic stochastic general equilibrium models make an attempt only to explain the sunny days without any storms or strong winds, dealing only in equilibrium calm, and do so by definition. Truly, they are the work of weather forecasters who do not understand storms. Economist Charles Goodhart, longtime member of the Bank of England's Monetary Policy Committee, summed up his practitioner's perspective on the dynamic stochastic general equilibrium approach: "It excludes everything I am interested in."

What we ought to be interested in goes well beyond patterns of human thinking as well. Several years ago, two neuroscientists ran an experiment on the trading floor of a major investment bank in London. Over eight consecutive business days, at both eleven A.M. and four P.M., they sampled saliva from the mouths of seventeen traders, and measured rising and falling levels of a number of steroid hormones, including testosterone, adrenaline, and cortisol. They found that when traders did well, they didn't do it solely through cleverness and cerebral dexterity. Guts, or rather "testicles," also played a role. Traders performed better on days in which they registered higher morning levels of the hormone testosterone, which is mostly produced in the testes.

This is actually quite unsurprising, as testosterone increases the level of hemoglobin in the blood, enabling it to carry more oxygen. For any animal, it generally boosts searching persistence, fearlessness, and appetite for risk, qualities that obviously help any trader exploit real opportunities in the market. Athletes preparing for a competition produce more testosterone.

The experiments also showed that levels of the hormone cortisol—often called the "stress hormone," because its levels rise in people experiencing psychological or physical stress—went up in direct proportion to the volatility of recent trading. The more wildly unpredictable the record of wins and losses, the more cortisol.

Now, why is this important? Because it is known that testosterone and cortisol, if their levels remain elevated over extended periods, have unfortunate side effects. Testosterone leads to overconfidence and a tendency to take excessive risks. The mental consequences of long-term exposure to heightened cortisol levels include anxiety, selective recall of disturbing memories, and a sense of danger lurking everywhere; people then become excessively risk averse. Last year Coates argued at length in his book *The Hour Between Dog and Wolf* that these simple facts should have big implications for how we think about markets.[21] Our bodies may well make us hardwired for episodes of financial boom and bust, fueled by testosterone on the way up and deepened by cortisol in the aftermath.

So it's time for theories in economics and finance to become more physiological and biological and turn away from the disastrous fixation on rationality.

Fortunately, aside from an entrenched core of economists, much of the current framework of rational, equilibrium-based economics is clearly destined, and soon, for the dustbin of intellectual history, despite the increasingly desperate efforts on the part of a few to preserve it. The task is to replace it with a real science of economic and financial weather, including its storms, whatever the driving factors may be. As we've seen in earlier chapters, it's possible to get considerable insight into disequilibrium dynamics with very simple models, as long as they capture key elements of reality. This seems to be the case with Blake LeBaron's very early model of Minsky's inherent market instability, although this is indeed nothing but a tentative first step.

10

Forecast

PITCHED COMPETITION BETWEEN HEDGE funds can wire up explosive feedbacks that destroy billions of dollars in a few minutes. Computer "algos" trading at the speed of light make markets fractious and prone to "sparks" on subsecond timescales. Markets and whole economies swoon through waves of excessive optimism or pessimism driven by feedbacks, some of which may even have a deep physiological basis. Stable self-correcting equilibrium is anything but the norm in economics and finance, even if Milton Friedman couldn't bear the thought—and he convinced several generations of economists to think the same.

Economics research journals today overflow with models of equilibrium applied to explain everything from persisting unemployment or poverty to corporate collusion or the stability (or lack thereof) of common currencies. There's nothing wrong with that, of course, as many of these phenomena do sometimes involve elements of balance among opposing forces, and equilibrium thinking can sometimes give a rough guide to how things work. What is unfortunate is the exclusivity of this equilibrium focus. Three quarters of a century ago, a few visionary economists tried to venture beyond equilibrium; their work has been systematically marginalized if not totally forgotten.

In the aftermath of the Great Depression, economists naturally found it hard to accept the rosy story of the invisible hand guiding economies inexorably to optimal outcomes. The British economist John Maynard Keynes argued that a temporary lack of economic demand may feed on itself, driving an economy into a stubborn period of stagnation, or even a self-sustaining depression. Before Keynes, and even more explicitly, the American economist Irving Fisher argued that markets and economies can get out of control in hundreds of ways, and that "only in imagination" can we expect to find a balanced equilibrium in economics; it should be as likely as finding an ocean without waves.[1] He pointed especially to waves of optimism, easy credit, and expanding debt that end naturally in "debt deflation" and long periods of tight money and economic depression (sound familiar?). In the 1940s, other economists such as Nicholas Kaldor and John Hicks built mathematical models demonstrating how economic activity might easily fluctuate up and down on its own, refusing to settle in any equilibrium.[2] These early works were fully in tune with the most advanced scientific thinking of the time, not only the recognition that fundamental instabilities drive our rich weather but many other things besides. In 1952, British mathematician Alan Turing—the inventor of the theory of computation—pointed out that positive feedbacks and instabilities lie at the foundation of life itself, especially the miracle of embryonic development as cells divide and specialize to take on different roles in the body. We now know he was right: biology does depend on positive feedbacks to create and control all the specialized neurons, blood cells, muscle tissues, and organs we need to live.[3]

But if the rest of science flowered from this insight, economics in the 1970s turned weirdly in on itself. Following the rational expectations revolution, it has remained stuck in its equilibrium shell, mostly treating the dynamics of markets as a topic unfit for serious study. Today, Fisher's and Keynes's insights about natural instability have been, if not rejected, then quietly co-opted into equilibrium models and effectively neutered. Economists, except for a small and determined minority, have virtually ignored the most profound scientific discoveries of the past few decades— chaos theory, for example, and the science of fractal structures we see in everything from landscapes to the distribution of galaxies in the universe, all of which arise through disequilibrium processes. Today the gradual reawakening of disequilibrium thinking has shown us that ongoing fluctuations in economic and financial systems are quite normal even in the absence of any external "shocks." We've learned to see the automatic efficiency of the invisible hand as the chimeric dream of a bygone era.

But in this final chapter, I want to consider another matter. Weather forecasters not only understand storms, but also predict them well enough to make a big difference. The tornadoes that sweep routinely through the plains of the United States each year don't cause as many deaths as they did a century ago, because the weather service can issue accurate warnings of the conditions likely to spawn them. This raises an obvious question: might we do something similar for economics and finance. Can we learn to make useful predictions of the future?

As I write in June 2012, a fever of speculation grips the financial press. Greece, Spain, Portugal, and Italy teeter on the brink of defaulting on their debts, threatening big banks in Germany, France, the U.K., and the United States. A nasty web of financial interdependence puts the entire European monetary union at risk. Yesterday, an e-mail alert in my in-box announced an op-ed by George Soros: THREE DAYS TO SAVE THE EURO. Will it be saved? Opinions range from sanguine faith that European leaders will not possibly let the Euro fail to the gloomier (and I think more realistic) view that the currency is probably doomed.[4] Readers of this book will know what happened next in this historical drama, but it is far from obvious right now.

There is no computer model of the European economy to which we can run to see what will unfold; the idea of accomplishing that is probably even preposterous. Come up with such a model, and its very existence would alter how people behave, rendering its predictions inaccurate. There's no arguing with it, this really is a problem with social science; its theories, when people learn of them, may act back to change reality, making those theories wrong.[5]

Many people see this kind of argument as the final word; that's it. We'll never do forecasting in economics and finance like we do for the weather. But that conclusion, I think, is rather too quick. "Forecasting" is a word with subtle shades of meaning.

History Doesn't Repeat Itself

At the time of the First World War, many meteorologists had all but given up on the idea of accurate and scientific weather forecasting. The field was as troubled as economics is now, its practical failure the focus of wide criticism. Robert Friedman, in writing a biography of Norwegian meteorological pioneer Vilhelm Bjerknes, described the state of weather forecasting in the early 1900s in terms that sound hauntingly familiar:

> The dream of finding simple laws for predicting weather faded by the end of the century . . . Many theories had been advanced: thermodynamics and hydrodynamics had been applied to idealized atmospheric problems, yet forecasting had become increasingly formalistic, divorced from any physical understanding of the processes responsible for weather change . . . By 1900 most meteorologists sought statistical patterns rather than physical or dynamic insights to predict weather. Disillusionment set in. Institutional conservatism towards new approaches tended to reinforce a sense of hopelessness.[6]

Perhaps it is no wonder, as meteorologists of the time were, in effect, hoping for a miracle.

The British Meteorological Office, for example, then maintained a huge and ever-growing index of weather maps recording air pressures, winds, humidity, and other atmospheric variables at stations scattered around the country, day by day, stretching well into the past. It was a history of the weather, and meteorologists consulted it as a "look it up" guide to what should happen next. The idea was simple. Whatever the current weather, scientists would scour the index of past weather looking for a similar pattern. Finding that conditions on, say, May 1, 1903, were close to those of today, they would page forward in the index to see what history recorded a day or two later, on May 2 and 3, 1903. If a calm and mostly sunny day on May 2 had given way to showers and strengthening winds on May 3, that's what they would predict—a day of sunshine followed by one of

showers and winds. Meteorologists hoped that weather history would repeat itself.

It didn't work very well, and Lewis Richardson—the man who had
wondered if the wind has a speed—thought he knew why. In 1916, Richardson had taken a position as superintendent of the British weather station in Eskdalemuir, Scotland, tasked with improving forecasting
methods. His first observation was that meteorologists weren't following
the example of other areas of science in which prediction was possible.
Astronomers, he noted, were able to predict the movements of planets
and stars with remarkable accuracy, even many years in advance, and
they never supposed that the exact history of the heavens would repeat
itself. Quite the contrary. As he commented, "It would be safe to say that
a particular disposition of stars, planets and satellites never occurs twice.
Why then should we expect a present weather map to be exactly represented in a catalogue of past weather?"[7]

The astronomers' success, instead, rested on an understanding of the
laws of motion for astronomical bodies, as first described by Isaac Newton and later developed by Leonhard Euler, Joseph Lagrange, and others.
Astronomers took the current positions of, say, Jupiter and Mars and
used the mathematics describing planetary motion under gravity to trace
the movement of each planet forward and predict where it would be in a
month, a year, in one hundred years, even if they found a combination of
planetary positions never before seen.

Prediction of anything, in Richardson's view, would always require
real understanding of the underlying laws of change, and weather scientists were trying to get by without it. Predicting the weather would "be
complicated because the atmosphere is complicated"; there could be no
shortcuts, no miracles. Richardson's subsequent efforts to prove his point
were at once tedious, dangerous, and disappointing, at least for a time.
He soon left Eskdalemuir to drive an ambulance in the First World War,
ending up with French troops in Northern France. Here, in spare moments between terrifying bouts rescuing the injured while under fire, he
undertook a momentous calculation, all by hand, sitting, as he later described it, "on a heap of hay in a cold wet rest billet." His aim was to calculate, by simulating the actual physics, the development of the weather
over a local zone of Europe over eight hours. In April 1917, during the
chaos of the battle of Champagne, his calculation—and a book manuscript

on which he was working—went missing. Finding them several months later under a heap of coal, he resumed calculating.

Finally, the calculation finished, Richardson checked his result against known observations of a change in air pressure over a spot in Germany one day in 1910. The results were totally wrong; his effort ended in failure. History, however, has vindicated everything Richardson did; he was wrong only because of a small arithmetical error.[8] His basic idea was correct, and weather forecasting centers around the globe now use variations of the technique with impressive predictive success, thanks to modern computers.

In Reading, England, for example, the European Centre for Medium-Range Weather Forecasts runs two supercomputers simulating a virtual atmosphere. The model forecasts the wind, the temperature, and the humidity at more than 20 million points from the earth's surface up to a height of about forty miles. In the United States, the National Centers for Environmental Prediction does much the same thing. These simulations (and similar ones undertaken in nations around world) lie behind the daily and weekly weather forecasts reported on the nightly news, as well as more specific prediction services for farmers, the airline and shipping industries, the military, and anyone else whose projects depend seriously on the weather. When an oil company charts a path for a tanker journey of several weeks, they save tens of thousands of dollars by routing away from strong winds and storms—but only because they can see into the future.

There are two lessons from this scientific success. First, technology vastly amplifies the power of the human mind. The philosopher Daniel Dennett once described the digital computer as "the most important epistemological advance in scientific method since the invention of accurate timekeeping devices," and he is probably right. Since its invention in the 1940s, the computer has allowed humans to simulate the workings of everything from jet aircrafts having millions of parts to traffic flows, even the complex neural firings of the human brain. We have created what historian George Dyson calls "a new universe" running in parallel with our own, and we have begun to populate that universe with a world of rich systems that we can use to understand our own universe. Second, success in weather forecasting demonstrates Richardson's main point—that power to predict the future comes directly from real understanding of the causal factors driving the present. It rarely comes through miraculous mathematical shortcuts or grand theories, however alluring they may be.

When multiple influences or forces interact, prediction demands some way to follow the interactions and trace the outcomes to which they lead, along pathways that are often circuitous. The resulting predictions are almost never exact or certain. But that's to be expected. Little in our world can be known with certainty.

The Entire Future of the Universe

Say "prediction" or "forecast" and most people imagine a precise claim about the future. An earthquake will strike Tokyo on Christmas Day 2015. The Cleveland Browns will win the next three Super Bowls in succession.[9] Exact prediction in this sense is indeed sometimes possible. We know[10] that the positions of sun, earth, and moon will be just right on May 1, 2804, to create a total eclipse of the sun. The moon will blot out the sun for a few minutes at every location along a path arcing across the Southern Hemisphere and intersecting Australia. The best place to see the eclipse will be a spot in the Coral Sea about six hundred miles northeast of Brisbane, Australia, where the darkness will last precisely five minutes and twenty-one seconds.

This exact prediction is possible because of the strict determinism of planetary motion as described by Newtonian laws, which inspired the French physicist Pierre-Simone Laplace to suggest that a sufficient intelligence could know the entire future of the universe. "To it," he imagined, "nothing would be uncertain, and the future as the past would be present to its eyes."[11] Of course, we shouldn't hope to do anything quite so exact in economics or finance, or pretty much anywhere else in science, as many problems get in the way.

When a pinball scatters through a pinball machine, its path is extraordinarily sensitive to any tiny influence it receives along the way. Fire the ball just a little harder and its path will change completely. This is known as deterministic chaos; it makes pinball fun, and in nature generally spoils Laplace's dream of perfect prediction. Because tiny accidents perpetually intrude on the course of events and knock history down different paths, perfect prediction is out, except over very short times. For fundamental mathematical reasons, even the most precise local weather simulations become useless after a few days. (For this reason, beware the ten-day forecast.)

In finance and economics, the same challenge stands. Even if psychologists (or roboticists) discovered tomorrow that people are actually machines following simple and predictable rules, the financial markets and most everything else in the social world would still be hugely unpredictable. Interactions between people would rapidly multiply any errors in our initial model of those individuals, and predictions from such models would soon be useless. It does not require the unfathomable complexity of individual human behavior and psychology to create an unpredictable system. Mathematics is enough. Of course, social reality *is* complicated by the complexities of behavior and psychology, which means we're really in trouble. If the fate of a banking system depends on the actions of individual bankers, as it often does, prediction of Laplace's kind is clearly impossible.

There is, furthermore, a true paradox at the heart of human efforts to understand human systems, a problem of self-reference to which I referred earlier. The financier George Soros refers to this paradox as "reflexivity." Our efforts to understand the social world, insofar as they actually make headway, inevitably feed back to alter and influence our actions. This is a peculiarity physical scientists don't have to deal with; it makes social science fundamentally different. Reflexivity is also another reason for unpredictability, as the philosopher of science Karl Popper once demonstrated in formal terms. The growth of human knowledge has a direct influence on human history. Look at the world-altering effects of the World Wide Web. We can't predict what we'll invent next or how our own knowledge will grow, because if we could, we would already know those inventions and that knowledge. A future discovery, predictable now, makes no sense. Hence, in some absolute way, our human future has to be unpredictable.

I certainly wouldn't argue with any of these points. But notice that each of these arguments establishes the impossibility of exact prediction, something that is actually quite rare in science. Epidemiologists, for example, have no hope of predicting exactly where and when an avian flu strain able to infect humans will evolve, as this depends on genetic accidents, and on the decisions of many people whose actions put them into contact with birds, giving the virus a chance to hop into a human host, where rapid evolution is more likely. But this complete ignorance doesn't prevent epidemiologists from making useful predictions about the likely paths of travel of such a virus, and those approximate insights could one day save millions of lives.

Short of perfect knowledge of the future there lies a vast world of partial understanding. Prediction and forecasting, in the engineering of ships, the launching of satellites, or in weather science, live quite comfortably in this world where exact prediction is impossible.

In economics and finance, merely predicting what is possible and likely can be hugely valuable, giving us warnings of specific dangers. We've seen that market competition fueled by leverage can push a market past a virtually invisible tipping point of instability. We've seen that the apparently sensible sharing of risks can, in some cases, make bankruptcies more likely, not less. An obvious target for socioeconomic forecasting is to anticipate the many devilish ways that markets can abruptly go haywire, and to identify the key factors that set up the driving feedbacks. In so doing, we can make our ignorance less dangerous than it would otherwise be.

Being realistic about potential hazards and surprises is where equilibrium thinking has been most damaging, as it has encouraged a deep complacency about the self-regulating properties of financial markets. Recognized ignorance is always preferable to deluded certainty. A pilot without an altimeter, in a metaphor used by Nassim Taleb, is better off than one who blindly trusts a faulty altimeter, as the former can at least look out the window. Yet the complexity of today's markets requires a different analogy: our pilot looks out the window and sees impenetrable fog, so if we want to fly at all, we're going to need the help of *something*. This is what explicit models of positive feedbacks are—tools to penetrate the fog, partially and imperfectly of course, and to get a glimpse of dangers before they take us down.

Fragility by Design—And How to Avoid It

Stefan Thurner and his colleagues' inquiry into the consequences of leverage in the hedge fund industry is a cousin of Norman Phillips's classic 1961 inquiry into the origins of the weather. Phillips wondered if heat driving warm air to flow on a rotating planet could be enough to stir up the chaotic weather we see in the real world. Thurner, Farmer, and Geanakoplos wondered if leverage, coupled with competition between funds, could lead inexorably to sudden violent episodes of deleveraging, as happened in the quant meltdown. Both inquiries answered yes. Neither phenomenon is really surprising, once you see the positive feedbacks at work.

The weather is what it is, and we generally don't try to change it.[12] In contrast, modern finance is a "demon of our own design"[13] and we can try to avoid the instabilities that make financial systems inherently fragile. In this sense, the model of leveraged competition offers a powerful illustration of what is possible with market models in which we can run experiments. This model, in particular, may be far more general than it seems.

In October 2008, John Geanakoplos gave a presentation to the Board of Governors of the Federal Reserve, including Chairman Ben Bernanke. He described what he called the "leverage cycle"—a natural tendency for economies to run through cycles of high and then low leverage, with episodes of the former being punctuated and terminated by explosive deleveraging events. He argued, in essence, that the model of hedge funds is really just a toy for a process of much broader importance. In the boom years leading up to the recent financial crisis, for example, credit was easy and key financial institutions came to be leveraged at levels in excess of thirty to one. The financial system became a time bomb wired to explode and just waiting for the right spark. The collapse of Lehman Brothers tipped off a subsequent deleveraging quite similar to that of the quant meltdown, only involving many more institutions on a vastly larger scale. This deleveraging is still going in the summer of 2012, nearly four years later.

As Geanakoplos pointed out, such feedbacks develop in any market using collateralized loans with margin calls. Use your credit card and you borrow without collateral; the bank issuing the card hopes to get paid because you are creditworthy. Collateralized loans work differently, with repayment guaranteed by some asset the borrower will lose if they do not pay. Banks borrow like this all the time, using stocks and other assets as collateral. Technically, these loans are often only for a day, yet contracts typically specify that the debt "rolls over" for another day as long as the ratio of outstanding loan to asset (stock) value remains below some threshold. This is where margin calls come in. Should the value of the stock fall, the borrower has to pay off part of the outstanding loan to stay within the agreed limit. Trouble comes because any borrower facing a margin call has to get cash from somewhere, and selling some of the collateral is often the easiest way. This creates a dangerous loop, as selling the asset drives its price down, triggering further margin calls, more sell-offs, and a self-reinforcing downward spiral.

Hence, the very nature of collateralized loans creates a fundamental instability threatening the economic peace at many levels. In his presentation, Geanakoplos argued that controlling leverage is as important to economic stability as controlling anything else, including interest rates. But almost nothing is actually known about the likely consequences of various possible measures to limit leverage. Eliminating it would be like banning electricity because houses occasionally burn down. Leverage lubricates the finance of everything from corporate payrolls to home mortgages, which take up decades of individual savings. Very little in our economy works without it. We only need to avoid *excess* leverage. But how much is too much? And how should we control it?

In answering such questions, forecasting exercises can help. Suppose we take this model of hedge funds in competition, think of it more generally as a model of financial firms in competition, and introduce a regulation limiting leverage to some maximum value—say 5, or 8 or 10. Two years ago, Thurner, Farmer, and Geanakoplos ran such experiments, and, to make the results even more relevant for policy, compared two particular cases. First, they ran the market with a simple cap on allowed leverage. Second, they also ran experiments with further regulations akin to the so-called Basel I and II rules of international banking. The banks in the model—the ones loaning money to the funds—were forced to keep some of their money aside, not loaning it out. The results show some tricky and counterintuitive outcomes.

An initial result will bring joy to free market fundamentalists. The experiments showed that letting the investment funds seek profits with no restrictions on leverage does indeed benefit the market, making it more "efficient" (in the economists' sense of lower volatility). Increasing the leverage cap lets the hedge funds pounce more aggressively on opportunities, and as a result they wipe out mispricings more effectively. The mean square price volatility drops with higher leverage. Again, this is in the absence of other regulations. In the regulated market, in contrast, the experiments showed that leverage has to become much higher to get the same reduction in volatility. So banking regulations get in the way of good market functioning.

But this isn't the whole story, of course. Higher leverage, as we know, increases the likelihood of violent collapse. In further experiments,

Thurner and colleagues looked at how often the funds in their simulations fail, finding that with a leverage cap only, the frequency rises rapidly with increasing leverage. With a relatively low leverage cap (around 5 in the model's units), the market already reaps the benefits of leverage; raising the cap higher only leads to more frequent collapse without any additional benefit. This happens because leverage pushes the market into a world of fat-tailed returns and positive feedback loops caused by such financial maneuvers as collateralized debt and margin calls. In contrast, the market with banking restrictions now works a little better, as the regulations reduce the number of failures with little cost in volatility.

These forecasts show that some limitation on leverage can bring benefits, while too much can be bad. They also illustrate that you can't test the idea of leverage limits without thinking about other regulations, too, as regulations interact in surprising ways. It bears repeating that no one—not banks, governments, or academic economists—was running anything like these models before the 2008 financial crisis. We were simply trying regulations and watching their effects on the real-world markets. In effect, we were doing our experiments in reality.

Fortunately, virtual forecasts of the kinds of things that might happen are becoming more common. Last year, researchers at the Bank of England took this study a little further to explore how the architecture of the financial system would influence this leverage-induced instability. Their experiments identified particular banks in a financial network as being the most likely to act as epicenters of funding crises. Other banks—those with links to many other institutions in the network—were the most likely to act as conduits to spread financial distress very rapidly. In reality, which banks play these roles? Not surprisingly, perhaps, but disturbingly, the study pointed to the large, complex, "too big to fail" institutions such as Goldman Sachs, J. P. Morgan, Citibank, and so on. The conclusion, as they put it, is that "the modern financial system seems to be almost designed for systemic trouble."

This is all just the beginning of a long, probably endless process of exploration. Of course, the very first lesson is that the natural evolution of markets tends to stir up instabilities—in excess leverage, too much complexity and interconnectedness, and so on. It's not enough to hope for miraculous, stable equilibrium. This idea is not at all new. It was the centerpiece of Irving Fisher's view of the economy in the 1930s, and has only been forgotten, with great difficulty, more recently. Thurner and his colleagues' model can be seen as giving a more specific scientific form to an accurate metaphorical picture that Fisher had even back then.

Storm Warnings

Positive feedbacks drive the most important and disruptive events in economics and finance, from financial bubbles to debt crises, bank runs, even waves of corporate corruption. It is a matter for sociologists and historians to explain why economists with few exceptions have tried so hard for fifty years to ignore this. Whatever the answer, that era does appear to be coming to a close. With ideas and techniques from other parts of science, we can explore market feedbacks and instabilities in detail never before possible. Economists no longer have to be like weather forecasters who do not understand storms.

In the not too distant future, it's easy to imagine a U.S. or European Center for Financial Forecasting, the technological equivalent of today's most advanced physics laboratories—the European particle physics center CERN, for example, or Los Alamos National Laboratory. Thousands of researchers would oversee massive simulations probing the developing network of interactions among the world's largest financial players, following the vast web of loans, ownership stakes, and other legal claims that link banks, governments, hedge funds, insurance companies, ratings agencies, and the like. The computers would test scenarios and calculate hundreds of indicators of systemic leverage, the density of interconnections, or the concentration of risk at single institutions or clusters thereof. Experts would probe models of the financial system, looking for weak points and testing its resilience, much as engineers now do with models of the electrical grid or other complex technological systems.

It's almost certain that facilities like this will spring up in the near future, vastly extending our ability to probe the financial system and gain insight into its likely future, and also to answer "what if" questions. What's currently missing—aside from the willingness of the economics profession—is data. To ensure the safety and stability of a nuclear reactor, engineers need access to every detail of its operations, and the ability to examine every component and its links to others. The same should be true of any agency trying to support the stability of the financial markets. Currently this just isn't the case, and authorities have historically collected financial data on an institution by institution basis, being less concerned by the links between them. This obviously makes it impossible to say anything about interconnections and the feedbacks they create, or about the overall dynamics and well-being of the financial system as a whole.

This is changing, as the crisis has spurred moves to collect much greater amounts of data on financial networks. In the United States, for example, the Dodd-Frank act created the new Office of Financial Research to bring better financial data to policy makers. Private hedge funds will soon be obliged to report information on their funds' exposure to different asset classes, their use of leverage, and their vulnerability to liquidity shortages. If regulators recognize the central role of positive feedbacks in creating systemic problems, and use this data to probe such feedbacks in an aggressive way, this could make a big difference.

A real data revolution might go much further. Modern sensor systems—as computerized components find their way into almost every object we use and own—will likely gather as much data in the next ten years as we have gathered in all of human history. No one yet has a clear vision of how all this data may feed into forecasting models, but let your imagination go. If excessive optimism or pessimism drive many market crises, these collective excursions from reality almost certainly show up in the physiology of the people involved. Economists have long argued about whether such episodes are real, or only seem excessive, but as John Coates and his colleagues have shown (in the experiments mentioned in chapter 9) clear signals of hormone-driven behavior can be found in the saliva. With networks of advanced sensors—think of a patch worn by volunteers that gathers physiological information and uploads it directly to some database—we may even gain a clear picture of hormonal changes as they sweep over a financial community.

Of course, none of the forecasts based on such data will meet the Laplacian ideal of a perfect knowledge of the future, which is a philosophical relic of little importance. Indeed, weather forecasters don't aim for this ideal, as they always have incomplete data on the atmosphere, and can only work with approximate equations. Making a strength of this uncertainty, atmospheric scientists run thousands of simulations, changing the data randomly to reflect their ignorance, and so generate thousands of possible forecasts about the future. The result is a cloud or "ensemble" of guesses about where the future will lie. Ensemble forecasting in finance and economics might work similarly, using slightly different possibilities for how the people and firms behave, also enabling those elements to have their own independent intelligence to try things and learn tricks the modeler may never see. The result would be not a single prediction, but a swarm of possibilities.

In pondering this future, delicate issues loom into view. As we develop large computational systems packed with masses of data monitoring the financial and economic system and projecting its likely future, this knowledge becomes extremely valuable. It should be treated as a public good—akin to clean air and water. Knowledge about our collective future, produced through the collective effort of many, should be the same. How can we keep this knowledge from being exploited by individual parties? As computer scientist Dave Cliff has suggested, it might be sensible for a government to invest in developing centers of such vast resources that no private party can possibly match them—as is the case with research on nuclear fusion or space exploration.[14]

These questions arise naturally in the context of serious efforts to understand the feedbacks at work in our socioeconomic world. Dealing with such questions is the price we pay for moving beyond the myth of the perfect self-regulating equilibrium. We shift to a perspective in which we expect to be surprised, and accept the need for persistent vigilance. Worst of all would be to replace the equilibrium delusion with a new fantasy, fooling ourselves into thinking we can build a complete theory of markets now that we appreciate positive feedbacks. We cannot eliminate fragility, only reduce it, and then only with persistent efforts to highlight our ignorance, our biases, our preconceptions about what can and cannot happen.

The Madoff Effect

For two decades starting around 1990, Bernie Madoff ran one of the most successful investment funds the world has ever seen. A former chairman of NASDAQ, Madoff's fund Fairfield Sentry year by year turned in an astonishingly consistent record of superior performance—roughly 15 percent per year on average, with very little fluctuation around that value. Madoff's success was so predictable that some people—just a few—thought it really looked, well, a little too good to be true. As finance journalist Michael Ocrant wrote in 2001, "Most of those who are aware of Madoff's status in the hedge fund world are baffled by the way the firm has obtained such consistent, nonvolatile returns month after month and year after year . . . What is striking to most observers is not so much the annual returns . . . but the ability to provide such smooth returns with so little volatility."[15]

As it turned out, of course, it was all too good to be true, a Ponzi scheme bigger than any in history, all just "one big lie," as Madoff admitted. But investors wanted to believe. We humans, for all our vaunted intelligence, are also gullible and gifted with a fantastically powerful mental apparatus for effective rationalization. Indeed, many psychologists and neuroscientists believe that rationalization is the primary skill of the conscious thinking mind—that its main job is to "keep our life tied together into a coherent story,"[16] whether this means bending logic and facts or not. "This time is different" always seems plausible for a reason; we like to believe that it really is different. As evolutionary biologists tell us, the human brain has not changed much in ten thousand years, and it probably won't any time soon. We're hardwired for errant thinking, and there will, as a result, be plenty of crises in the future.

To avoid any misunderstanding, I want to be absolutely clear that no amount of better economic science will prevent financial crises in the future. Science and understanding aren't enough. Indeed, crises often arise from a human propensity to deactivate safeguards just in time to let the next crisis happen. The 1986 nuclear accident at Chernobyl, for example, wasn't a case of sloppy stupidity. There were multiple distinct safety systems in place and functioning properly. They would have prevented the disaster. But a key automatic shutoff was deliberately disabled so plant operators could test running the reactor at low power, and this is when the disaster struck. Even with a perfect understanding of financial dynamics, we may waltz into the next crisis just because we think we're safe and that we can relax, just when we really shouldn't.

But there's another problem that is even more serious. Not everyone wants a stable functioning financial system. Crises through history have often been linked not only to poor thinking but also to corruption and political failure. In the late eighties and early nineties, about 20 percent of all the savings and loans in the United States went bankrupt—not through any external disaster, but as the result of a wave of greed fueled by tax incentives that let the managers of these banks plunder their funds. In the wake of this crisis, economists George Akerlof and Paul Romer wrote a paper of lasting profundity. In the paper, entitled "Looting: The Economic Underworld of Bankruptcy for Profit," Akerlof and Romer argued that it's often possible for managers of banking institutions to run their firms into the ground for their own personal profit: they loot the bank, even legally. Note their final two paragraphs:

> The S&L fiasco in the United States leaves us with the question, why did the government leave itself so exposed to abuse? Part of the answer, of course, is that actions taken by the government are the result of the political process. When regulators hid the extent of the true problem with artificial accounting devices, when congressmen pressured regulators to go easy on favored constituents and political donors, when the largest brokerage firms lobbied to protect their ability to funnel brokered deposits to any thrift in the country, when the lobbyists for the savings and loan industry adopted the strategy of postponing action until industry difficulties were so large that general tax revenue would have to be used to address problems instead of revenue raised from taxes on successful firms in the industry—when these and many other actions were taken, people responded rationally to the incentives they faced within the political process.
>
> The S&L crisis, however, was also caused by misunderstanding. Neither the public nor economists foresaw that the regulations of the 1980s were bound to produce looting. Nor, unaware of the concept, could they have known how serious it would be. Thus the regulators in the field who understood what was happening from the beginning found lukewarm support, at best, for their cause. Now we know better. If we learn from experience, history need not repeat itself.

That was 1993, and their argument can be made again today, as very similar dynamics led to the current crisis. This entails real, serious costs for all of us. As Andrew Haldane of the Bank of England estimates, the U.S. and U.K. governments pay about $2–3 billion per year to prop up each of the largest five or so banks. This comes from a careful analysis of the long-term costs of the occasional, but recurrent financial crises.[17] Looting is effectively ongoing on a vast scale.

I've argued that we need better science to forecast the kinds of instabilities to which our systems are prone—and this should include those involving corruption. We face a constant struggle between market regulators seeking clarity and individual investors whose strategies work best when they are obscure. In this regard, the equilibrium delusion has been a willing ally, seeing instability as the exception rather than the norm, and giving too much support to naïve arguments about self-regulation. Fortunately, the crisis seems to have convinced many people of this, even many in the economic mainstream.

In November 2010, the president of the European Central Bank, Jean-Claude Trichet, gave an address at the ECB's 2010 Central Banking Conference, which brought together central bankers from around the world. In the speech, Trichet aimed to identify "some main lessons to be learned from the crisis regarding economic analysis." First, he admitted some of the obvious shortcomings of current finance theory:

> When the crisis came, the serious limitations of existing economic and financial models immediately became apparent . . . Macro models failed to predict the crisis and seemed incapable of explaining what was happening to the economy in a convincing manner. As a policy-maker during the crisis, I . . . felt abandoned by conventional tools.
>
> In the absence of clear guidance from existing analytical frameworks, policy-makers had to place particular reliance on our experience . . . In exercising judgement, we were helped by one area of the economic literature: historical analysis. Historical studies of specific crisis episodes highlighted potential problems which could be expected . . . Most importantly, the historical record told us what mistakes to avoid.

Trichet went on to describe the kinds of ideas he thinks finance theory needs to turn to if it is going to improve. In brief, he pointed to four things: get past the idea that economic agents must be rational and optimizing, take note of human learning, include financial markets in the models used by central banks, and bring economic theories up to date with advanced ideas coming from physics and other sciences linked to the study of complex systems. As he put it:

> In this context, I would very much welcome inspiration from other disciplines: physics, engineering, psychology, biology. Bringing experts from these fields together with economists and central bankers is potentially very creative and valuable. Scientists have developed

sophisticated tools for analysing complex dynamic systems in a rigorous way. These models have proved helpful in understanding many important but complex phenomena: epidemics, weather patterns, crowd psychology, magnetic fields. Such tools have been applied by market practitioners to portfolio management decisions, on occasion with some success. I am hopeful that central banks can also benefit from these insights in developing tools to analyse financial markets and monetary policy transmission.

This is quite an extraordinary statement coming from the president of the European Central Bank to central bankers from around the world. Having the courage of one's convictions, Nietzsche said, is a very popular error. It is even more courageous, he noted, to question one's convictions.

In this regard, William Dudley, president and chief executive officer of the Federal Reserve Bank of New York, also deserves great credit. I quoted some of his embarrassing proclamations about the wonders of the free market at the beginning of this book—for example, that derivatives and other financial innovations facilitate "greater risk-taking, but this increased risk-taking does not destabilize the economy." But the crisis has convinced Dudley that he was wrong and in fact had been seriously deluded by efficient market thinking. Speaking before the Economic Club of New York in April 2010,[18] he noted that

> I am going to be a bit of a heretic and argue that there is little doubt that asset bubbles exist and that they occur fairly frequently. By an asset bubble, I mean price increases (or declines) that become unmoored from fundamental valuations . . . Recent experience has underscored the fact that poorly regulated financial systems are prone to such bubbles and that the costs of waiting to respond to an asset bubble until after it has burst can be very high . . . Despite the fact that it is hard to discern bubbles, especially in their early stages, I conclude that uncertainty is not grounds for inaction.

This, too, is remarkable, especially given the conservative economic audience to whom Dudley was speaking. In his speech, Dudley made other important and insightful points. For example, he pointed out that there are bubbles of different kinds, and that those involving leverage and credit are typically vastly more damaging and dangerous when they deflate than those simply involving stock prices. After all, debt is typically held by banks and highly leveraged investors, so a deflating bubble can take much of the financial system with it. Equity ownership is typically unleveraged and less of a problem. Second, Dudley recognized the inherent difficulties not only of recognizing bubbles but also of finding means for making their consequences less likely. As he put it, "None of this is going to be easy. A lot more work will be required to develop a portfolio of tools that could be used, that would be effective and would not be subject to significant evasion or unintended consequences."

This is where ideas from other areas of science may be a big help.

The ideas of equilibrium and self-regulating markets started out as an inspiring vision of what decentralized market activity can achieve. Markets indeed do wonderful things, but the narrow-minded interpretation of this idea has over time become a principal weapon in the fight against good thinking.

Humans have overcome facile assumptions in our thinking about many of the natural systems around us, from wind dynamics to earthquake sizes to patterns of flowing liquids. Economics is no different, and it's time we let ourselves see it.

Acknowledgments

Many people have helped me with various portions of this book, directing me to relevant research, explaining delicate points of logic, taking the time to broaden my view on important issues, reading and critiquing chapters, or supplying figures from their own work. These include physicists, economists, and many others in between.

My profound thanks to (in alphabetical order) Robert Axelrod, Stefano Battiston, Alex Bentley, Jean-Philippe Bouchaud, William Brock, Guido Caldarelli, Silvano Cincotti, Kim Christensen, Doyne Farmer, Vidar Frette, Xavier Gabaix, Tobias Galla, Mauro Gallegati, Dirk Helbing, Jeff Johnson, János Kertész, Imre Kondor, Paul Ormerod, Esteban Perez, Luciano Pietranero, Eric Hunsader, Neil Johnson, Alan Kirman, Blake Lebaron, Sander van der Leeuw, Shengtai Li, Andrew Lo, Matteo Marsili, Alex Pentland, Fabio Pammolli, Tobias Preis, Erik Reinert, Ole Røgeberg, Barkley Rosser, Enrico Scalas, Didier Sornette, George Soros, Gene Stanley, Stefan Thurner, Paul Umbanhowar, Frank Westerhoff, Paul Wilmott, Matias Vernengo, and Yi-Cheng Zhang. If I have failed to remember others—and this is likely—my sincere apologies.

As always, my agent, Lisa Adams at the Garamond Agency, helped me immensely in working to clarify my vision for the book before the writing began. Thanks also to my editors at Bloomsbury, Benjamin Adams (U.S.) and Michael Fishwick (U.K.), who had great confidence in the idea of the book and put their energy behind it. Benjamin took every chapter apart and put it back together in a much improved form.

Finally, infinite thanks to my wife, Kate, who suffered through a year and a little more of living with my blank looks and vacant stares, my erratic and irritating "I'm-occupied-elsewhere" behavior. Without her unending patience and encouragement—and her occasional deadlines, firmly enforced—this book would never have been completed.

Notes

Chapter 1: The Equilibrium Delusion

1. This is clear from a postmortem of events on May 6, 2010, conducted well after the crash. See Andrei Kirilenko et al., "The Flash Crash: The Impact of High Frequency Trading on an Electronic Market." Available at http://papers.ssrn.com/sol3/papers.cfm?abstract_id=1686004.

2. "Findings Regarding the Market Events of May 6, 2010," Report of the Staffs of the CFTC and SEC to the Joint Advisory Committee on Emerging Regulatory Issues. September 30, 2010

3. Graham Bowley, "Lone $4.1 Billion Sale Led to 'Flash Crash' in May," *New York Times*, October 1, 2010. www.nytimes.com/2010/10/02/business/02 flash.html.

4. In 2002, economist Vernon Smith shared (with psychologist Daniel Kahneman) the Sveriges Riksbank Prize in Economic Sciences in Memory of Alfred Nobel. (This is actually not a prize established in 1895 by the will of Alfred Nobel, but was created by Sweden's central bank the Sveriges Riksbank in 1968, in memory of Nobel.) In his lecture upon receiving this prize, Smith says that "I urge students to read narrowly within economics, but widely in science. Within economics there is essentially only one model to be adapted to every application: optimization subject to constraints due to resource limitations, institutional rules and/or the behaviour of others, as in Cournot-Nash equilibria. The economic literature is not the best place to find new inspiration beyond these traditional technical methods of modelling."

5. I learned of a peculiarity in the culture of economics several years ago at a meeting in Budapest bringing together central bankers with physicists and other natural scientists. I gave a general talk showing how even the simplest natural systems—some sand in a box, for example—can do wildly

surprising and perplexing things. Shake the box up and down and at certain frequencies a world of mysterious patterns will emerge on the surface. Surely, I suggested, economic and financial systems are immeasurably more complex than this and we shouldn't expect simple equilibrium theories to capture much if anything about their behavior. An economist from the Federal Reserve told me later that this kind of "emergence" is fine in natural science, but it's not what economists like to see in their models. "If an economic theorist gives a talk and ends up pulling a rabbit out of a hat," I recall him saying, "then you can be sure he or she will have shown very clearly along the way how they put the rabbit in the hat. We don't like surprises." This floored me. In other words, economists want to work with simple models that won't throw out any surprises and give the illusion of complete understanding, even if those models tell them absolutely nothing about the real world, which, of course, throws out surprises quite frequently.

6. Nanex publishes its research on the website www.nanex.net/FlashCrash /OngoingResearch.html

7. Mark Buchanan, "Meltdown Modeling," *Nature* 460 (August 5, 2009): 680–682.

8. Matt Taibbi, "Why Isn't Wall Street in Jail?" (February 16, 2011), www.rolling stone.com/politics/news/why-isnt-wall-street-in-jail-20110216.

9. David Colander et al., "The Financial Crisis and the Systemic Failure of Academic Economics," report of the working group on "Modeling of Financial Markets," the 98th Dahlem Workshop, December 2008.

10. Quentin Michard and Jean-Philippe Bouchaud, "Theory of Collective Opinion Shifts: From Smooth Trends to Abrupt Swings," *European Physical Journal B*, 47 (2005): 151.

Chapter 2: A Marvelous Machine

1. Adam Smith, *The Wealth of Nations*, chap. 2, book 4.

2. Alan Greenspan, The Adam Smith Memorial Lecture, Kirkcaldy, Scotland (February 6, 2005). Available at www.federalreserve.gov/boarddocs/speeches /2005/20050206/default.htm.

3. I thank economist Alan Kirman for pointing this out to me. *Lettre no. 1454 to Hermann Laurent in* William Jaffe, ed. *Correspondence of Leon Walras and Related Papers*, Vols. I–III (Amsterdam: North Holland, 1965).

4. John Geanakoplos, "The Arrow-Debreu Model of General Equilibrium," in *The New Palgrave Dictionary of Economics*, Steven N. Durlauf and Lawrence E. Blume, eds., 2nd ed. (New York: Palgrave Macmillan, 2008).

5. Franklin Fisher, "The Stability of General Equilibrium—What Do We Know and Why Is It Important?" chap. 5, in *General Equilibrium Analysis: A Century After Walras*, ed. by Pascal Bridel (London and New York: Routledge, 2011), 34–45.

6. Binyamin Appelbaum and Eric Dash, "S. & P. Downgrades Debt Rating of U.S. for the First Time," *New York Times*, August 5, 2011. Available at www.nytimes.com/2011/08/06/business/us-debt-downgraded-by-sp.html.

7. Holbrook Working, "The Investigation of Economic Expectations," *American Economic Review* (May 1949): 158–60.

8. Alfred Cowles, "Stock Market Forecasting," *Econometrica* 12 (1944): 206–214.

9. Paul Samuelson, "Proof That Properly Anticipated Prices Fluctuate Randomly," *Industrial Management Review* 6, no. 2 (Spring 1965): 41.

10. Joseph de la Vega, *Confusion of Confusions* (Boston: Baker Library, 1957). First published in 1688.

11. Frederic Morton, *The Rothschilds: A Family Portrait* (London: Secker and Warburg, 1962), 69.

12. Eugene Fama, "Mandelbrot and the Stable Paretian Hypothesis," *Journal of Business* 36, no. 4 (1963): 420–429.

13. Eugene Fama, "Efficient Capital Markets: A Review of Theory and Empirical Work," *Journal of Finance* 25 (1970): 383–417.

14. Andrew Lo, "Efficient Markets Hypothesis," in *The New Palgrave Dictionary of Economics*, Steven N. Durlauf and Lawrence E. Blume, eds., 2nd ed. (New York: Palgrave Macmillan, 2008).

15. Greg Smith, "Why I Am Leaving Goldman Sachs," *New York Times*, March 14, 2012. www.nytimes.com/2012/03/14/opinion/why-i-am-leaving-goldman-sachs.html?_r=1.

16. For a short review, see Esteban Pérez Caldentey and Matías Vernengo, "Modern Finance, Methodology and the Financial Crisis," *Real-World Economics Review* 52 (2010): 69–81.

17. Michael Lewis, "Betting on the Blind Side," *Vanity Fair* (April 2010). www.vanityfair.com/business/features/2010/04/wall-street-excerpt-201004.

18. Robert C. Merton and Zvi Bodie, "Design of Financial Systems," *Journal of Investment Management* 3 (2005): 1–23.

19. R. Glenn Hubbard and William Dudley, "How Capital Markets Enhance Economic Performance and Facilitate Job Creation" (New York: Goldman Sachs Global Markets Institute, 2004).

Chapter 3: Notable Exceptions

1. See the 2011 speech of Andrew Haldane, Bank of England. "Control Rights (and Wrongs)," Wincott Annual Memorial Lecture, Westminster, London (October 24, 2011). Available at www.bankofengland.co.uk/publications /speeches/2010/speech433.pdf.

2. For example, consider the views of Edward Conard of Bain Capital, as described in Adam Davidson, "The Purpose of Spectacular Wealth, According to a Spectacularly Wealthy Guy," *New York Times*, May 1, 2012. Available at www.nytimes.com/2012/05/06/magazine/romneys-former-bain-partner -makes-a-case-for-inequality.html?pagewanted=all.

3. From a scientific point of view, this statement deserves some clarification. Unstable equilibria are also important. Even if a system tends not to spend much time near such states, their existence may influence its dynamics most of the time. Deterministic chaos—erratic and unpredictable motion that arises even in simple dynamical systems—can even be seen as reflecting the existence of an infinite set of unstable equilibria. Rather than having a stable equilibrium state, the system wanders close to and then away from all of the unstable states, never alighting on any, only getting close enough to be repelled and driven toward another. The mathematical analysis of chaos can often be reduced to an analysis of what happens near each of these unstable states. So unstable equilibria are not unimportant in a fundamental sense, but they are certainly not states in which a system is likely to be found.

4. The key papers were Hugo Sonnenschein, "Do Walras' Identity and Continuity Characterize the Class of Community Excess Demand Functions?," *Journal of Economic Theory* 6 (1973): 345–354; Gérard Debreu, "Excess Demand Functions," *Journal of Mathematical Economics* 1 (1974): 15–21; Rolf Mantel, "On the Characterization of Aggregate Excess Demand," *Journal of Economic Theory* 7 (1974): 348–353.

5. Quoted in Alan Kirman, *Complex Economics* (New York: Routledge, 2010).

6. Further work—characterized by increasing desperation, I would say— has come up with some recipes by which an economy can find equilibrium, but at the expense of being more or less wholly implausible. They assume, for example, that people in the economy aren't adjusting prices on their own, but that the whole thing is carried out by some wise "auctioneer" who monitors prices as well as the excess demand in every market and adjusts prices according to a complicated scheme. Read the following example and see how much this brings to mind real-world economics:

The behavior of the auctioneer is governed by the total excess demand expressed by the individual agents. Initially, the auctioneer decreases the prices of all commodities with negative excess demand and increases the prices of all commodities with positive excess demand in such a way that the ratio between any two prices with either positive or negative excess demand is kept constant. Prices are adapted in this way until one of the markets attains equilibrium. Then the auctioneer adjusts the prices in order to keep the excess demand of this commodity equal to zero. In general, the auctioneer keeps, with respect to their initial values, . . . the relative prices of the commodities with positive (negative) excess demand maximal (minimal) and allows the relative prices of the commodities with zero excess demand to vary between these two bounds. As soon as one of the markets with positive (negative) excess demand attains equilibrium, the corresponding price is decreased (increased) away from the relative upper (lower) bound and the auctioneer adjusts this price simultaneously with the other prices of the commodities with zero excess demand in order to keep these markets in equilibrium. On the other hand, if one of the prices of the commodities with zero excess demand reaches the relative upper (lower) bound, then this market is no longer kept in equilibrium, but the corresponding price is kept equal to the current relative upper (lower) bound. In this way, the auctioneer traces a path of prices leading to an equilibrium price system.

> From G. van der Laan and A. J. J. Talman, "Adjustment
> Processes for Finding Economic Equilibria,"
> *Economics Letters* 23 (1987): 119–23.

So that's it. Having started with the idea that markets all on their own find states superior to what any central planner could possibly find, we find that the only way the system can find this wonderful equilibrium is through the concerted effort of an auctioneer holding immense quantities of information and acting like a central planner!

7. Donald Saari, "Mathematical Complexity of Simple Economics," *Notices of the American Mathematical Society* 42 (1995): 222–30.

8. Frank Ackerman, "Still Dead After All These Years: Interpreting the Failure of General Equilibrium Theory," *Journal of Economic Methodology* 9, no. 2 (2002): 119–139.

9. The textbook Ackerman cites is Andreu Mas-Colell, Michael Whinston, and Jerry Green, *Microeconomic Theory* (New York: Oxford University Press, 1995).

10. See Mark Rubinstein, "Rational Markets: Yes or No? The Affirmative Case," *Financial Analysts Journal* 57, no. 3, (May/June 2001). The story is told in S. Sontag and C. Drew, *Blind Man's Bluff: The Untold Story of American Submarine Espionage* (London: HarperCollins, 1998).

11. Francis Galton, "Vox Populi," *Nature* 75 (1907): 450–51.

12. James Surowiecki, *The Wisdom of Crowds* (New York: Anchor, 2005).

13. See Daniel Ariely, *Predictably Irrational* (London: HarperCollins, 2008).

14. See Stanislas Dehaene et al., "Log or Linear? Distinct Intuitions of the Number Scale in Western and Amazonian Indigene Cultures," *Science* 230 (2008): 1217–20.

15. Jan Lorenz et al., "How Social Influence Can Undermine the Wisdom of Crowd Effect," *PNAS* 108, no. 22 (2011): 9020–25.

16. Harrison Hong, Jeffrey Kubik, and Jeremy Stein, "Thy Neighbor's Portfolio: Word-of-Mouth Effects in the Holdings and Trades of Money Managers," *Journal of Finance* 9, no. 6 (2005).

17. Olivier Guedj and Jean-Philippe Bouchaud, "Experts' Earning Forecasts: Bias, Herding and Gossamer Information," *International Journal of Theoretical and Applied Finance* 8 (2005): 933–46.

18. In 1953, American economist Milton Friedman even suggested that this arbitrage process should impose a kind of evolutionary selection in the market and act to eliminate irrational people from it. After all, if irrational people make unwise trades and create imbalances in the market, smarter people will step in to take advantage and will profit from the imbalance. That profit has to come from somewhere, and that somewhere, Friedman suggested, is the pockets and bank accounts of the irrational investors, who will eventually, if they persist in their silly behavior, be driven from the market.

19. Andrei Shleifer and Robert Vishny, "The Limits of Arbitrage," *Journal of Finance* 52, no. 1. (March 1997): 35–55. Available at http://pages.stern.nyu.edu/~cedmond/phd/Shleifer%20Vishny%20JF%201997.pdf.

20. Bob Woodward, *Maestro: Greenspan's Fed and the American Boom* (New York: Simon and Schuster, 2000).

21. See "Remembering the Crash of 1987," CNBC at www.cnbc.com/id/20910471.

22. See Annelena Lobb, "Looking Back at Black Monday: A Discussion with Richard Sylla," *Wall Street Journal Online*, October 15, 2007, at http://online.wsj.com/article/SB119212671947456234.html?mod=US-Stocks. Retrieved October 15, 2007.

23. See www.lope.ca/markets/1987crash/1987crash.pdf.

24. David M. Cutler, James M. Poterba, and Lawrence H. Summers, "What Moves Stock Prices?" *Journal of Portfolio Management* (Spring 1989): 15, 3.

25. Ray Fair, "Events That Shook the Market," *Journal of Business* 75, no. 4 (October 2002), www.bis.org/publ/bppdf/bispapo2b.pdf.

26. Graham Bowley, "The Flash Crash, in Miniature," *New York Times*, November 8, 2010. Available at www.nytimes.com/2010/11/09/business /09flash.html?pagewanted=all.

27. See www.nanex.net/FlashCrash/OngoingResearch.html.

28. Susanne Craig, "Bank Stocks Get a Boost from Geithner," *New York Times*, October 6, 2011. Available at http://dealbook.nytimes.com/2011/10/06 /bank-stocks-get-a-boost-from-geithner/.

29. In the language of economic finance, stock prices should be equal to "the present value of rationally expected or optimally forecast future real dividends discounted by a constant real discount rate." Investors estimate the dividend payments they will likely get from the company next year, the year after, and so on into the future, and add them up, also taking into account that payments they will get in the future have a reduced or "discounted" value. If you can earn 5 percent in the bank, then $95 in one year becomes roughly $100; hence, today's present value of $100 a year in the future is only $95.

30. Andrew Lo, "Efficient Market Hypothesis," *The New Palgrave Dictionary of Economics*, in Durlauf and Blume, eds., 2nd ed. (New York: Palgrave Macmillan, 2008).

31. Armand Joulin et al., "Stock Price Jumps: News and Volume Play a Minor Role," *Wilmott* (September/October 2008).

32. In principle, there is one final way out for an efficient markets devotee. Perhaps these big movements take place when some big market player brings their own private information into play by making a big trade. Goldman Sachs makes a big trade on things only they know and prices respond, moving back toward their fundamental values, just as the EMH would say.

    This also doesn't appear to be true, although the evidence showing this is a little technical. If big players making big informative trades cause big movements, then big price changes in the market should be associated with trades involving a high volume of traded stocks. Looking at the biggest price changes, you should find that many of them involved high-volume trades. This isn't the case. Farmer and his colleagues looked at this a couple years ago and found that for large price changes, there is very little link at all between the price change and the volume of stocks traded. "Large jumps," as they put it, "are not induced by large trading volumes." See J. Doyne Farmer et al., "What Really Causes Large Price Changes?," *Quantitative Finance* 4 (2004): 383–97.

33. See http://delong.typepad.com/sdj/2011/10/calibration-and-econometric -non-practice.html.

34. See http://ineteconomics.org/video/conference-kings/efficient-market -theory-jeremy-siegel.

35. Robert Lucas, "In Defence of the Dismal Science," *The Economist* (August 6, 2009). Available at www.economist.com/node/14165405. To be fair to Lucas, he did clarify in the article that the "efficiency" he was talking about had nothing to do with optimal market function in any sense, only the difficulty of predicting markets.

36. Sometimes people refer to this as "information efficiency," but this use of the word is also somewhat peculiar. Paul Samuelson may have proven that if investors pounce on all available information they'll make markets unpredictable, but this doesn't imply that an unpredictable market is one in which all information is being properly used. Any number of things could make a market unpredictable. Just suppose (to make the point) that investors in some market make their decisions to buy and sell by flipping coins. Their actions would bring absolutely no information into the market, yet prices would fluctuate randomly and the market would be hard to predict.

37. "What Went Wrong with Economics," *The Economist* (July 16, 2009). Available at www.economist.com/node/14031376?Story_ID=14031376.

38. "Lucas Roundtable," *The Economist* (August 6, 2009). Available at www .economist.com/blogs/freeexchange/2009/08/lucas_roundtable.

39. Emanuel Derman, *My Life as a Quant: Reflections on Physics and Finance* (Hoboken, NJ: Wiley, 2004).

40. www.nobelprize.org/nobel_prizes/economics/laureates/2002/smith -lecture.pdf.

Chapter 4: Natural Rhythms

1. R. J. Geller, "Earthquake Prediction: A Critical Review," *Geophysical Journal International* 131 (1997): 425–50.

2. Rudiger Dornbush, "Growth Forever," *Wall Street Journal*, July 30, 1998.

3. Beno Gutenberg and Charles Richter, *Seismicity of the Earth and Associated Phenomena*, 2nd ed. (Princeton: Princeton University Press, 1954).

4. For a short overview of power laws in science, see the good article on Wikipedia: www.en.wikipedia.org/wiki/Power_law.

5. Even if several buses serve one route, and start out evenly spaced to begin with, they won't remain that way. A natural dynamic tends to bring them together. Imagine two buses separated initially by ten minutes. At hours of peak demand, the leading bus finds stops with many passengers, and has to linger at each as they load. The bus slightly behind will tend to find the stops with fewer passengers, as the leading bus has depleted the num-

bers. The trailing bus doesn't have to stop for as long, and so tends to catch up to the leading bus over time.

6. Jim Andrews, "Japan Aftershocks: How Long Will They Go On?", Accu Weather.com, April 13, 2011. Available at www.accuweather.com/en/weather -news/japan-aftershocks-how-long-wil-1/48298.

7. Omori visited San Francisco following the great earthquake of 1906, and seems to have had an interesting time, among other things being attacked several times by anti-Japanese thugs. He was quite forgiving, later writing "referring to some trouble I had with hoodlums in San Francisco . . . It did me no injury and I bear no malice. There are hoodlums in all countries. The people of California treated me extremely well and I am very much pleased with my trip." See "Hawaii Is Safe from Earthquakes," *Hawaii Gazette*, August 14, 1906.

8. Fabrizio Lillo and Rosario Mantegna, "Power-Law Relaxation in a Complex System: Omori Law after a Financial Market Crash," *Physical Review E* 68 (2003): 016119.

9. See www.lope.ca/markets/1987crash/1987crash.pdf.

10. You can see a map showing quakes in California over the most recent week on the U.S. Geological Survey site at http://earthquake.usgs.gov/earthquakes/map/.

11. Some business school professors in the U.K. have given a nice discussion of the actual likelihood of events drawn from a normal distribution. See www.ucd.ie/quinn/academicsresearch/workingpapers/wp_08_13.pdf. As they conclude, "the estimate of a 25-sigma event being on a par with Hell freezing over is probably about right."

12. Xavier Gabaix, "Power Laws in Economics and Finance," *Annual Review of Economics* 1 (2009): 255–93.

13. The most entertaining discussion on this point is certainly Nassim Taleb's *The Black Swan* (New York: Random House, 1997).

14. Edward Hallett Carr, *What Is History?* (New York: Penguin Books, 1990), 57.

15. The history of research into fat tails is long and rather confusing. Soon after he first noted fat tails in market movements, Mandelbrot also noticed something else—that the pattern of market returns also looks much the same on different timescales. That is, take a record of price movements over one month and shrink it down by a factor of about thirty, and it will look much like a typical record of prices over one day. This presents a puzzle, as Mandelbrot recognized, if we're to think of price changes as being independent at different times. What happens in the market over longer times is, of course, just the result of a sequence of happenings over

shorter times. Hence, the probabilities on shorter times must determine the probabilities on longer times. Is there any way it could work to produce this delicate self-similarity?

Mandelbrot showed that there is, but only if the distribution of returns belongs to a special class of probability distributions originally studied by the mathematician Paul Lévy. These distributions not only have fat tails, but if you add a bunch of them together, the sum is a quantity that also has fat tails—and with precisely the same fat-tail exponent. Just the recipe required. For several decades, this idea produced both interest and controversy in economics. To begin, it implies some things about price movements that are pretty weird. For example, it suggests that the variance of prices—the mean square measure of how much they fluctuate—should be literally infinite.

Many economists found this too much to swallow. However, the appeal of what Mandelbrot called his "stable Paretian hypothesis" for the distribution of market returns was equally strong—primarily that it offered one natural way to account for the existence of fat tails, and did so in a way that seemed to make sense of fluctuations on shorter and longer scales and the link between them in a single go. All this with a theory that's only a minor tweak of the original random walk theory, too, with changes at different times being independent.

But alas, it was not to be, and Mandelbrot's idea we now know isn't actually right at all. That much is proved by the recent studies with massive data. As it turns out, Lévy's mathematics of combination only works if the fat tail has an exponent between 0 and 2. These are distributions that have infinite second moments. That is, the standard deviation of price movements in mathematical terms is infinite; calculate it over time and the average value you get will simply keep growing and growing. Real markets aren't like that, the fat-tail exponent actually being close to 3. Hence, the data rules out an entire class of possible pictures of market fluctuations, notably those based on the independence of movements at different times.

But the trouble with the stable Paretian hypothesis was evident even well before modern data, and even hinted at by Mandelbrot in his original paper. The idea that market moves over different time intervals is actually quite preposterous, and flies in the face of everything we know about markets. Markets have a kind of memory, which makes them rich and much more complex than any constant probability fluctuation can account for.

16. Zhuanxin Ding, Clive Granger, and Robert Engle, "A Long Memory Property of Stock Market Returns and a New Model," *Journal of Empirical Finance* 1 (1993): 83–106. Available at www.netegrate.com/index_files

/Research%20Library/Catalogue/Quantitative%20Analysis/Long-Range
%20Dependence/A%20Long%20memory%20property%20of%20Stock
%20Returns%20and%20a%20new%20Model%28Ding,Granger
%20and%20Engle%29.pdf.

17. Economists had known about volatility clustering at least since the 1960s,
but the importance of the phenomenon only seems to have been appreciated in the 1990s. Andrew Lo and A. Craig MacKinlay, in their 1991 book
A Non-Random Walk Down Wall Street, note that "there is already a growing consensus among financial economists that stock market prices are
not independently and identically distributed." The long memory effect
reported by Ding, Granger, and Engle had been noted earlier in 1986 by
economist Stephen Taylor as well. See Stephen Taylor, *Modelling Financial
Time Series* (New York: John Wiley and Sons, 1986).

18. Lillo and Mantegna, "Power-Law Relaxation in a Complex System: Omori
Law After a Financial Crash," *Physical Review* 68 (2003): 016119.

19. See Alexander Peterson et al., "Quantitative Law Describing Market Dynamics Before and After Interest-Rate Change," *Physical Review E* 81 (2010):
066121. Available at http://polymer.bu.edu/hes/articles/pwhs10.pdf.

20. See, for example, Ary Goldberger et al., "Fractal Dynamics in Physiology,"
PNAS 99 (2002): 2466–72.

21. See Klaus Linkenkaer-Hansen et al., "Long-Range Temporal Correlations
and Scaling Behavior in Human Brain Oscillations," *Journal of Neuroscience* 21 (2001): 1370–77. Available at www.jneurosci.org/content/21/4/1370
.full.pdf.

22. Mark Buchanan, *Ubiquity* (New York: Crown, 2001).

23. See A. Lo and A. C. MacKinlay, "When Are Contrarian Profits Due to Stock
Market Overreaction?," *The Review of Financial Studies* 3 (1990): 175–205.

24. See Bence Tóth and János Kertés, "Increasing Market Efficiency: Evolution
of Cross-Correlations of Stock Returns," *Physica A* 360 (2006): 505–15.
Available at http://arxiv.org/PS_cache/physics/pdf/0506/0506071v2.pdf.

Chapter 5: Models of Man

1. For an excellent review of market universals, see Lisa Borland et al., "The
Dynamics of Financial Markets—Mandelbrot's Multifractal Cascades,
and Beyond," *Wilmott Magazine*, June 10, 2009. Available at www.wilmott
.com/pdfs/0503_bouchaud.pdf.

2. Benoit Mandelbrot, Adlai Fisher, and Laurent Calvet, "A Multifractal Model
of Asset Returns," Cowles Foundation Discussion Paper #1164 (1997).
Available at http://users.math.yale.edu/~bbm3/web_pdfs/Cowles1164.pdf.

Also see Benoit Mandelbrot and Richard Hudson, *The (Mis)behaviour of Markets* (Hoboken, NJ: Wiley, 2004).

3. J. P. Bouchaud, A. Matacz, and M. Potters, "The Leverage Effect in Financial Markets: Retarded Volatility and Market Panic," *Physical Review Letters* 87 (2001): 228701.

4. Robert Axelrod, "Advancing the Art of Simulation in the Social Sciences," in *Simulating Social Phenomena*, ed. Rosaria Conte, Rainer Hegselmann, and Pietro Terna (Berlin: Springer, 1997), 21–40.

5. Milton Friedman, "The Methodology of Positive Economics," in *Essays in Positive Economics* (Chicago: Chicago University Press, 1953). Available at http://dieoff.org/_Economics/TheMethodologyOfPositiveEconomics.htm.

6. William Sharpe, "Capital Asset Prices: A Theory of Market Equilibrium," *Journal of Finance* 19 (1964): 425–42.

7. Richard Thaler, "From *Homo economicus* to *Homo sapiens*," *Journal of Economic Perspectives* 14, no. 1 (2000): 133–41.

8. For further discussion of the philosophical mess that is Friedman's argument, see chapter 7 of Steve Keen, *Debunking Economics* (Sydney: Zed Books, 2002). Keen draws on the much more detailed analysis of the philosopher Alan Musgrave.

9. Duncan Foley, "Rationality and Ideology in Economics," *Social Research* 71 (2004): 329–342. Available at http://homepage.newschool.edu/%7Efoleyd/ratid.pdf.

10. Nick Goodway, "Bailey Hedge Fund Closes After Slump," posted at www.thisismoney.co.uk/money/markets/article-1591207/Bailey-hedge-fund-closes-after-slump.html (June 20, 2005).

11. http://bigpicture.typepad.com/comments/files/AQR.pdf.

12. http://bigpicture.typepad.com/comments/files/renaissance_technologies.pdf.

13. http://bigpicture.typepad.com/comments/files/Barclays.pdf.

14. Quoted in Jack Schwager, *Market Wizards: Interviews with Top Traders* (Columbia, MD: Marketplace Books, 2006), 128.

15. Economists have of course noticed deviations from rational behavior in games. One interesting finding is that the predictions of classical game theory do tend to be born out in situations in which the game is simple enough and all the players smart enough so that each one can figure out the rational strategy and believe that others will figure it out as well. In a simple game known as the centipede game, for example, 70 percent of professional chess players chose the rational strategy while only 5 percent of other subjects did. Moreover, every chess grand master chose the rational strategy when they were told that their opponent was another chess

player. When playing students, they choose that strategy less frequently. See Steven Levitt, John List, and Sally Sadoff, "Checkmate: Exploring Backward Induction Among Chess Players," *American Economic Review* 101 (2011): 975–90. Available at www.fieldexperiments.com/uploads/133.pdf.

16. That real people often don't play according to the rational ideal has been known since the early days of game theory. In 1957, two researchers at the RAND corporation in California, Merrill Flood and Melvin Dresher, ran a simple experiment to see if Nash's idea really captured how people played a simple game. The Nash equilibrium in this game isn't too hard to calculate, so the two could easily have played rationally if they wanted to. In the experiments, however, the two players worked in a very different way. In particular, they never settled into any kind of equilibrium strategy, but instead waged a complex game of cat and mouse in which their behavior continued to evolve and fluctuate. Floyd and Dresher also had the players write down comments along the way, reflecting their shifting emotions when surprised by the other's actions. The players tried through their actions to encourage their opponent to be more cooperative, sometimes being pleasantly surprised by the other's actions, "Goodness me! Friendly!," at other times angered, "To Hell with him," and at other times puzzled and frustrated, "This is like toilet training a child—you have to be very patient." See William Poundstone, *Prisoner's Dilemma* (New York: Anchor Books, 1993), p. 106–16.

17. Interview with Dave Cliff. Available at http://physicsoffinance.blogspot .com/2011/12/interview-with-dave-cliff.html.

18. Erik Reinert manages a website organizing materials on the topic. See www.othercanon.org/index.html.

19. John Maynard Keynes, *The General Theory of Employment, Interest and Money* (Cambridge: Cambridge University Press, 1936). Available at http:// www.newschool.edu/nssr/.

20. Peter Lynch, *Beating the Street* (New York: Simon and Schuster, 1993).

21. Martin Pring, *Technical Analysis Explained: The Successful Investor's Guide to Spotting Investment Trends and Turning Points*, 4th ed. (New York: McGraw-Hill, 2002).

22. Christopher Neely and Paul Weller, "Technical Analysis in the Foreign Exchange Market," working paper 2011-001B, Federal Reserve Bank of St. Louis. Available at http://research.stlouisfed.org/wp/2011/2011-001 .pdf.

23. Juli Creswell, "Currency Market Expects Rate Cut by Bank of Japan," *Wall Street Journal*, September 5, 1995, C16.

24. Schwager, *Market Wizards*, 26.

25. John Conlisk, "Why Bounded Rationality?" *Journal of Economic Literature* 34 (1996): 669–700. Available at http://teaching.ust.hk/%7Emark329y/EconPsy/Why%20Bounded%20Rationality.pdf.

26. See A. Dijksterhuis et al., "On Making the Right Choice: The Deliberation Without Attention Effect," *Science* 311 (2006): 1005–7.

27. See P. Umbanhower, F. Melo, and H. L. Swinney, "Localized Exertations in a Vertically Vibrated Granular Layer," *Nature* 382 (1996): 793–96.

Chapter 6: Ecologies of Belief

1. Robert Nelson, *Economics as Religion* (University Park: Penn State University Press, 2001).

2. Explaining why the rational expectations perspective has been so influential and hard to displace is not easy. It reflects a strong cultural inertia holding that good theories should be wrapped up in elegant equations and demonstrated through formal proofs. Rational expectations theories lend themselves to such results. Economists themselves have been hard pressed to explain the phenomenon. See, for example, Willem Buiter, "The Unfortunate Uselessness of Most 'State of the Art' Academic Monetary Economics," *Financial Times* (March 3, 2009). Available at www.voxeu.org/article/macroeconomics-crisis-irrelevance.

3. William Chase and Herbert Simon, "Perception in Chess," *Cognitive Psychology* 4 (1973): 55–61.

4. This result is consistent with the famous finding of psychologist George Miller that seven is a kind of "magic number" expressing something important about our short-term memory. We can remember about seven things—numbers, words, chess pieces—at a time, but not many more. See George Miller, "The Magical Number Seven, Plus or Minus Two," *Psychological Review* 63 (1956): 81–97.

5. See, for example, George Evans and Seppo Honkapohja, "Learning and Macroeconomics," *Annual Review of Economics* 1 (2009): 421–51. What this paper does is explore what happens in some of the common rational expectations models if you suppose that agents' expectations aren't formed rationally but rather on the basis of some learning algorithm. The paper shows that learning algorithms of a certain kind lead to the same equilibrium outcome as the rational expectations viewpoint. This is interesting and seems very impressive. However, it's not as impressive as it first seems, as the learning algorithm is of a rather special kind. Most of the models studied in the paper suppose that agents in the market already know *the right mathematical form* they should use to form expectations

about prices in the future. All they lack is knowledge of the values of some parameters in the equation. This is a little like assuming that people who start out trying to learn the equations for, say, quantum theory, already know the right form of Schrödinger's equation, the central equation of that theory, with all the right space and time derivatives, though they are ignorant of the correct coefficients. This is quite a spectacular assumption. I thank Ivan Sutoris for pointing me to this paper.

6. See Jennifer Whitson and Adam Galinsky, "Lacking Control Increases Illusory Pattern Perception," *Science* 322 (2008): 115–17.

7. An economist might want to object that people choosing at random to go to the bar 60 percent of the time is indeed a solution from game theory, a so-called mixed strategy. But this, too, is not what goes on here. By following adaptive, evolving strategies, the agents in Arthur's game do better (end up satisfied more frequently) than they would by playing the purely random strategy. Game theory doesn't cut it.

8. I should emphasize that Arthur wasn't the first economist to consider market models with adaptive agents. For example, important earlier work by Alan Kirman showed how spontanous fluctuations in markets might be understood by thinking of market participants as "trend followers" or "fundamentalists," and who might switch from one kind of behavior to another depending on what has recently happened. In a bull market, for example, more fundamentalists tend to become trend followers, which helps drive prices higher. Kirman drew his inspiration from the foraging behavior of ants. See Alan Kirman, "Epidemics of Opinion and Speculative Bubbles in Financial Markets," in M. Taylor, ed., *Money and Financial Markets* (London: Macmillan, 1991).

9. Blake LeBaron, "Building the Santa Fe Artificial Stock Market," working paper, Brandeis University (June 2002). Available at http://people.brandeis .edu/~blebaron/wps/sfisum.pdf.

10. Blake LeBaron, "Agent-Based Financial Markets: Matching Stylized Facts with Style," in D. Colander, ed., *Post Walrasian Macroeconomics: Beyond the DSGE Model* (Cambridge: Cambridge University Press, 2006). Available at http://people.brandeis.edu/~blebaron/wps/style.pdf.

11. Damien Challet and Yi-Cheng Zhang, "Emergence of Cooperation and Organization in an Evolutionary Game," *Physica A* 226 (1997): 407.

12. R. Savit, R. Manuca, and R. Riolo, "Adaptive Competition, Market Efficiency and Phase Transitions," *Physical Review Letters* 82 (1999): 2203.

13. "Interview: Cliff Asness Explains Why He Started a Managed Futures Fund," *Business Insider* (March 5, 2010). Available at http://articles.businessinsider .com/2010-03-05/wall_street/29960522_1_trend-inflows-trading-places.

14. Yi-Cheng Zhang, "Why Financial Markets Will Remain Marginally Inefficient." Available at http://arxiv.org/abs/cond-mat/0105373.

15. This isn't the only way to get a fluctuating volume. Another way to allow for a fluctuating volume is to let the agents accrue wealth over time, and let the volume of their trading grow in proportion to that wealth. Again, this is an obvious step toward reality, and again leads to market fluctuations with many of the rich statistical features seen in real markets, even in such simple models.

16. G. Berg, M. Marsili, A. Rustichini, and R. Zecchina, "Statistical Mechanics of Asset Markets with Private Information," *Quantitative Finance* 1, no. 2 (2001): 203–11.

17. See, for example, C. H. Keung and Y. C. Zhang, "Minority Games," in R. Meyers, ed., *Encyclopedia of Complexity and Systems Science* (Berlin: Springer, 2009).

18. Vince Darley, *Nasdaq Market Simulation: Insights on a Major Market from the Science of Complex Adaptive Systems* (New York: World Scientific, 2007).

19. As an aside, you can't use ordinary hydrogen, but need its isotopes, deuterium or tritium, the nuclei of which contain a proton and either one or two neutrons. These things can fuse together into unstable nuclei, which decay, ultimately creating nuclei of the stable element helium, with two neutrons and two protons.

20. To learn more about the program on inertial confinement fusion see https://lasers.llnl.gov/programs/nic/target_physics.php.

21. Technically this is known as the Rayleigh-Taylor instability.

22. Interestingly, what happens in inertial confinement fusion during implosion is very close to what happens during a supernovae explosion, only in reverse. Now the flow is outward, not inward, but similar instabilities drive the growth of waves and eventual turbulence.

23. For a partial list, Wikipedia can help. See http://en.wikipedia.org/wiki/Plasma_stability#Plasma_instabilities.

Chapter 7: Perils of Efficiency

1. See Stephen Peter Rigaud, *Biographical Account of John Hadley, Esq. V.P.R.S., the Inventor of the Quadrant, and of His Brothers, George and Henry* (London: Fisher, Son & Co., 1835).

2. The physical effect behind this is known as the Coriolis force, which is a consequence of the conservation of angular momentum in the atmosphere on a rotating planet. Think of a ring of air, at high altitude, drifting toward the North Pole. As it approaches the pole, this ring naturally moves in closer to the axis of the earth's rotation (that axis runs through the

poles). For the angular momentum of the ring to remain fixed, the ring must spin faster as it drifts northward. This is what makes high altitude air at midlattitudes move in an easterly direction relative to the earth. By the same argument, a ring of low-altitude air drifting back toward the equator must slow down the further it goes, and therefore move in a westerly direction relative to the earth. This explains the trade winds.

3. The idea was so natural that within a few decades it had sprung up independently in the minds of the German philosopher Immanuel Kant and the English chemist John Dalton, before either even heard of Hadley's original paper. See Edward Lorenz, "A History of Prevailing Ideas About the General Circulation of the Atmosphere," *Bulletin of the American Meteorological Society* 64 (1983): 730.

4. No one person can be credited with this discovery. Rather it emerged from the work of a number of meteorologists including Austrian Albert Defant, Norwegian Vilhelm Bjerknes, Brit Eric Eady, and American Jule Gregory Charney, the latter of whom had a long and distinguished career as a meteorologist at MIT. In 1979, he chaired a committee of the National Research Council looking into the link between atmospheric carbon dioxide and climate. The groups' report is one of the first scientific assessments of global warming, and gave an estimate for the likely temperature rise expected for a doubling of CO_2 as "near 3°C with a probable error of ± 1.5°C." Remarkably, this is pretty close to the assessment by international scientists three decades later. The IPCC Fourth Assessment Report (2007) estimates that "equilibrium climate sensitivity is likely to be in the range 2°C to 4.5°C, with a best estimate value of about 3°C. It is very unlikely to be less than 1.5°C. Values substantially higher than 4.5°C cannot be excluded, but agreement with observations is not as good for those values."

5. For an illuminating discussion of Phillips's experiment and its historical impact see John Lewis, "Clarifying the Dynamics of the General Circulation: Phillips's 1956 Experiment," *Bulletin of the American Meteorological Society* (1998). Available at www.aos.princeton.edu/WWWPUBLIC/gkv/history/Lewis-on-Phillips98.pdf.

6. Friedman said this in conversation with MIT economist Franklin Fisher. See his paper, "The Stability of General Equilibrium—What Do We Know and Why Is It Important?," in P. Bridel, ed., *General Equilibrium Analysis: A Century After Walras* (London: Routledge, 2011). Available at http://economics.mit.edu/files/6988.

7. Lukas Menkhoff and Mark P. Taylor, "The Obstinate Passion of Foreign Exchange Professionals: Technical Analysis," *Journal of Economic Literature* 45, no. 4 (2007): 936–72.

8. Many researchers have explored simple models along these lines. See, for example, Thomas Lux and Michele Marchesi, "Scaling and Criticality in a Stochastic Multi-Agent Model of a Financial Market," *Nature* 397 (February 11, 1999): 498–500.

9. Amir E. Khandani and Andrew W. Lo, "What Happened to the Quants in August 2007? Evidence from Factors and Transactions Data," *Journal of Financial Markets* 14 (2011): 1–46.

10. See, for example, a nice paper by Lasse Pederson, "When Everyone Runs for the Exit," *International Journal of Central Banking* 5 (2009): 177–99, available at pages.stern.nyu.edu/~lpederse/papers/EveryoneRunsForExit.pdf.

   This is logically a minor variant of a bank run—although the bank run is purely driven by expectations, people fleeing to save their own money. The leverage case is a bit different; the sales happen in a forced way through the need to make payments, whatever the expectations.

11. Stefan Thurner, J. Doyne Farmer, and John Geanakoplus, "Leverage Causes Fat Tails and Clustered Volatility," *Quantitative Finance* 12 (2012): 695–707.

12. See the blog of Rick Bookstaber, http://rick.bookstaber.com/2007/08/can-high-liquidity-low-volatility-high.html.

13. You can see a nice video illustrating the phenomenon at http://web.mit.edu/newsoffice/2009/traffic-0609.html.

14. Robert Merton and Zvi Bodie, "Design of Financial Systems: Towards a Synthesis of Function and Structure," *Journal of Investment Management* 3 (2005): 1–23.

15. Report from the *Ninth Annual OECD/World Bank/IMF Bond Market Forum*, May 22–23, 2007. Available at www.oecd.org/dataoecd/49/45/39354012.pdf.

16. S. Battiston, D. D. Gatti, M. Gallegati, B. C. N. Greenwald, and J. E. Stiglitz, "Liaisons Dangereuses: Increasing Connectivity, Risk Sharing, and Systemic Risk," *Journal of Economic Dynamics and Control* 36 (2012, 1121–1141).

17. See William Brock, Cars Hommes, and Florian Wagener, "More Hedging Instruments May Destabilize Markets," Working Paper, Center for Nonlinear Dynamics in Economics and Finance (May 2009). See also Fabio Caccioli and Matteo Marsili, "Efficiency and Stability in Complex Financial Markets," Economics Discussion Papers, No. 2010-3, Kiel Institute for the World Economy (2010).

18. John Cochrane, "Lessons from the Financial Crisis," *Regulation* (Winter 2009–2010): 34–7. Available at www.cato.org/pubs/regulation/regv32n4/v32n4-6.pdf.

19. See the blog *Economics of Contempt* at http://economicsofcontempt.blogspot.fr/2010/02/mind-boggling-nonsense-from-john.html.

20. Robert Nelson, *Economics as Religion* (University Park: Pennsylvania State University, 2002).

21. See Frank Westerhoff, "The Use of Agent-Based Financial Market Models to Test the Effectiveness of Regulatory Policies." Available at www .uni-bamberg.de/fileadmin/uni/fakultaeten/sowi_lehrstuehle/vwl_ wirtschaftspolitik/Team/Westerhoff/Publications/2011/P45_JfNS_FW .pdf.

Chapter 8: Trading at the Speed of Light

1. Lauren La Capra, "How P & G Derailed One Investor," The Street (May 17, 2010). Available at www.thestreet.com/story/10757383/5/how-pg-plunge -derailed-one-investor.html.

2. Joe Pappalardo, "New Transatlantic Cable Built to Shave 5 Milliseconds off Stock Trades," *Popular Mechanics*, October 27, 2011. Available at www.pop ularmechanics.com/technology/engineering/infrastructure/a-transat lantic-cableto-shave-5-milliseconds-off-stock-trades.

3. A. D. Wissner-Gross and C. E. Freer, "Relativistic Statistical Arbitrage," *Physical Review E* 82, (2010): 056104.

4. Paul Wilmott, "Hurrying into the Next Panic?" *New York Times*, July 28, 2009. Available at www.nytimes.com/2009/07/29/opinion/29wilmott .html.

5. Carol Clark, "Controlling Risk in a Lightning-Speed Trading Environment," *Federal Reserve Bank of Chicago Financial Markets Group*, Policy Discussion Paper Series PDP 2010-1 (2010).

6. Terrence Hendershott, Charles Jones, and Albert Menkveld, "Does Algorithmic Trading Improve Liquidity?" *Journal of Finance* 66 (2011): 1–33.

7. Ibid. These authors were careful to point out the limitations of their study. As they noted, "A couple of caveats are in order, however. Our overall sample period covers a period of generally rising stock prices, and stock markets are fairly quiescent during the 2003 introduction of autoquote. While we do control for share price levels and volatility in our empirical work, it remains an open question whether AT and algorithmic liquidity supply are equally beneficial in more turbulent or declining markets."

8. David Easley, Marcos Lopez de Prado, and Maureen O'Hara, "The Microstructure of the Flash Crash," *Journal of Portfolio Management* 37 (2011): 118–28.

9. CFTC-SEC, *Findings Regarding the Market Events of May 6, 2010*, September 30, 2010.

10. See testimony of Chris Nagy, TD Ameritrade Holding Corp's Managing Director of Order Routing, cited in "Panel Urges Big Thinking in 'Flash Crash' Response," Reuters, August 11, 2010.

11. Reginald Smith, "Is HFT Inducing Changes in Market Microstructure and Dynamics," working paper (2010).

12. Andrew Haldane, "The Race to Zero." Speech given at the International Economic Association Sixteenth World Congress, Beijing, China, July 8, 2011.

13. Neil Johnson et al., "Financial Black Swans Driven by Ultrafast Machine Ecology," See preprint at http://arxiv.org/abs/1202.1448.

14. See Tapani N. Liukkonen, "Human Reaction Times as a Response to Delays in Control Systems." Available at www.tol.oulu.fi/fileadmin/kuvat/Kajaani/ReactionTime-ALMA.pdf.

15. Louise Story and Graham Bowley, "Market Swings Are Becoming New Standard," *New York Times*, September 11, 2011.

16. See www.nanex.net/FlashCrashFinal/FlashCrashAnalysis_Theory.html.

17. Dave Cliff and Linda Northrop, "The Global Financial Markets: An Ultra-Large-Scale Systems Perspective." Review of the U.K. Government's Foresight Project, The Future of Computer Trading in Financial Markets.

18. www.nanex.net/StrangeDays/06082011.html.

19. http://blogs.progress.com/business_making_progress/2011/02/beware-the-splash-crash.html.

20. S. V. Buldyrev et al., "Catastrophic Cascade of Failures in Interdependent Networks," *Nature* 464 (2010): 1025–28.

21. Robin Banerji, "Little Boy Lost Finds His Mother Using Google Earth," (April 13, 2012). Available at www.bbc.co.uk/news/magazine-17693816.

22. Sander van der Leeuwe, "The Archeology of Innovation: Lessons for Our Times," Athens Dialogues, Harvard University. Available at http://athensdialogues.chs.harvard.edu/cgi-bin/WebObjects/athensdialogues.woa/wa/dist?dis=83.

23. Paul Wilmott, "Hurrying into the Next Panic?" *New York Times* July 28, 2009.

Chapter 9: Twilight of the Idols

1. Gordon Winston, quote in Ole Røgeberg and Hans Olav Melberg, "Acceptance of Unsupported Claims about Reality: A Blind Spot in Economics," *Journal of Economic Methodology* 18 (2011): 1, 29–52.

2. Ole Røgeberg and Hans Olav Melberg, "Acceptance of Unsupported Claims about Reality: A Blind Spot in Economics," *Journal of Economic Methodology* 18 (2011): 1, 29–52.

3. Bertrand Russell, *My Philosophical Development* (London: Routledge, 1995).

4. Robert Lucas, "Econometric Policy Evaluation: A Critique," in K. Brunner and A. Meltzer, *The Phillips Curve and Labor Markets*, Carnegie-Rochester Conference Series on Public Policy, 1 (New York: American Elsevier, 1976), 19–46.

5. M. H. R. Stanley, L. A. N. Amaral, S. V. Buldyrev, S. Havlin, H. Leschhorn, P. Maass, M. A. Salinger, and H. E. Stanley, "Scaling Behavior in the Growth of Companies," *Nature* 379 (1996): 804–6.

6. The comment is the first one appearing on the blog post: http://mainlymacro .blogspot.fr/2012/03/microfounded-and-other-useful-models.html.

7. Ray C. Fair, *Testing Macroeconometric Models* (Cambridge: Harvard University Press, 1994).

8. See George Evans and Seppo Honkapohja, "An Interview with Thomas J. Sargent," *Macroeconomic Dynamics* 9 (2005): 561–83.

9. See F. Brayton and P. Tinsley, eds., "A Guide to FRB/US" (Washington: Federal Reserve Board, 1996). Available at www.federalreserve.gov/pubs /feds/1996/199642/199642abs.html.

10. See Paul Ormerod and Craig Mounfield, "Random Matrix Theory and the Failure of Macro-Economic Forecasts," *Physica A* 280 (2000): 497–504.

11. See Volker Wieland and Maik Wolters, "Macroeconomic Model Comparisons and Forecast Competitions." Available at www.voxeu.org/index.php ?q=node/7616.

12. Narayana Kocherlakota, president of the Federal Reserve Bank of Minneapolis, quoted in James Morley, "The Emperor Has No Clothes," *Macro Focus* 5, no. 2 (June 24, 2010).

13. Tobias Preis, Johannes J. Schneider, and H. Eugene Stanley, "Switching Processes in Financial Markets," *Proceedings of the National Academy of Sciences* 108 (2011): 7674–78.

14. George Soros, *The Alchemy of Finance* (New York: Simon and Schuster, 1987).

15. Casey Selix, "Financial Meltdown: Hyman Minsky Warned Us This Would Happen," *Minnesota Post*, September 17, 2008.

16. Hyman Minsky, *Stabilizing an Unstable Economy* (New York: McGraw-Hill Professional, 2008).

17. See Mauro Gallegati, Antonio Palestrini, and J. Barkley Rosser, Jr., "The Period of Financial Distress in Apeculative Markets: Interacting Heterogeneous Agents and Financial Conditions," *Macroeconomic Dynamics* 15 (2011): 60–79.

18. David Colander et al., "The Financial Crisis and the Systemic Failure of

Academic Economics," discussion papers 09-03, University of Copenhagen, Department of Economics.

19. Robert E. Lucas Jr., "Asset Prices in an Exchange Economy," *Econometrica* 46, no. 6 (1978): 1429–45.

20. William Buiter, "The Unfortunate Uselessness of Most 'State of the Art' Academic Monetary Economics," *Financial Times*, March 3, 2009.

21. John Coates, *The Hour Between Dog and Wolf* (New York: Penguin, 2012).

Chapter 10: Forecast

1. Irving Fisher, "The Debt-Deflation Theory of Great Depressions," *Econometrica* 1 (1933): 337–57.

2. Nicholas Kaldor, "A Model of the Trade Cycle," *Economic Journal* 50 (1940): 78–92.

3. Alan Turing, "The Chemical Basis of Morphogenesis," *Philosophical Transactions of the Royal Society of London* 237 (1952).

4. For an argument in this direction from late May 2012, see Simon Johnson, "The End of the Euro: A Survivor's Guide," available at http://baselinescenario .com/2012/05/28/the-end-of-the-euro-a-survivors-guide/.

5. Human responses may also make theories right, in some cases. Indeed, many studies suggest that some theories can also act as self-fulfilling prophecies, encouraging people to act in a way that makes them more true. Rather depressingly, this seems to be the case with the economists' model of individual human behavior based on narrow self-interest. Experiments with students, for example, show that those in, say, psychology or computer science care to some extent about fairness, as well as what they can get for themselves (this is also true of people more generally also). There is, however, one exception—graduate students in economics, who are systematically more self-interested than their colleagues in other fields. The reason seems to be that they have absorbed the predictions of the self-interest model and so expect to encounter such behavior from others. As a consequence, they act that way themselves. See, for example, Robert Frank, Thomas Gilovich, and Dennis Regan, "Does Studying Economics Inhibit Cooperation?," *Journal of Economic Perspectives* 7 (1993): 159–71. This self-fulfilling dynamic can be quite damaging, of course, as it can undermine cooperation in a wide variety of settings.

6. Robert Friedman, *Appropriating the Weather* (Ithaca: Cornell University Press, 1989).

7. Lewis Fry Richardson, *Weather Prediction by Numerical Process* (Cambridge: Cambridge University Press, 1922).

8. It turns out that Richardson overlooked the application of a mathematical smoothing technique that would have suppressed the development of unrealistic atmospheric changes. Later calculations suggest that had he used it, his result would have been fairly accurate even though the calculation was carried out by hand.

9. I've been a loyal fan of the Cleveland Browns for nearly half a century. I am allowed to dream.

10. We "know," that is, barring any act of God interventions such as the catastrophic collision of an asteroid or comet with the earth or moon.

11. Pierre Simone Laplace, "A Philosophical Essay on Probabilities," (New York: Dover, 1953).

12. Actually, this is no longer true. China, in particular, has a large scientific program in weather modification. See www.guardian.co.uk/environment /blog/2009/oct/01/china-cloud-seeding-parade.

13. Rick Bookstaber, *A Demon of Our Own Design* (Hoboken: Wiley, 2007).

14. U.K. Government's Foresight Project, The Future of Computer Trading in Financial Markets, "The Global Financial Markets: An Ultra-Large-Scale Systems Perspective." Available at www.bis.gov.uk/assets/foresight/docs /computer-trading/11-1223-dr4-global-financial-markets-systems-perspec tive.

15. Michael Ocrant, "Madoff Tops Charts; Skeptics Ask How," *MarHedge* 89 (May 2001).

16. Joe LeDoux, *The Emotional Brain* (New York: Touchstone, 1996).

17. Andrew Haldane, "The $100 Billion Question," comments given at the Institute of Regulation and Risk, Hong Kong, March 30, 2010. Available at www.bankofengland.co.uk/publications/speeches/ . . . /speech433.pdf.

18. William Dudley, "Asset Bubbles and the Implications for Central Bank Policy," remarks at the Economic Club of New York, New York City, April 7, 2010. Available at www.newyorkfed.org/newsevents/speeches/2010 /dud100407.html.

Index

Ackerman, Frank, 48
aftershocks, 74, 82
agent-based models, 136
Akerlof, George, 219
algorithmic trading, 102–103, 157–158,
    160–162, 164–165, 168–175
American International Group (AIG),
    146–147
animal spirits, 189–192
applause, 15–16
Apple, 6
apps, for Apple devices, 25–26
AQR Capital Management, 10, 97–99,
    123, 137
arbitrage, 49, 53–55, 141, 158
Ariely, Daniel, 50
Arrow, Kenneth, 30–32, 39–40, 42,
    46, 135
Arrow-Debreu equilibrium, 46–48
Arthur, Brian, 117–120
Asch, Solomon, 190
Asness, Cliff, 97–99, 106, 123, 124, 137
asset bubbles, 136–137, 180–181, 196–197,
    221–222
assumptions, inaccurate, 92–97
atmosphere, 134–135, 140
autocorrelation, 80–81
automated trading, 4, 56, 173
    See also computerized trading
Axelrod, Robert, 91–92

Bachelier, Louis, 37, 80
Bailey, Jonathan, 97–98
Bailey Coates Cromwell Fund,
    97–98
Baker, Howard, 56

banking networks, 20
banking regulations, 20, 213
Bank of America, 64, 151
baroclinic instability, 134–135
Basel I, 213
Basel II, 213
Basel III, 20
Bates, John, 173, 174
Battiston, Stefano, 147
Becker, Gary, 178–179
behavioral economics, 50, 109–111
bell curve, 72–73, 80
Bernanke, Ben, 212
Berns, Gregory, 191
bias, 50
bid-ask spreads, 164–165, 175
Bjerknes, Vilhelm, 206
black swan events, 166–167
Bodie, Zvi, 41, 145
Bookstaber, Rick, 142–143
Bouchaud, Jean-Philippe, 55, 61, 177
brain waves, 83
Brecht, Bertolt, 114
Brierley, Saroo, 175
Brock, William, 149
Brouwer, Luitzen, 31
Browning, Iben, 71
bubbles, 19, 136–137, 180–181, 196–197,
    221–222
Buffett, Warren, 146, 147
Buiter, William, 178, 201
Burry, Michael, 41

Caccioli, Fabio, 149
California, electricity market
    deregulation in, 21

capital asset pricing model, 94–95
Capital Fund Management, 61
capitalism, 32
Carr, Edward Hallett, ix, 80, 151
causal pathways, 127
cause and effect, 150–153
Challet, Damien, 119–120, 123, 126
change, laws of, 48
chaos theory, 205
chartists, 136
Chase, William, 115–116
Cheng, Minder, 99
chess, 115–116, 167
Chesterson, Gilbert Keith, 89
Chicago school of economics,
    112–113
Citigroup, 64, 151
Cliff, Dave, 102–103, 171–172, 217
Clower, Robert, 200
Coates, Stephen, 97–98, 202, 216
Cochrane, John, 150–151, 152
cognitive psychology, 117–119
Colander, David, 199–200
collateralized debt obligations
    (CDOs), 63
collateralized loans, 212–214
collective behavior, 16, 109–111, 143–145,
    194
competition, 21
competitive equilibrium, 32
complete markets, 40–41
compound interest, 2
computerized trading, 20, 42, 56,
    102–103, 157–162, 169–175
computers, 208
computer simulations, 140–143, 197–198,
    208
corruption, 12, 218–220
cortisol, 202
Countrywide Financial, 156
Cournot, Antoine Augustin, 29
Cowles, Alfred, 34
Craven, John, 49
creative destruction, 105
credit bubble, 40–41
credit default swaps, 41, 147, 149, 177
Cutler, David, 57

Dahlem Conference, 14
Darwin, Charles, 80
Debreu, Gérard, 30–32, 39–40, 42, 46,
    47, 135
decision making, 108–109, 117–119

de Groot, Adriaan, 115
de la Vega, Joseph, 35–36
deleveraging, 99, 198, 212
DeLong, Brad, 64
demand
    excess, 47
    supply and, 47
Dennett, Daniel, 208
deregulation
    electricity market, 21
    financial, 41–42, 137
derivatives, 4, 20, 41–43, 63, 137,
    146–150, 177
Derman, Emanuel, 67
Deutsche Bank, 151
Devons, Ely, 112
Ding, Zhuanxin, 81
Dirac, Paul, 192
Direct Edge, 42
disequilibrium systems, 83, 205
    metaphors for, 84
    rice avalanche and, 84–85
disequilibrium thinking, 14, 17–23,
    105–108
Dodd-Frank act, 216
Dornbush, Rudiger, 72
dot-com bubble, 72
Dow Jones Industrial Average, 5, 60, 75
Dudley, William, 43, 66–67, 221–222
dynamics, 104–105, 181, 203
dynamic stochastic general equilibrium
    (DSGE) model, 187–189, 192, 201
Dyson, George, 208

earthquakes, 70–74, 76–77, 82
    Gutenberg-Richter law for, 73–76, 80
    predicting, 71
ecological perspective, 126–128
economic bubbles, 19
    See also bubbles
economic forecasting
    failures of mainstream, 186–189
    future of, 205–222
economics
    behavioral, 50, 109–111
    equilibrium thinking in, 6–9, 83–88,
        135–137, 203–205
    failures of mainstream, 13–14, 22
    forecasting problems in, 22–23
    influence of, 13
    intellectual crisis in, 199–200
    mathematics in, 7, 26, 29, 67–68,
        200–201

positive feedbacks in, 6–9, 19–20, 132, 215
economic shocks, 114
economic theory, ix–x, 67–68, 88, 91–92, 100, 128, 182–186, 201
economic thinking, ix
economists
    social pressures on, 199–200
    work of, 12–13
Edelson, Micah, 191
efficiency
    information, 38–42, 181
    meaning of, 64–66, 95
    vs. stability, 145–150, 173–174
efficient atmosphere hypothesis (EAH), 87–88
efficient frontier, 153–155
efficient market hypothesis, 17, 21, 27–29, 35–40
    continued belief in, 63–67, 180–182
    evidence contradicting, 57–60, 63, 86
    strong form of, 64
    support for, 46, 86
    various meanings of, 64–67, 95
    weak form of, 64–66, 124–125
Einstein's theory of relativity, 158
electric grid, 173–174
electricity market deregulation, in California, 21
El Farol bar, 117–120
E-mini stock index futures, 4, 161, 169–170
Engle, Robert, 81
Enron, 21
Enstar, 59
equilibrium
    Arrow-Debreu, 46–48
    competitive, 32
    general, 30–32, 46–48, 135
    of human body, 82–83
    market, 6–9, 29–32, 48–49, 53–55
    Nash, 100–105
    rational expectations, 40–41, 46–47, 60
    stable, 46–48
    unstable, 46
equilibrium price, 29–31
equilibrium theory, 30–32
equilibrium thinking, 17, 20–21
    in economics, 6–9, 83–88, 135–137, 203–205
    flaws in, 86–88, 174–175, 211

mathematics of, 29–32
origins of, 28–29
persistence of, 83–84
Euler, Leonhard, 200, 207
Euler equation, 200–201
European Central Bank, 187
European debt crisis, 205
European monetary union, 4
excess demand, 47
expectations, 40, 113, 183, 191
    market, 33–34, 57, 60, 113, 183
    rational, 113–117, 184–189, 192, 197, 199, 204–205
    self-fulfilling, 57
extremes, 78
extreme weather, 1–2

Fair, Ray, 58–59, 61, 75
false metaphors, 21, 83–84
Fama, Eugene, 35–38, 42, 180–181
Farmer, Doyne, 65, 102–104, 140, 145, 211, 213
fat tails, 78, 80, 84, 125
Federal Reserve, 18, 56, 187
Feynman, Richard, 139, 178
finance, physics of, 15–17, 131–132
financial acceleration, 149
financial crises, 8–9, 14, 218–219
    See also global financial crisis (2007–2008)
    disequilibrium view of, 18–19
    history of, 68
financial deregulation, 41–42, 137
financial innovations, 41–43, 145–146
    See also derivatives
financial institutions, 196–197
financial models, 89–111
financial transactions, tax on, 154–155
Fisher, Franklin, 32
Fisher, Irvin, 71–72, 204, 214
5 percent problem, 33–34
flash crashes, 4–8, 12, 59, 156–162, 165–172, 173
fluid turbulence, 86
Foley, Duncan, 97
forecasting
    economic, 205–222
    financial market, 33–35, 65, 79–82
    models, 186–189
    weather, 206–208
Foxwell, Herbert, 105
fractals, 90
fractures, 165–169

FRB/US model, 187
free market, 24–26, 32
Friedman, Milton, 24, 28, 49–50, 92–97, 135, 203
Friedman, Robert, 206
F-twist, 93–97
Fukuyama, Francis, 21
fundamentalists, 136, 155, 198, 213
fundamental value, 55, 60
futures market, 3–5

Galla, Tobias, 102–104
Galton, Francis, 49
game theory, 100–105, 118
Gaussian distribution, 72–73, 80
Geanakoplos, John, 31, 140, 145, 211–213
Geithner, Timothy, 59
Geller, Robert, 71
general equilibrium, 30–32, 46–48, 135
generalizable causes, 151–152
geology, 79–80
Global Alpha, 97
Global Equity Opportunities Fund, 10
global financial crisis (2007–2008), ix, 196, 199–200
    causes of, 23, 45–46
    costs of, 45
    efficient market hypothesis and, 180–182
    lessons learned from, 220–221
    positive feedbacks and, 8
    predicting, 78–79, 188
global warming, 2
Goldberger, Ary, 83
Goldman Sachs, 10, 12, 38–39, 43, 78–79, 97
Goodhart, Charles, 201
government policy, market theory and, 41
Granger, Clive, 81
Gray, Charles, 195
Great Depression, 204
Greece, debt crisis, 4
greed, 12, 53–55
Greenspan, Alan, 28, 45, 55–56, 58
Grossman, Sanford, 124
group behavior, 16, 109–111, 143–145, 194
group influences, on behavior, 190–192
Gutenberg, Beno, 73–74
Gutenberg-Richter law, 75–76, 80
gut feelings, 109, 194

Hadley, George, 133–134
Haldane, Andrew, 164–165, 219
Hamilton, William Peter, 24
Hamilton, William Rowan, 29
Hayek, Friedrich von, 28, 105
heartbeats, 82–83
hedge funds
    computer simulations of, 140–143
    leverage and, 211–212, 213
    quant meltdown, 9–12, 54–55, 97–100, 123, 137–139
    strategies of, 137–138
herding behavior, 52
herding cats, 128
heuristics, 109
Hibernia Atlantic, 158
Hicks, John, 204
Hindenburg, 151–152
high-frequency trading, 20, 157–165, 168–175, 177
Hildenbrand, Werner, 47
history
    of markets, 81–82
    in natural science, 80
homeostasis, 82–83
Hommes, Cars, 149
Homo economicus, 109
Hormats, Robert, 56
housing bubble, 40–41, 52, 177, 180, 191–192, 196–197
Hubbard, R. Glenn, 43, 66–67
human behavior, 91–92, 97, 108–111, 113
    group influences on, 190–192
    irrational, 55
human body, equilibrium of, 82–83
Hunsader, Eric, 165, 170–171
hurricanes, 87–88
Hurts, Harold Edwin, 162–163
Hutton, Will, 1
hydrogen atom, 119
hypotheses
    assumptions and, 93–95
    testing, 92–93

imbalances, spotting, 53–54
Industrial Revolution, 27, 29
Inforeach, 157
information, market response to, 57–63, 82
information efficiency, 38–42, 181
information seeking, 36
instability, 6, 8–9, 14, 20, 129–131, 134–137, 177, 197

interactions, 144
Internet stock bubble, 8
intertemporal utility, 91
intrinsic value, 55, 60
intuition, 84
investment strategies, 106–108, 124,
    137–138, 167–168
investor confidence, 125, 150–151
investors
    information seeking by, 36
    irrational behavior by, 55
invisible hand, 7, 17, 25, 27, 30, 32, 42, 48,
    58, 204
irrational behavior, 55

January Effect, 65
Jazz Pharmaceuticals, 59
Jensen, Michael, 63
jet streams, 134–135
Jevons, William Stanley, 30
Johnson, Neil, 165–166, 167
Jones, John Tudor, 57, 75, 99
Joulin, Armand, 61
Journal of Post-Autistic Economics, 186
J. P. Morgan, 12

Kahneman, Daniel, 109
Kaldor, Nicholas, 91, 204
Kay, John, 114
Keen, Steve, 203
Kertész, János, 86
Keynes, John Maynard, 13, 55, 105, 119,
    183, 191, 204
Keynesians, 183
Khandani, Amir, 137–139, 142
Kindleberger, Charles, 68, 192
Kirman, Alan, 47
Knight, Frank, 112–114
Kocherlakota, Narayana, 188–189
Koning, John Paul, 57
Krugman, Paul, 200

Lagrange, Joseph, 29, 207
Lanchester, John, ix
Laplace, Pierre-Simone, 209
learning, 116–117
least action principle, 29
LeBaron, Blake, 119, 197–198, 202
Lefèvre, Augustin, 61
Lehman Brothers, 150–153, 212
leverage, 10, 11, 139, 141–143, 177, 198,
    211–214
leverage cycle, 212

Lewis, Michael, ix
Linkenkaer-Hansen, Klaus, 83
liquidity crises, 11
Lo, Andrew, 38, 65, 86, 128, 137–139, 142
long/short equity strategies, 137–138
Long-Term Capital Management (LTCM),
    54–55
Lorenz, Jan, 51, 52
Lucas, Robert, 40, 42, 64, 66, 67,
    183–186
Lyell, Charles, 79–80
Lynch, Peter, 106

MacKinlay, Craig, 65, 86
macroeconomic theory, 128,
    182–186, 192
Madoff, Bernie, 12, 217–218
Magellan Fund, 106
Mandelbrot, Benoit, 75–76, 80
Mantel, Rolf, 47
Marcus, Michael, 107
margin calls, 10, 139, 212–214
market efficiency
    illusion of, 142–143
    notable exceptions to, 45–69
    vs. stability, 145–150
    theory of, 17, 21, 27–29, 35–43, 48–49
market equilibrium, 6–9
    greed and, 53–55
    mathematics of, 29–32
    theory of, 48–49
market expectations, 33–34, 57, 60, 113,
    183
market failure, 26
market fluctuations
    fractal properties of, 90
    leverage and, 141–143
    minority game and, 125–126
    prediction of future, 79–82, 121–122
    statistical analysis of, 75–76
market liquidity, 159–162, 177
market makers, 4, 164–165, 170
market models, 117–126, 136, 140–143,
    167, 197–198
market norms, 21
market prices, randomness of, 36–37
markets
    See also stock market
    complete, 40–41
    computer simulations of, 140–143,
    197–198
    crowded to uncrowded transitions, 98,
    106, 123–124, 167–169

markets *(continued)*
   disequilibrium view of, 17–23
   ecological perspective on, 126–128
   efficiency of, 17, 21, 25, 27–29, 32,
      35–42
   excess volatility in, 60
   false metaphors of, 21
   greed and, 53–55
   instability of, 8–9, 20, 177, 182, 197
   as machines, 24–26
   mathematics of, 26
   memory of, 81–82, 89
   movements in, 57–63
   predictability of, 65–66, 71–72,
      124–125
   price movements in, 192–193
   response to information, 57–63, 82
   as self-regulating, ix–x, 8, 26, 45, 66,
      170, 211
   structure of, 119–123
   unpredictability of, 32–37, 66, 80–82,
      122–125
market shocks, 75–76
market signals, 65, 80–81
market theory
   efficiency and, 43
   government policy and, 41
market universals, 89–90
market volatility, 60–63, 89, 90, 163–164
Markowitz, Harry, 153
Marshall, Alfred, 28
Marsili, Matteo, 149
Marx, Karl, 27
mathematics
   in economics, 7, 26, 29, 67–68,
      200–201
   of equilibrium, 29–32
   power-law, 77–79
McCarthy, Mike, 156–157, 161
Medallion Fund, 9–10, 97
megathrust earthquakes, 70–71
Melberg, Hans, 179, 180, 181
memory, 116, 191
Merton, Robert, 41, 54, 145
metastability, 19
meteorology, 22, 86–88, 90, 135,
   206–208
microfoundations, 182–189
Mill, John Stuart, 70
minority game, 119–127, 136,
   167, 192
Minsky, Hyman, 195–198
mixed strategies, 104–105

momentum, 193, 198
momentum investing, 124–125
monetary incentives, 21
Morgan Stanley, 59, 64
Morgenstern, Oskar, 70, 100
mortgage-backed securities, 63, 147
multi-fractals, 90
Muth, John, 113

Nanex, 8, 59, 165
NASDAQ stock exchange, 127–128
Nash, John, 100–102, 104, 118
Nash equilibrium, 100–105
negative feedbacks, 7
Nelson, Robert, 154
neoclassical economics, 13, 178
networked systems, 173–174
network engineering, 173–174
news events, causing market movements,
   57–63
Newton, Isaac, 28–29
Newtonian physics, 28–29, 96
New York Stock Exchange, 42
   automatic protection rules, 5
   flash crash, 4–7
Nile river, 162–163
nonmarket relations, 21
normal distribution, 72–73, 80
Northrop, Linda, 171–172
nuclear fusion, 129–131

Ocrant, Michael, 218
Office of Financial Research, 216
oil market, 29–30
Omori, Fusakichi, 74, 82
Ormerod, Paul, 188
Other Canon, 105–108
Overdahl, Jim, 156
Overland Park, Kansas, 1–3

Pareto optimal, 32
Pentland, Alex, 189–190
Pescatori, Andrea, 186
Phillips, Norman, 135, 211
physics, 128
   applications of, 15–16
   of finance, 15–17, 131–132
   Newtonian, 28–29, 96
   plasma, 128–131
planetary motion, 96, 207
plasma, 128–131
politics, 44
Popper, Karl, 210

portfolio insurance, 56–57
positive feedbacks
    among hedge funds, 10–11, 143
    in biology, 204
    concept of, 2–3
    in economics, 6–9, 19–20, 132, 215
    models of, 211
    in stock market, 4–6, 165
Poterba, James, 57
power laws, 74–79, 89
predictability, 24–25, 65–66, 71–72,
    80–82
Prediction Company, 65
predictions. See forecasting
Preis, Tobias, 192–194
Prescott, Edward, 184, 186
prices
    autocorrelation of, 80–81
    equilibrium, 29–30, 31
    market, 36–37
privatization, blind faith in, 21
Procter and Gamble, 5, 157
Progress Energy, 59
Progress Software, 173
psychological insights, as investment
    strategy, 107–108
Putnam, Harvey, 21

quant meltdown, 9–12, 19, 97–100,
    137–139, 177
quantum theory, 183–184

Rabi, Isidor, 1
Radner, Roy, 40, 42
random walk, 80
rational addiction, 179–182
rational behavior, 91, 108–109
rational choice theory, 91–92, 97, 101
rational expectations, 113–117, 184–189,
    192, 197, 199, 204–205
rational expectations equilibrium, 40–41,
    46–47, 60
rational optimization, 178–179
Rayleigh-Taylor instability, 130
Reed, Cameron, 3
reflexivity, 210
Reinert, Erik, 105, 132
Reinhart, Carmen, 68
relativistic arbitrage, 158
Renaissance Technologies, 9, 99
representative agent, 144
resource allocation, 39–41
Ricardo, David, 28

rice avalanche, 84–85
Richardson, Lewis Fry, 157, 207–208
Richter, Charles, 73–75
Rickards, James, 133
risk, 145–150
    sharing, 147–149
    transfer of, 43
    vs. uncertainty, 112–113
river flooding, 162–163
Rodriguez, Jorge, 107
Røgeberg, Ole, 179, 180, 181
Rogoff, Kenneth, 68
Romer, Paul, 219
Rothschild, Nathan, 36

Saari, Donald, 48
Samuelson, Paul, 34–36, 42, 94,
    154
San Francisco earthquake (1906), 77
Santa Fe model, 119
Sargent, Thomas, 184, 186
savings and loans crisis, 218–219
Scholes, Myron, 54
Schrödinger's cat, 183–184
Schumpeter, Joseph, 105
Schwager, Jack, 107
science, disagreements in, 179–180
scientific thinking, shifts in, 22
Securities and Trade Commission (SEC),
    investigation of May 6, 2010, market
    events by, 5–7
self-fulfilling expectations, 57
self-interest, 53–55
self-regulating markets, ix–x, 8, 26, 45,
    66, 170, 211
Sharpe, William, 94–95
Shiller, Robert, 60, 133
Shleifer, Andrei, 54
Siegel, Jeremy, 64
Simon, Herbert, 89, 115–116
Simons, James, 9, 97, 99
Smets, Frank, 187
Smith, Adam, 7, 17, 25, 27–28, 42,
    48, 53
Smith, Greg, 38–39
Smith, Reginald, 163–164
Smith, Vernon, 67–68
social conformity, 199
social influence, 51–52
social norms, 21
social sciences, 93
social trust, 21
Sonnenschein, Hugo, 47

Soros, George, 107–108, 194–195,
    205, 210
South Sea bubble, 197
speculation, 136, 154
speculators, 197–198
spikes, 165–169
spin glasses, 121
stability
    vs. efficiency, 145–150, 173–174
    vs. liquidity, 161
stable equilibrium, 46–47, 48
Standard and Poor's, downgrading of
    U.S. credit rating by, 33
Standard and Poor's Stock Index, 3–5,
    33, 60
standard deviation, 72, 78–79
Stanley, Eugene, 76, 174
states of matter, 128–129
statistical analysis, 72–79
Stiglitz, Joseph, 124, 147
stock futures, 3–5
stock market
    See also markets
    crash of 1929, 75, 197
    crash of 1987, 55–58, 75
    first, 35–36
    flash crashes, 4–8, 12, 59, 156–162,
        165–173
    on May 6, 2010, 4–7, 20, 59, 156–159,
        161–162, 169–172
    patterns in, 90–91
    positive feedbacks in, 4–6, 165
    quant meltdown, 9–12, 19, 97–100,
        137–139, 177
    reasons for large movements in, 57–59
    spikes and fractures in, 165–169
    unpredictability of, 33–35
    U.S., 42, 43
stock prices
    capital asset pricing model of, 94–95
    reasons for large fluctuations in, 57–59
stocks, intrinsic value of, 55, 60
strategic thinking, 100–108, 118
stress, 202
stylized facts, 91
subprime mortgage crisis, 40–41,
    146–147
Summers, Larry, 57
superconductivity, 179–180
supply and demand, 29–32, 47
Surowiecki, James, 50
switching events, 193–195
Sylla, Richard, 56–57

Taibbi, Matt, 12
Taleb, Nassim, 78, 211
technical strategies, 106–107
technology, 175–177, 208
testosterone, 201–202
Tett, Gillian, ix
Thaler, Richard, 100, 101, 109
theories
    assumptions and, 92–97
    descriptively false, 95–97
    testing, 178, 186
thinking
    disequilibrium, 14, 17–23, 105–108
    equilibrium. see equilibrium thinking
    psychology of, 115–117
    strategic, 100–108, 118
Thurner, Stefan, 140, 145, 182, 211–212,
    213
Tobin, James, 154
Tōhoku earthquake, 70–71
tornadoes, 1–2
Tóth, Bence, 86
trade winds, 134
traffic, 143–145
Transparency International, 12
Trichet, Jean-Claude, 220–221
Tukey, John, 112
Turing, Alan, 204
Twain, Mark, 203

uncertainty, 40, 54, 63, 89, 112–113
United East India Company, 35
United Kingdom, capital markets
    in, 43
United States
    capital markets in, 42–43
    credit rating of, 33
unpredictability, 72, 112–113
    of markets, 36–37, 80–82, 100,
        122–125
    reflexivity and, 210
unstable equilibrium, 46–47
USS Scorpion, 49

value investors, 106
van der Leeuw, Sander, 176,
    177
Veblen, Thorstein, 105
Viniar, Davod, 78–79
Vishny, Robert, 54
volatility
    leverage and, 141–143
    market, 61–63, 89, 90, 163–164

von Moltke, Helmuth, 102
von Neumann, John, 70, 100

Waddell, Chauncy, 3
Waddell and Reed Financial, Inc., 3–4, 6,
    161, 169–170, 171
Wagener, Florian, 149
Wall Street, environment on, 52
Walras, Léon, 29, 30, 47–48
Wealth of Nations (Smith), 27
weather forecasting, 206–208
weather models, 19, 208
weather science, 22, 86–88, 90, 134–135
welfare theorems, 32, 135

Westerhoff, Frank, 155
Wharton School, 64
Wilmott, Paul, 158–159, 177
Winston, Gordon, 179
wisdom of crowds, 17, 48–52, 55
Working, Holbrook, 33–34
Wouters, Raf, 187
Wren-Lewis, Simon, 185

Yodzis, Peter, 126–127

Zaman, Saeed, 186
zero latency, 157
Zhang, Yi-Cheng, 119–120, 123, 126

A NOTE ON THE AUTHOR

Mark Buchanan is a physicist and science writer. He is the author of three previous books, *Ubiquity*, *Nexus*, and *The Social Atom*, and has been an editor of the science journal *Nature* as well as *New Scientist*. His articles have appeared in *Science*, *Wired*, the *New York Times*, the *Independent*, and the *Harvard Business Review*. He currently writes monthly columns for the financial media outlet Bloomberg View, as well as for *Nature Physics*. He lives in Dorset, England, with his wife and two dogs.